AUSTRALIAN
COMMENTARIES

AUSTRALIAN COMMENTARIES

Select Articles
from the *Round Table* 1911 – 1942

Edited and with an Introduction by

L. L. ROBSON

Senior Lecturer in History
University of Melbourne

MELBOURNE UNIVERSITY PRESS
1975

First published 1975

Printed in Hong Kong by
Dai Nippon Printing Co. (H.K.) Ltd for
Melbourne University Press, Carlton, Victoria 3053
U.S.A. and Canada: ISBS Inc., Portland, Oregon 97208
Great Britain, Europe, the Middle East, Africa and the Caribbean:
International Book Distributors Ltd (Prentice-Hall International), 66 Wood
Lane End, Hemel Hempstead, Hertfordshire HP2 4RG, England

© Melbourne University Press 1975

National Library of Australia Cataloguing in Publication data
Robson, Leslie Lloyd
    Australian commentaries: select articles from the 'Round
    Table' 1911-1942/edited and with introduction by L. L.
    Robson.—Carlton, Vic.: Melbourne University Press, 1975.
    Index.
    Bibliography.
    ISBN 0 522 84077 9.
    1. Australia–Politics and government–1911–1942–Addresses,
    essays, lectures. 2. Australia–History–1911–1942–Addresses,
    essays, lectures.
    I. Title.
    994.04

PREFACE

Following their work in the creation of the Union of South Africa in 1909, Lord Milner, the British high commissioner for South Africa, and certain of his followers—known as Milner's kindergarten—became preoccupied with the future of the British empire, a subject that dominated Milner's life thereafter. It has been stated, indeed, that his whole career after South Africa was animated by an ardent belief in the empire's destiny and civilizing influence.[1]

In September 1909 a number of these Edwardians formed the Round Table group, or moot; the object was to organize influential citizens in the dominions and Britain for discussion of the empire and its future.[2]

Lionel Curtis and John Dove, the one a former assistant colonial secretary to the Transvaal and the other a former chairman of the Transvaal land settlement board, both visited Australia in 1910 to assist in the formation of local discussion groups. Similar visits had been made to Canada and New Zealand. The project met with some suspicion in Canada where it was feared that the visitation was a thinly disguised attempt to impose and retain London-based control of the dominion, but in general the plenipotentiaries from the metropolis were well received and aroused the enthusiasm of responsible and politically effective people.

To stimulate discussion, to educate the public on world politics and familiarize the groups with developments in Britain and abroad, the *Round Table* journal, 'a quarterly Review of the Politics of the British Empire' was launched in London in November 1910 ('Empire' was changed to 'Commonwealth' in the issue of March 1919 and remained so for the period covered by this book).

The coming of the 1914–18 war, however, spelt doom to the notion of a community of nations as the Round Table group envisaged it. The development of nationalism both in the white dominions and in India led to the movement becoming a rather more informal club than had been anticipated, though its power still appears to have been formidable.

Accounts of the reception Curtis and Dove received in Australia have not survived in their papers or in extensive first-hand accounts but it may be assumed that, as in New Zealand, the movement was brought to the attention not only of academics, lawyers and politicians but businessmen and representatives of the main professions. From its inception, each issue of the *Round Table* contained an article from each of the self-governing nations within the empire, together with other articles on imperial matters as a whole. Though the format of the journal changed in the course of time, it has continued to be published since 1910 and its reports form a very coherent and consistently intelligent commentary on empire and British commonwealth affairs.

Until July 1966 the Round Table made it a fixed rule not to record in the journal the names of the individuals or groups who wrote for it. Revelation of the identity of the authors whose work is here reproduced would no doubt illuminate their analyses of events, though the Round Table principle stressed that articles be the fruit of free and wide discussion, but their chief value must reside in their quality as informed journalism.

As such they are presented, preceded by a commentary on the history of Australia and the *Round Table* pieces during the period from the establishment of the journal to the 1940s when, with prime minister John Curtin's appeal to the U.S.A. for assistance against the Japanese forces moving south towards Australia and New Zealand, the relations between Great Britain and her southern dominions were seen to be changed and the early aims of the Round Table movement either destroyed or fundamentally altered. One war (that in South Africa) had led to the Round Table's early hopes and optimism; two others brought about their drastic alteration.

Yet perhaps the most valuable part of the ideals formed and expressed by the members of Milner's kindergarten remains— the journal they brought into being has continued to provide a forum for intelligent commentary on world affairs. They might be remembered better for their liberal belief in the value of an exchange of ideas by which men would surely perceive the truth than for attempts to spar with national and other forces beyond their ability to shape.

The *Round Table* between 1911 (there was no article on Australia in the first issue of November 1910) and 1942 published about five hundred articles on Australian affairs totalling perhaps a million words. In selecting which of these to reproduce I have been guided by what appears most significant at the federal as opposed to the state level (articles on the various states have therefore not been considered for inclusion) and by an effort to isolate the commentaries that appear best to reveal and illuminate the significant aspects of Australia's development.

It is a great pleasure to record my thanks to the Round Table moot for so readily agreeing to republication of articles on Australia. In particular I wish to thank the honorary secretary, Sir Neil Pritchard, who so courteously and helpfully put his knowledge and services at my disposal. D.H. Simpson, the librarian at the Royal Commonwealth Society greatly helped me in conversation and by permitting me to utilize his library. I must also thank Dr Trevor Reese and the staff at the Institute of Commonwealth Research for their hospitality, and the director and officers of the Institute of Historical Research in the same way. The University of Melbourne granted me valuable short-term leave.

The largest debt of all I owe to Margot Beever who did so much work in elucidating reference notes and offering the most useful suggestions on how the articles might be brought out in book form. I wish also to thank the staff of Melbourne University Press for the editing and production of the book.

The articles are reproduced as they originally appeared. Inaccuracies discovered in quotations have been retained but are corrected in the editorial notes. Note numbers have been added and the occasional footnotes incorporated into the editorial notes. Original running headings and page numbers have been deleted. Of the two dates given for each article, the one at the start is the time of publication in the *Round Table* journal and the one at the end the time of writing.

The Round Table consistently used the spelling 'labour' whether it referred to the British Labour Party, the Australian

Labor Party or the labour movement. This was despite the fact that the 1908 Commonwealth conference established the spelling 'Australian Labor Party'. The British party has continued to use the spelling 'Labour'.

CONTENTS

Preface   v
Conversion Factors   xi
Introduction   1

ix

Contents

CONVERSION FACTORS

1 yard	0.91 metre
1 mile	1.61 kilometres
1 acre	0.40 hectare
1 ton	1.02 tonnes
£1	$2
1s	10c
1d	0.83c

INTRODUCTION

In the period between the Boer War and the outbreak of the Great War, Australian sentiments towards Britain and the empire had strengthened as a growing sense of isolation and danger emerged in relation to the rise of Germany and the presence of Japan. The passage of the Immigration Restriction Act of 1901 showed the determination of Australia's first federal politicians to develop a white nation and to strengthen its defences in collaboration with the British navy.[1]

Other factors too played a part in keeping Australia in close touch with Britain. As the writer in the *Round Table* mentions, various bodies such as the 'Imperial' leagues [p. 24] encouraged Australians to think of themselves as an integral part of the empire. It was most pleasing and reassuring to be told that one was part of the greatest empire since Rome.

The 1911 imperial conference revealed that the centralists in the empire—those who sought to solve the 'imperial problem' by forging strong links among the members—were swimming against the tide of dominion nationalism, but the conference was also noteworthy for the manner in which the dominions were taken into a closer embrace by the mother country: they were given a confidential insight into British foreign policy and plans to deal with any future threat to the empire.

This threat was mainly from Germany whose vigorous policy of trade expansion and ship building threatened the hegemony of Britain, and it was against this background that the *Round Table* commentator was able to report a quickening of Australian resolve to play her part in the defence of the empire [p. 24].

Devotion to the ideals of the British empire was not only the prerogative of the Liberal protectionists, led by Alfred Deakin, and the free-traders, led by George Reid, but was perhaps equally shared by most leaders of the third Australian federal political group, the Labor party. During the first years of federation, Labor supported the Liberal protectionists in return for concessions. This period of the 'lib-lab' coalition saw the passage of a good deal of liberal and progressive legislation including age and invalid pensions, a system of arbitration and other measures which reflected the liberal bourgeois character of the Australian people.

Increasing industrialization flowing in part from protectionist policy led, however, to the diminution of support for the Liberals and in 1909 Deakin led his party to join forces with the free-traders. Labor was thus left isolated, but such was its leadership under Andrew Fisher and the energetic and fiery W. M. Hughes and so attractive and widely based its appeal to the electorate, that it was able to form a government after the general election of 1910. To Labor, effective federation demanded rather more central power than the constitution permitted, but referenda seeking such further control were rejected. Labor's policy thenceforward was said to have been hampered but, as threshed out at the conference held in Hobart in January 1912, it at least appeared to be coherent. The *Round Table* writer considered, however, that it was less doctrinaire than it appeared on paper [p. 35]: Labor leaders were practical men who simply wished to give everyone a larger share of the results of his work.

The state of political parties in the period after the formal coalition of the groups opposed to Labor led to a situation where at the federal level and in the two main states of New South Wales and Victoria the political forces were more or less in balance. Theoretically it was a two-party system, reflected the *Round Table* [p. 34], but in reality there were three political ideologies represented in the Australian community. These were conservative, progressive and socialist, and the commentator noted that at the state level this situation had led to a Labor government under W. A. Holman in New South Wales and a non-Labor administration in Victoria under W. A. Watt. The parties were, however, closely balanced in the federal parliament: the lower house had a non-Labor government by a narrow majority whereas Labor had a huge majority in the senate.

In these circumstances the work of government was frustrated and in mid-1914 the Liberals under Joseph Cook secured a double dissolution of the two houses. An election campaign was in full swing when events in Europe suddenly diverted the attention of Australia, its politicians and people to the outbreak of the war with Germany.

Australians had been preoccupied with defence from earliest settlement, and the Crimean War in particular was the signal for impressive demonstrations of solidarity with Britain and the empire.[2] As the *Round Table* noted when it came to describe Australian reaction to the outbreak of war in Europe [p. 39], Australian soldiers had already fought on behalf of the empire in the Sudan in 1886, following the death of General Gordon, in China during the Boxer War and in South Africa during the Boer War.

The Labor party easily won the general election of 1914, partly due to the ever-increasing prestige and prominence of Hughes and his association in the public mind with military training and preparation to defend the nation. The tone of the *Round Table* in its discussion [p. 39] of the outbreak of war reveals how the writer is pleased with the active part taken by the federal government up to that point in the war, and especially the role of the navy in covering the New Zealand expedition to capture Samoa and the Australian force which invaded German New Guinea. Hardly less important was the sinking of the *Emden* by the *Sydney* during the passage of the Australian contingent to Egypt in 1914. The most significant aspect of the *Round Table*'s observations to its influential readership, however, is the announcement about Germany's unscrupulous ambition and the belief that that nation had deliberately started the war to enslave Europe and bring the British empire to its knees. Stressing the ideological background to the war, the writer draws attention not only to the philosophy of Nietzsche but to the writings of others who it was said had influenced their fellow-citizens to believe that Germany's national destiny involved the leadership of Europe and the colonies controlled by the nations of that continent [p. 45].

Early in the war then, the calculated culpability of Germany had been stressed; the public was conditioned to steel itself to a war against evil which would ensure that Germany's unconditional surrender would ensue. The invasion of Belgium and the destruction of Louvain made such sentiments readily acceptable, and the co-operation of labour in prosecuting the war was rendered logical also by reference to German opposition to claims put forward by organized working forces and trade unions. The *Round Table* piece as a whole is characterized by an enthusiasm for the war, reflected in the country at large by the belief that should Germany be permitted to win the war, Australia would become the vassal of a state whose evil philosophy was that might was right.

Much of the outburst of pride that accompanied news concerning the landing of units of the AIF at Anzac Cove on 25 April 1915 may be related to the adulatory despatch from Ellis Ashmead-Bartlett,[3] the British war correspondent and, possibly, the lengthy period of time (nine months) the Australian people had to wait before their soldiers first went into action. Gallipoli came to have a special significance and importance for the Australian people. The reasons for this are related to the fact that the Australian troops were clearly distinguished from other troops, the Dardanelles campaign was characterized by dramatic hand-to-hand fighting, the propaganda concerning the campaign was fed very forcefully into the home front, and it appeared that the Australian soldiers had performed bravely and well in their first encounter with the enemy. In addition the emotional poverty of Australian history had suddenly and substantially been enriched with drama for the first time. The association of Anzac Day in 1916 and in the later years of the war with pleas to enlist in the AIF also had an effect in driving home the belief that the Gallipoli campaign represented a high-point in Australia's life. According to the *Round Table* writer [p. 48], the nation had been given not only her tradition but a fuller meaning of imperial fellowship. He meant that Australia had now been equipped with a blood-letting event which permitted her to hold up her head in company with those countries whose gaining of nationhood had been associated with war.

Such was one result of worship of the nineteenth-century nation-state, and the conclusion of the *Round Table* article [p. 50] suggests that it did not really matter what grand strategy had in store for the Australian forces on the Gallipoli peninsula because the AIF had done its best. In a manner very reminiscent of C.E.W. Bean's later writing on the war, the writer draws comfort from the fact that the Dardanelles campaign had been similar to Australian droughts and bushfires in a way—war also might be a form of natural disaster which is not overcome at once but calls for renewed and unflagging efforts.[4]

As the build-up of forces on the western front continued, the battles of the Somme began in July 1916. Here the AIF suffered severe losses, a fact that led Hughes to seek the conscription of Australian men to keep up the numbers said to be necessary to sustain and expand the AIF. The opposition of Labor members of parliament especially induced Hughes to conduct a referendum on the question in October 1916.[5] The campaign was savage, as the article in the *Round Table* indicates, caused a distinct form of polarization in relation to capital and labour, and reduced the writer of the article to a sense of deep shame [p. 62] in which he accused the Australian people of lack of sincerity and intelligence in their political life compared with the high spiritual plane reached in Britain. He went further and, in an outburst of breast-beating, stated that Australians had proved themselves lacking in what he described as the faithfulness that the British masses had always shown to the highest ideals of the race and without which the 'island story' could not have been written. The sense of a corporate feeling among members of the empire, as envisaged by the founders of the Round Table movement, could not have been better exemplified.

Those supporting and opposing conscription were closely identified with non-Labor and Labor political forces respectively and, when the conscription referendum was rejected, the departure of Hughes and conscriptionists from the Labor party was completed. A group of ex-Labor men joined the non-Labor ranks under Hughes as the 'Win the War Party' and in April 1917, after Labor had lost New South Wales, fought and decisively won a general election. The Australian people wanted Hughes to lead them to victory in the war but were not prepared to adopt conscription and put up with the inconvenience of fighting a total war.

Increases in the cost of living, the strengthening of the militant element in the labour movement, and anger at the breakup of labour solidarity in the conscription referendum of

1916 put labour into an ugly mood. Thus when procedures designed to speed up work by industrial efficiency in the government tramway and railway workshops in Sydney were introduced in 1917, the workers there found this so distasteful that they came out on strike, leading to similar action throughout Australia.[6] The *Round Table* correspondent viewed the events with gravity, to the point of heading his article 'The Great Strike'.

Volunteer labour defeated the strikers, together with what the *Round Table* termed exceedingly strong public opinion and distress among families of the workers. It was remarked also [p. 64] that the New South Wales government, left unfettered by the federal power, treated the strike as an organized rebellion, both in its defiance of constitutional authority and its callous neglect of the pressing needs of war time. Other factors, too, were at work and in a lengthy and reflective analysis of the strike, the *Round Table* writer singled out a number of points [p. 65] the first of which was the general situation of Australian politics. Here he drew attention to the defection from labour of perhaps 25 per cent of trade unionists who had voted for conscriptionists, and to the financial weakness of the unions after their expenditure on the campaign against Hughes's proposals. Secondly he attributed the strike to an award made twelve months previously to coal miners after a big strike, which gave the workers an exaggerated sense of their power. Another factor in the strike was the increased cost of living and especially the knowledge that huge stockpiles of wheat sold to the imperial government were being destroyed by mice. Over and above that, the conscriptionist governments at state and federal levels aggravated feelings by not very subtly suggesting that strikers and their supporters were virtual traitors.

In short, the government's obsession with winning the war by sending men to Europe led it to crack down extremely hard on the unions' demands, and this gave the *Round Table* the chance to analyse industrial and political conditions in Australia as they had emerged by 1917. In answering the question 'Why should such a wealthy working class be so class-conscious?', a rather puzzled commentator stressed what he described as the disproportionate influence of Marxist theorists and drew

6

attention to the Industrial Workers of the World (IWW) as well as the reality of class war which flowed from the characteristics of modern capitalism. The attraction of this view of society, he said, could be attributed mainly to the lack of intelligent men to oppose it, together with the power of shrewd but uncultured people who learned their politics through the arbitration system.

Not only the workers, however, came under fire in this analysis: the employers knew practically nothing of the workers' motivations and desires, declared the *Round Table*, and failed to understand that employees were voicing a deeply felt frustration at becoming more and more wage-slaves who wanted a full share in control of industry. The exigencies of the war had brought such feelings to the surface because there was proof that some capitalists were doing well out of the war, and yet calls for further loyalty and sacrifice were being made to workers suffering from inflation of prices [p. 66]. In this frame of mind, and forming his views against the background of Bolshevik revolution in Russia, the correspondent gloomily feared a great increase in IWW influence, to be followed by something in the nature of social revolution.

Such a revolution did not occur, but violence did during the government's second attempt to introduce conscription after heavy losses of Australian soldiers at the front in the battles of 1917, the success of the German U-boat campaign in cutting off supplies to Britain, the collapse of the Russian army on the eastern front and Italian setbacks. Hughes's government decided not to conduct a general election on the issue of conscription, though Sir William Irvine, a prominent Victorian Liberal, considered such an action the correct and constitutional procedure. With characteristic boldness and the apparent certainty that everyone in the nation saw the issues exactly as he did, Hughes opened the campaign at Bendigo on 12 November 1917, a cabinet meeting in the train from Melbourne to Bendigo having evidently decided that the government should stand or fall on the decision of the people. 'I tell you plainly', announced Hughes, 'that the government must have this power [to conscript]. It cannot govern the country without it, and will not attempt to do so.'

The course of the conscription campaign was characterized

by a series of events that gave the impression that the prime minister was at the end of his tether: he regarded all his opponents as rogues, he attempted to censor statements made by the Labor premier of Queensland, T. J. Ryan (and succeeded only in drawing attention to what appeared to be authoritarian and crude proclivities on the part of the federal government and its chief) and he suddenly created a commonwealth police force, thereby further undermining any credibility he might have had for constitutional and cool procedure.

The campaign to vote 'no' was said to have been helped by letters from soldiers at the front urging such a decision and also by the line taken by archbishop Mannix. That prelate was the subject of a very strong attack by the *Round Table* correspondent who had accused Mannix of stopping the flow of Roman Catholic recruits. This, however, is without foundation[7] though evidently believed at the time [p. 80]. Nor can it be shown that the archbishop's voice and influence were largely responsible for the failure of the government's proposals. Perhaps more influential was the manner in which the government seemed undecided about precisely how many soldiers were needed to reinforce the AIF. In 1916 the number had been stated as 16 500 a month, yet in 1917 the figure had fallen to 7000, even though the war situation was described as one of the utmost gravity. Such was one result of accepting the reinforcement figures worked out in 1916, and the *Round Table* correspondent was not the only one presumably who was exceedingly uneasy on the matter [p. 81].

Behind the anti-conscription case was distrust of the Hughes government and what it might do. Labour men feared that the Nationalists, if granted power to conscript, would go the whole way and utterly destroy the working conditions and pay established by the trade union movement and enshrined in the arbitration system. They had logic on their side, given Hughes's conviction that the war had to be won at all costs. The prime minister had overreached himself in trying to convince the population that danger to Australia was as immediate as that. The danger was not as clear-cut as he said; unionists and others considered that there were other dangers as well as a German victory, and that those dangers—such as decline in living standards and the reduction of union strength—were as immediate as the threat from the Kaiser. In this way the cutting edge of Hughes's arguments were blunted.

The *Round Table* might well wring its hands in despair at the selfishness of the Australian people in refusing to conscript themselves, but much worse was to come and one of the most interesting articles in the journal describes with muted anger and disappointment the transactions that followed the referendum [pp. 83–8]. Those events appeared to justify the warnings of the anti-conscriptionists that Hughes and his cronies could not be trusted, for the prime minister proceeded to wriggle out of his clear-cut pledge not to govern the country if conscription were rejected. Only Irvine, in the opinion of the *Round Table*, took the honourable and logical course of announcing that either the government must resign or go to the country on the issue of conscription. It did neither. In an unedifying manner the party chose to cling to power by prevarication and casuistry. Hughes went through the motions of resigning but declined to offer the governor-general any advice about a successor. In this course of action the prime minister emerged with no credit, but it was enough for him and some of his supporters that Labor was kept out of office and prevented from putting its case to the people at an election.

When the armistice was signed on 11 November 1918, Hughes was in Britain for the purpose of attending the imperial conference. The return and demobilization of the AIF proceeded smoothly and during this period Hughes and Sir Joseph Cook, who had accompanied him to Europe, concerned themselves with securing a voice for Australia at the conference table and the peace conference, especially in regard to German possessions in the Pacific, the matter of reparations and the establishment of the League of Nations.

The Nationalist government which had emerged from the debacle of the 1917 conscription referendum said little of the proceedings at Versailles and earned the animosity of the *Round Table* writer [p. 90]. Plainly and understandably disillusioned with Hughes and his conduct, the correspondent pleaded for more open diplomacy and noted that governments from now on would need to have the knowledge and understanding of their people behind them. On this point, it should be observed that the crucial question of former German and

9

existing Japanese-occupied territory in the Pacific had not been discussed publicly during the war due to censorship. What form of control was to be exercised over the former German territories? Here there was no instant agreement that Australia should attempt to take on such responsibilities. The labour press denounced claims for annexation as immoral and regarded them as further proof, were any more needed, of the capitalistic and imperialistic character of the war. The non-labour press, too, was doubtful whether Australia should attempt to take over the territories in question, on the grounds that the federal government did not have the resources. On the other hand the importance to all Australians of their white Australia policy made it logical that they should either control the territories referred to or else have the final voice in whether or not such territories should be the scene of Asian immigration and influence.

The League of Nations and the principles and ideals that led to its emergence were supported in Australia when it was seen that the projected organization was being taken seriously by European statesmen, but the *Round Table* commentator found some cause for alarm in the implications of separate dominion membership of the league. Would it not be possible, he argued, that members of the empire might be placed in a state of hostility towards each other if one of their number were branded by the league as an aggressor, or otherwise fell under unfavourable notice? These and other matters should be the subject of an imperial conference, he concluded [p. 96].

In the meantime that most imperial of nationalists, Hughes, had returned to Australian soil. The heat of the conscription campaigns and their political sequel appeared to have gone and everywhere the prime minister was greeted with cheers. The forces favouring Hughes were his standing as a symbol of Australian nationalism and its close relationship with the record of the AIF, the fact that he had rubbed shoulders with the mighty at Versailles and stood up for Australia, his support by the returned soldiers—based partly on his exertions on their behalf in France in 1918 and partly on their admiration for Hughes's pugnacity and cheek—and the lack of any other dominant personality on the Australian political scene. In the opinion of the *Round Table* correspondent, however, the most potent element in the prime minister's popularity and standing was his record at the peace conference which, if the papers were to be believed, revealed that he had stood virtually alone against the rest of the civilized world in protecting the white Australia policy by securing islands in the Pacific as a buffer against Asia.

Australia's safety was indeed a cause for concern. Japan had been the nation insisting on recognition of racial equality and, though her views had been overruled by President Wilson, it was unlikely, predicted the *Round Table*, that she would accept this decision as final; there were dangers ahead in the posture of independence assumed by small nations [p. 100]. In the meantime Hughes was in a position in which he could either continue to lead the Nationalists or, theoretically, form a fresh political party altogether. But the war had thrown him beyond the boundaries of Australian political parties and there he was to remain.

The decade of the 1920s in Australia was dominated by a conservative government which concentrated on strengthening and extending the sale of Australian primary produce and was preoccupied with fear of communism and its foreign agents following the consolidation of the Bolshevik revolution. It was essentially a holding administration of Nationalists and the newly formed Country party, presided over most of the time by S. M. Bruce,[8] an ornament of the Melbourne Club whose slogan was 'men, money and markets'. But Hughes still led the Nationalists till 1923 and the emergence of the Country party,[9] a group that turned out to be lethal to Australia's war-time leader.

The Country party was formed by rural interests who became dissatisfied with war-time controls over such products as wool, wheat and butter and irritated at attempts to impose price control and a tariff designed to foster Australian manufactures. A good deal of the party's later success has been attributed to the preferential voting system. It transpired that Bruce was permitted to stand for the Nationalists unopposed in his first election for the constituency of Flinders in Victoria on condition that the preferential system was introduced.[10] The Country party was a sectional party pure and simple which supported the Nationalists at both federal and state levels in return for concessions, somewhat as Labor had done in the case of Deakin's Liberals in the period to 1909. The leader of the federal Country party was Dr Earle Page, a physician.[11] In conjunction with Bruce, he headed the Bruce-Page government of 1923–9.

The Country party was always concerned at the low population density in the hinterland from which it drew its strength, and so was nearly everyone else, though for different reasons. When the Australian thought of the rest of the world, one comparison always struck him and that was the extremely low population density of his country, the emptiness of the northern part of the continent, and the large number of people everywhere else in the world. Australia's population was approximately 5.5 million in 1921 and during that decade the Nationalist government sought to encourage immigration from Britain especially. It became an unarguable proposition that Australia was under-populated and hence virtually defenceless, but the addition of a few more millions would not have seriously altered her ability to defend herself by the conventional means available in the 1920s—army personnel, an air force and navy.

The *Round Table* [p. 108] argued that the minute population garrisoned in Australia was uneconomic because it was so scattered and Australia would be much better off if her population were concentrated on the south-east coast. This was true. Capital was dispersed over too wide an area, and railways and public works were a heavy burden to carry for the sake of a handful of individuals who chose to live in the back-blocks. The undoubted importance of the wool industry, however, made such a dispersal of settlement necessary up to a point and hence he who would criticize the vast spread of population was compelled to urge extensive immigration policies to 'normalize' the economy and the demographic structure of the nation. In this predicament the *Round Table* observed that immigration would need to be carefully controlled because land was too dear for many of the required new settlers, and when it was not too dear, was no good.

The 'men' for Bruce's 'men, money and markets' were therefore needed. Markets also might be tapped in Asia as Australian industrial enterprises began to develop their potential for sales, and Australia harnessed her resources in the form of Victorian brown coal and Tasmanian water power.

In 1922 the parliamentary representatives of many of the people who lived in the rural areas, which appeared empty of inhabitants to some urban eyes, played a decisive part in the downfall of Hughes. In the election of 16 December the Nationalist representation fell from 38 to 29, Labor rose from 23 to 29, and the Country party retained 14 seats. There were 2 Liberals and 1 Independent, and thus the Country party held the balance of power. It refused to bargain with any party that included Hughes and, fearing that a fresh election would increase the power of Labor, the non-Labor forces were thereby compelled to contemplate a coalition.

The Country party objected to Hughes because he had recently led a party that lost seats, because he was autocratic and still tainted with Labor ideology, because he loathed the Country party, and because he was a personal enemy of Dr Page whom he had attacked relentlessly. In these circumstances the Country party was unswervingly hostile to Hughes who, sensing he was losing control of the party, had sought and gained promises from his cabinet before the election not to join any Country party-Nationalist coalition.[12] Such promises proved to be worthless. Hughes resigned the leadership, and a fresh government was formed under the leadership of Bruce, his young lieutenant and ex-treasurer. The new prime minister's deputy was Dr Page who was able to drive a hard bargain and secure virtual cabinet equality with the Nationalists. Obsessed with retaining a separate identity, the Country party secured all the advantages of partnership and few of the drawbacks. The new government set its face against 'socialization' and the intervention of government in trade and industry. Bruce took an early opportunity to announce that the coalition government stood for a vigorous national policy [p. 116].

To think, see and be seen to act nationally, but within the framework of the empire, really broke no new ground in terms of earlier governments' aims and conduct; that sense of nationalism had led Hughes to stress at the peace conference the crucial role of the Pacific islands formerly held by Germany, and it was one result of the deliberations at Versailles that Australia ultimately came to exercise a mandate, under the League of Nations, over German New Guinea.[13] Following the abortive attempt by Queensland to control a portion of the territory of New Guinea in 1886, Britain had reluctantly stepped in until, in 1906, Australia had been granted control over Papua. This southern part of the huge island was found to produce gold but attempts to induce gold seekers to take up coconut plantations were unsuccessful. Neither rubber nor copra were found to pay very well and development was extremely slow. In an article on the subject, the *Round Table* correspondent attributed this tardy economic growth partly to world price fluctuations but mainly to the operation of the Australian navigation act, the provisions of which meant that practically all New Guinea shipping was confined to one Australian company trading between the island and Sydney. He considered the government of Papua essentially a benevolent dictatorship, but one that wisely attempted to retain the native way of life and as many Papuan customs as possible. Casting his thoughts ahead, however, he pondered what would ultimately replace the native way of life as it inevitably changed in relation to European customs. The substitution of an industrial for a military ideal among the tribesmen was sought, and all kinds of sports encouraged, cricket being designed to replace cannibalism. The ultimate replacement of native religious practices by forms of Christianity was predicted. Technical education existed but, concluded the *Round Table*, the encouragement of native agriculture formed the most important aspect of Australian attempts to encourage education which, however, had an uphill battle against the deep conservatism of the native people [p. 124].

Conservatism in the style practised by the Bruce-Page government was also lodged on the Australian mainland, and the general election of 1925 showed its strength: Labor's number of seats fell to 23 whereas the Nationalists secured 38 and the Country party 14. This election was fought on the issue that the five Labor states (only Victoria was non-Labor) had failed to suppress the growth of communism as manifested in a series of strikes, and further failed to co-operate with the federal government for that purpose. In these circumstances Bruce was enabled to fight an election on the issue that he should be given more power to control the growth of communism. This was in part precipitated by a series of seamen's strikes which led to an act of July 1925 by which foreign-born persons might be deported for hindering good government. Two leaders of seamen's unions that had gone on strike were summoned under this legislation, but J. T. Lang, the premier of New South Wales, refused to co-operate with Bruce in serving the necessary writs, whereupon the federal authority managed to use federal police agents, and alleged that the Labor government of New South Wales had shown sympathy with communists.

This seamen's strike continued during the election campaign. There were occasional outbreaks of violence and enough threats of it and intimidation to present the government with the beginnings of a case for strengthening their power to deal with such strikes on a national basis. The government could then show that state Labor administrations evidently were unable or unwilling to restore normal conditions. Bruce in reality ran a 'Red scare' campaign with ill-defined details of the fresh powers he sought, but with emphasis enough given to the influence of Moscow in Australia.

In addition the prime minister announced an elaborate social services policy, national insurance, improvement of country communications and increased defence expenditure. The government also announced its adherence to the British empire and painlessly presented rhetoric concerning the suppression of communism and realization of Australia's destiny.

The Labor opposition, under Matthew Charlton, sensed the Australian fear and distrust of any 'ism' and especially communism, and steered clear of this, though assertions were made that Labor was better able to deal with strikes than Bruce and his colleagues were, that Bruce should have ensured that warships ordered in Britain were built in Australia, and that Australian industry had not been adequately protected.

As a result of a private member's bill, this election was the first one with compulsory voting. The *Round Table* was not happy about this at all and doubted the wisdom of compelling the apathetic and the ignorant to vote. It also drew attention to the absurd system of voting for the senate under which government candidates could win every seat contested despite the fact that Labor had polled 4 out of every 10 votes cast [p. 136].

Bruce's political ideology and programme were approved by

15

the people and, two years after the election of 1925, the government's distrust of state-run enterprises became evident when the decision was made to sell the commonwealth shipping line, on the ground that it was losing money. To what extent the line had been successful in keeping down other freight rates was a matter for strong debate and difference of opinion about the principles of accounting procedures. The *Round Table*, for its part, considered it significant that the Country party, which might have been expected to voice the opinion of primary producers who felt that the line kept down freight rates, whole-heartedly supported the proposal to sell the line. Possibly Bruce's statement that if the ships were kept, parliament would have to vote a considerable sum of working capital for them, had the desired effect [p. 141]. The buyer of the line subsequently defaulted in payment.[14]

In 1928 the Bruce-Page government suffered considerable losses at the general election, losses that may be traced to ill-considered tampering with the arbitration system and related closely to Bruce's inability to compromise so that he might receive favourable publicity for his sympathy with both employers and employees. Bruce was losing his touch. He seemed incapable of understanding that the welfare of Australia was in the final analysis the welfare of everyone in it and not merely those with the most wealth, breeding or brains, and he went beyond Australians' parameters of expectation when he announced that the federal government would abandon the field of arbitration, on the ground that the state-federal conflicts in the field were intolerable.

This apparent blow to the sacred Harvester judgment of 1907 and its implications was too much for the people to accept, and Hughes found his long-nursed resentment of Bruce, the man who had replaced him six years previously, about to be gratified with revenge. In September 1929 the government was defeated by one vote in committee on a motion by Hughes to postpone withdrawal from industrial arbitration until after an appeal to the electors [p. 145]. The government went to the country and was struck down. The *Round Table* thought Bruce would be remembered for his stimulation of scientific research and the financial agreement he had been able to conclude with the states [p. 146].

The victory of Labor was related to the onset of the economic depression, its pledge to maintain the commonwealth arbitration court, and the alarming indications of increases in unemployment. The party had promised unemployment insurance, aid to the poorer states, a shipping service to Tasmania and protection to all industries. The new prime minister was J. H. Scullin and the treasurer was E. G. Theodore, who was generally regarded as the most able man in the ministry.

The incoming government was now faced with economic problems it was unable even to diagnose, let alone begin to solve, as the economic depression that struck the western world brought and continued to bring the misery of unemployment and the degradation of the dole to Australian workers. Scullin's government threshed around, hopelessly split from within by the belligerent conduct of Lang in New South Wales and his instinctive rejection of orthodox capitalistic nostrums, and by grave doubts among others concerning the propriety of Theodore's actions: when premier of Queensland he had, it appeared, been guilty of fraud in relation to some mining leases. When the hapless Scullin restored Theodore to the treasurership before he had been cleared of criminal charges, J. A. Lyons and J. E. Fenton withdrew from the party in disgust and doubt. The prime minister was too bourgeois to resist Sir Robert Gibson, the conservative head of the Commonwealth Bank, and in a welter of faction fighting, confusion and anger, the Labor party was brought down by the newly formed United Australia Party (UAP), led by Lyons and J. G. Latham and apparently controlled by powerful business interests.[15]

The *Round Table* correspondents found a great deal to describe in these stirring times but paused to deplore the fact that the term 'Liberal' had not been revived as a description of the anti-Labor forces. As one writer observed, it was notorious that very few political parties could survive a term in office during times of economic distress [pp. 155–6]. Labor's downfall was spectacular: Scullin went to the polls with 35 supporters and lost 23 of them. Lyons's landslide win was a measure of the conservativeness and fear of the Australian people. The *Round Table* commentator concluded that the election was an example of the old adage that in times of trouble the elector votes not so much for men and policies as against them [p. 163].

The UAP's victory was so complete that it could afford the luxury, very rare among anti-Labor parties, of governing without the Country party. That situation did not last, however, in the election of 1934 the Country party once again held the balance of power and was able to take up its accustomed role in coalition.

In the years that followed, the UAP-Country party allies concentrated on revision of the tariff, in the hope that the unimaginative though apparently sensible steps in reviving trade would set Australia on the path to prosperity. Lyons saw before him no guiding beacon in the form of a coherent aim and policy related to social justice for his stricken country, but presided over a cautious nation, ever ready to count its blessings after the trauma of the depression, an experience made worse by the non-existent or primitive forms of social welfare inherited from the 1920s.

The trade diversion policy bore all the marks of a businessman's government. Its aims were to increase Australian exports of her great primary products such as wool, wheat and meat, expand secondary production and divert to good trading customers some of the goods currently going to nations that bought little in return. Britain in particular was to be treated favourably; motor vehicle chassis were to be imported solely from that nation, if they had to be imported at all, and efforts were made to increase the imports of British cotton and rayon piece goods.

By these actions Australia struck a blow against Japan's textile industries and their exports to Australia. Japan retaliated by placing similar duties on Australian goods and refused to come to an agreement with Australia unless she gave Japan a chance to compete with Britain. The *Round Table* correspondent examined the problem [pp. 166–74] and was moved to question L. S. Amery's view that the British empire was a unit that had a common ideal and might enlist the forces of economic nationalism for the mutual benefit of all members. Was it realistic for Australia to alienate Japan even if, as it was held, she was able to mass-produce goods on the basis of cheap labour and undersell Britain? Britain denied having had anything to do with Australia's economic attack on Japan but L. F. Giblin, Ritchie professor of economics at the

University of Melbourne, evidently suspected otherwise and spoke darkly of 'log-rolling' and 'interested parties'. Someone was behind the times. While Lyons referred fulsomely to the 'British empire', the *Round Table* had since 1919 referred to itself as 'a quarterly review of the politics of the British Commonwealth'.

The aggressive search for markets by Japanese industry rendered Australia uneasy, but she had little room for manoeuvre due to her dependence, by convention, sentiment and economy, upon the mother country. Britain did not reciprocate when the chips were down in her relations with Germany, and the *Round Table* correspondent in 1938 found himself reporting that Australia had been virtually disregarded during the turmoil in the British cabinet relating to the resignation of Anthony Eden and British negotiations with Nazi Germany. The leader of the Australian Labor party was now John Curtin, elected to that position in 1935, and he considered that the challenge of the fascists in Europe was a ground for calling the Australian parliament together. The press supported him, a factor suggesting that Lyons was getting out of touch with his allies. Lyons's decline had started; events were now so shaping themselves that a rather old-fashioned and dignified gentleman would find the world too far out of joint for him to cope with it. Or perhaps he had done the work for which he had been made leader of the UAP.

Lyons, continuing to use the relatively new device of nation-wide wireless broadcasts, announced a £25 million increase in defence expenditure during the next three years and the *Round Table* writer reported that the strength of the defences at Singapore could easily be exaggerated [p. 177]. The resources of Britain had been stretched too far, and Australia began to feel chilly. It received with astonishment and some pain the news of British official reaction to Hitler's aggressive statements and action, and again Curtin drew attention to what appeared to be a disturbing breakdown of communication between Britain and Australia in these anxious days. It was significant that the Labor leader again received support from an unexpected quarter. The attorney-general, R. G. Menzies, made a calculated comment concerning Lyons's leadership when he observed that parliament had been kept too much in the dark concerning foreign affairs.

The prime minister was a sick man. With no great originality he had presided over revival of the natural forces inherent in the Australian economy following the worst days of the depression, and the electors recognized his homely virtues at a time when people were nursing their wounds. But Lyons began to pine; he did not thrive on the wheeler-dealing offered by the men of Canberra, Sydney and Melbourne. He discovered he had no true mates and compared his situation unfavourably with the early days in Tasmania[16] where the economic stakes were low. He died of a heart attack on 7 April 1939.

Lyons's successor was R. G. Menzies who was called upon to preside over Australia during war time. He declared that when Britain was at war, Australia was at war. There was no essential difference in the attitude of Menzies to that of Fisher or Cook in 1914. Indeed a special force of infantry was raised and given the same name as its parent body of 1914–18—the Australian Imperial Force (AIF). The names of the new divisions marked the continuity of war, for they were known as the 6th to 9th divisions.

Menzies' party, the UAP-Country party coalition, fell to pieces as the result of factionalism, the prime minister's arrogance and the narrow majority he had in parliament, and in October 1941 a stop-gap administration led by A. Fadden collapsed to be replaced by a Labor government under the leadership of John Curtin. Curtin appealed to America to defend Australia following the attack on Pearl Harbor and the swift advance of the Japanese forces through south-east Asia. His request was answered and when in May 1942 the *Round Table* correspondent closed his report to London, American forces had virtually occupied Australia. The report mentioned that the Americans laughingly pointed out that the best place to defend the U.S.A. was in someone else's country. It also noted that Australia was suffering the consequence of past neglect of defence, poverty, industrial relations and education [p. 198], but did not allocate blame for that neglect.

PART ONE

1911 – 1914

AUSTRALIA AND THE EMPIRE

August 1911, vol. 1, pp. 497–500

THE student alike of Federal and Imperial questions, will find plenty to interest him in the happenings in Australia during the last few months. But in view of the meeting of the Imperial Conference,[1] before reviewing recent events in Australia, it may, perhaps, be of interest briefly to supplement certain remarks made by the writer of the article "The Australian Position" in a recent number of THE ROUND TABLE, concerning the present general attitude of the Australian people towards Imperial affairs.[2] It must at once be admitted that a great change has come over public opinion during the last few years. There are many people in Queensland, for instance, who have a vivid recollection of the bitter criticism levelled against the then Premier of that State, Sir Samuel Griffith (now Chief Justice of the High Court of Australia),[3] for his share in bringing about, some twenty years ago, what was contemptuously styled the "Naval Tribute"; an arrangement by which the six Australian colonies, as they then were, agreed to pay a total annual subsidy of £126,000 to the Home Government, in return for the maintenance in these waters of an additional special Australian squadron, consisting of five third-class cruisers and two torpedo gun-boats. Queensland's share in this "tribute," on a population basis, was about £12,000. Those were the days when "Imperialist" was synonymous with "Jingo" as a term of reproach, and a writer or speaker could count upon a sympathetic audience when he declared that "Australia was being dragged into European complications to serve England's own greedy and selfish ends"— "European" complications, since the "portent of the East" had hardly yet appeared above the horizon. It was even hinted that the real reason for the presence of the English warships on our coasts was that they might overawe the people of Australia, should they show any signs of resenting the mother country's insolent over-lordship. But now, England's quarrels, England's interests, are ours also, and Queensland, which once grudged the payment of a few thousands of pounds a year to the British Admiralty for its protection, is proud, in common with all the other States, to form part of a Commonwealth which cheerfully faces an expenditure of millions

23

in order to furnish its quota of a great Imperial fleet, and even considers this as only the first instalment of its task. No doubt the people of Australia look upon their ships as primarily designed to protect their own coasts, but the leaders of all political parties in the Commonwealth have made it clear that in case of need they will be available for the defence of the Empire as a whole, wherever their services may be required.

It would be difficult, if not impossible, to give a categorical list of all the reasons for this remarkable change of sentiment. Some perhaps, are apparent enough, others lie below the surface, and are not so easily measured or understood. No doubt the South African War (at the close of last century) exercised a powerful influence in this direction. English regular and Australian volunteer fought side by side against a common enemy, and each bore himself as befitted his country and his race. The effect was increased by the fact that even if the Boers had been victorious they could never have invaded either Great Britain or Australia. The attack ostensibly was upon the colonists of the sub-continent, but in reality upon the prestige of the Empire at large, and it was to uphold this that both British and Australian rallied. Another potent factor may be found in the rapid rise during the last few years, of two military and naval powers, Germany and Japan, the one apparently challenging the mother country's supremacy on the sea, and forcing her to concentrate a large proportion of her defensive strength in her own waters; the other a possible menace to white civilization throughout the whole Eastern world. Australia, virtually an outpost, peopled by a mere handful of Europeans, facing the teeming millions of a newly awakened Asia, cannot close her eyes to the grave peril of isolation, and the absolute need of union with her fellow Europeans of her own race, who will aid her to hold her own.

Of less importance, yet by no means without their influence, have been the, perhaps, rather artificial methods which have been largely resorted to of late for the purpose of fostering a spirit of unity and mutual interest between the different parts of the Empire. The various "Imperial" Leagues, the correspondence societies, the regular salute to the Union Jack practised in many schools; the interchange of flags and courtesies between schools in Australia and Great Britain; the circulation of standard English authors among the younger generation of Australians by means of state aided school libraries; the patriotic numbers of the "school papers" issued for Empire Day by the Education Departments of all the states—all these have played their part, if only a small one, in moulding public opinion as it is in Australia to-day.

But even after allowing for all this, it must in honesty be confessed that speaking generally, the average citizen of the Commonwealth troubles himself very little about Imperial affairs at all. Not infrequently, it is true, with a mental attitude, or perhaps merely a trick of speech derived from an older generation, he speaks of England as "Home," although he himself may never have set foot on its shores. But as a rule the mother country is, after all, a far land, even a foreign land, to the majority at least of the native-born, while Australia is the real "Home," where their work and their interests lie. As for the other Dominions, for the most part they attract little attention, and in some instances only as possible rivals for the trade of the United Kingdom or for the emigrants who year by year leave it to seek new homes across the sea. The Empire is there, certainly, and we are proud of it, loyal to it, in a very real if vague fashion. But, except in the time of some stern crisis, or when some great world event, such as the death of the late King Edward, catches at the nation's heart-strings, it is too distant, too formless, to excite any very strong enthusiasm in our minds. What we know as "Imperial Federation," the ideal of a concrete political union between the mother country and the scattered Dominions, may occasionally furnish matter for discussion, more or less academic, in the columns of newspapers and magazines; but these excite, as a rule, only a passing interest, and neither reflect nor influence, to any appreciable extent, the general trend of public thought. The question is not considered as within the present range of practical politics. And not only so, but in so far as it is believed to involve the creation of a central Executive, probably located in London, and charged with the control of the general affairs of Homeland and Dominions alike, it is, perhaps, not too much to say that any small amount of opinion that may exist upon the subject is distinctly inimical to the idea. Australians are very strong Home Rulers—that is, so far as Australia is concerned—and they are apt to look with suspicion upon any proposal which may seem to carry with it any curtailment of their power to govern themselves, or any check, however insignificant, upon the free exercise of the legislative or administrative functions of either Commonwealth or States. But this statement must not be mis-understood. It is not meant to assert that there is in this country no regard for the Empire, no Imperialism, in the true sense of the words. Australian loyalty, as already pointed out, if vague and unformed, is yet very real; we are proud of our Empire, and of our citizenship therein; of the glories, the traditions and the memories in which we, in common with all Britons, have our part.

May 1911

LABOUR POLICY IN THE
COMMONWEALTH PARLIAMENT

September 1912, vol. 2, pp. 664–77

THE evolution of the Labour policy in the Commonwealth Parliament has been favoured by the comparative freedom of its supporters from local precedents, traditions, and inter-State jealousies, and the consequent sympathy of the Party with the national idea of federation. Trade-union congresses and the early proposals made for the federation of labour organizations bore fruit indirectly, inasmuch as they accustomed the labour leaders to think from a national point of view at the time when the older parties were grouped in single states on party lines. With the advent of federation, the Conservative parties of New South Wales and Victoria were ranged in opposition in the National legislature, and entirely new questions, which parties organized on local lines were not prepared to meet, appeared on the political horizon. Amidst these conflicting interests, so perplexing to the older parties, the course of labour ran comparatively smoothly. Several years prior to this—after their first experience in the New South Wales Parliament—the party had agreed to subordinate the tariff to strictly labour issues. Moreover their policy as to State control of industries was consistent with the idea of a protectionist tariff, especially with Protection as a National, rather than a local State policy. The party was already organized on an inter-state basis, so that questions of personal leadership had been settled. Furthermore, it was gradually realized that the chief reforms advocated by the party could be more effectively secured through a National Government than through the local legislatures.

The most recent Commonwealth Labour platform was formulated at the labour conference held in Hobart in January last.[4] The results of this conference will furnish the political texts for the Labour party for the next two years, and in view of the fact that the party is now charged with the responsibility of office in the Federal Government, and further that, no matter what the result of the next General Elections may be, the party must be the controlling factor in the Senate, the Hobart Conference is viewed by the delegates as the most important labour gathering yet held in Australia. Turning to the amended platform we find that its eleven planks are

26

as follows: 1. Maintenance of white Australia; 2. Graduated tax on unimproved land values; 3. Effective federation; 4. The new protection; 5. Nationalization of monopolies; 6. Arbitration Act amendment; 7. Navigation laws; 8. Commonwealth freight and passenger steamers; 9. Restriction of public borrowing; 10. General insurance department; and 11. Commonwealth sugar refining. In the official report of the conference it is specially mentioned that the following planks of the previous platform had been made law: 1. White Australia; 2. Old-age and invalid pensions; 3. Graduated tax on unimproved land values; 4. Citizen defence force, with compulsory military training and Australian-owned and controlled navy; 5. Commonwealth bank; and 6. Electoral reform. With the exception of four planks relating respectively to the new protection, nationalization of monopolies, Arbitration Act amendment, and navigation laws (replaced as Nos. 4, 5, 6 and 7 in the new platform), these comprise the whole of the legislative policy put forward by the party in their previous platform of 1908. And it should be observed that the realization of the first two exceptions mentioned was dependent upon the approval of the proposed laws at the Referenda last year,[5] while bills relating to the last two have been introduced but not yet passed. It is obvious, therefore, that at any rate as regards legislative action a good deal has been accomplished, and in fact it is now asserted that in view of the failure to obtain enlarged constitutional powers at the Referenda last year, the party has, so far as useful legislation is concerned and more particularly as regards industrial matters, come to a "dead end." Hence it is not altogether surprising, even in view of the large majority against the proposed amendments in April, 1911, that the Conference unanimously decided that another appeal must be made to the people and that the same powers should be sought by referenda to be submitted at the next general elections. This resolution is now embodied in the third plank of the new platform under the title of "effective federation." The form of the questions will be decided by the caucus, and it is probable that they will be split into five or six instead of being lumped together as on the last occasion.

Though the amended platform will not strictly come into operation until after the next general elections, since the present Labour members have not signed it, it will be of interest to examine briefly the various planks in the light of past events, and of certain statements issued as a result of the caucus meetings, which, at the time of writing, were being held.

The "White Australia" policy is to be interpreted literally, and means the reservation of the whole Commonwealth territory for the exclusive occupancy of people of European stock. At present the most important practical phase of the question is the development of the tropical territories with white labour, and in view of the taking over by the Commonwealth from South Australia of the Northern Territory at the commencement of 1911, the Commonwealth Labour Government is now brought face to face with this problem. The Labour party is beginning to realize that, in view of the growing demand which modern nations make on the material resources of the world, it will be difficult for any nation to lock up perpetually large tracts of productive country. For defence purposes, too, it is recognized that the settlement of the Northern Territory is a matter of urgency. The Commonwealth Government has recently formulated a land policy on the leasehold system for the settlement and development of the territory; in the meantime an Administrator[6] and other officers have been appointed; exploration parties, including men of high scientific attainments, have been sent out, and the capacities of the country are being tested in various directions. A Government-owned steamer is to be provided for the use of settlers on the Daly River, and a Bill is to be introduced next session providing for a settlers' bank. The idea is that a man will be able to go to the Territory, work for wages for a few months, then go to the bank and be started on a leasehold block with cattle, a house, and implements. Whether the progress of science and invention, as applied to tropical industries, and a more rapid physiological adaptation to climatic conditions than is now anticipated, will enable the ideal to be realized, yet remains to be proved. In the meantime the "White Australia" policy will remain a leading question.

The beginning of the extension of the existing railway as far as the Katherine River (about sixty miles) is intended this year, but no general scheme of railway construction will be adopted until a committee of three experts, to be appointed shortly, have gone over the ground and furnished recommendations.

In regard to the building up of an agricultural population, the attitude of the Labour party in the Commonwealth legislature has been one of *laissez faire*. The professed reason for this policy, while containing a certain amount of truth and justification, is largely a false pretence. The Party allege that it is useless, and even dangerous, to invite people to come to the country under present conditions, that there is now no land available, that the only suitable areas, within reasonable distances of railway lines or any areas in remoter portions on which a settler could hope to make a living or bring up a family, except under conditions of unendurable hardship, are alienated in freehold, and their ownership concentrated into large holdings. Hence the third Labour Government imposed in 1910 a progressive land tax, with an exemption, except in the case of absentee holders, of £5,000 unimproved value. As a result of the first year's operation of this tax it is now claimed that it is achieving its main purpose, that of breaking up big estates. The assessments for the second year's tax show a falling off of about 10 per cent, which is stated to be largely due to the effect of the first year's tax in breaking up estates.

The third plank in the new platform, entitled "Effective federation," provides for the resubmission, by referendum, of the proposal submitted in 1911, and has already been alluded to. This was probably the most important matter which demanded the attention of the Conference, since not only has the Commonwealth Government under the existing Constitution no power to nationalize any industry, but also practically the whole realization and development of the Labour policy is dependent upon whether the party can succeed in obtaining the sanction of the people to the enlarged powers sought. Thus we find that in the absence of such powers it will be impossible for the Labour party to realize any of the fourth, fifth, eighth, or eleventh planks of the new platform.

What is known as the "new protection" is the subject of the fourth plank and is a proposal which originated with the Labour party at an early stage in Federal politics. The object of this system is stated to be to guarantee the Australian market to Australian manufacturers, on the understanding that they would pay fair and reasonable wages, and that they would not enter into combines and trusts, nor overcharge the consumers for their goods. The principles of this system were embodied in the Excise Tariff (Agricultural Machinery) Act, 1906, which imposed an excise duty on a scheduled list of agricultural implements manufactured in Australia, and then proceeded to declare that the duty should not be payable on goods manufactured under the prescribed conditions as to remuneration of labour and other matters. This Act, after nearly two years of dislocated industry and expensive litigation, was declared unconstitutional on the grounds (*a*) that it was an attempt to regulate the internal trade and industry of the States, (*b*) that it discriminated between States and parts of States, and (*c*) that it contained provisions dealing with matters other than the imposition of taxation. Though the policy of the party in respect of this matter is indefinite, it was stated by the Prime Minister[7] at the Hobart Conference that, if the constitutional amendments are carried, the system will be brought into effect.

The fifth plank, relating to nationalization of monopolies, may be considered in connexion with the eighth and eleventh planks relating respectively to Commonwealth freight and passage steamers

and to a Commonwealth sugar refinery. Though various proposals
for the nationalization of industries have been made, and two or
three of these expressed in the form of resolutions in one or other of
the Federal Houses of Parliament, no definite scheme for such a step
has ever been officially brought forward by the Labour Government.
The objective of the party in this direction may be gauged from the
propaganda put forward in the manifesto issued in March, 1910,
prior to the last General Election. In that document it was stated
that the nationalization of monopolies demanded the urgent attention of the people; that the capitalistic system was developing on the
same lines as in America, and that nothing short of nationalization
would prevent the exploitation of the people. The sugar monopoly,
tobacco combine, coastal shipping, and the coal vend were specially
mentioned. In addition to the planks relating to Commonwealth
steamers and to a Commonwealth sugar refinery, two other
resolutions dealing with the subject of nationalization were passed by
the Conference in January last, viz.: (1) That publicly owned
ironworks are an urgent necessity, and (2) that the sale of alcoholic
liquors in the Federal territory (i.e. in the Northern Territory and
in the Federal Capital Territory) be nationalized.

As regards the Arbitration Act amendment (plank 6), the only
resolution passed by the Conference specifically relating to this
matter was to the effect that the Act should be amended so as to
prohibit members of the legal profession from appearing before the
court for either party. It was stated that a recent case, in which a
union composed mainly of pastoral workers was concerned, cost
no less than £26,000 in lawyers' fees for both parties. The question
of amending the Act has, however, two other important bearings—
first in regard to "effective federation," since the power of the
Commonwealth to make laws in regard to conciliation and arbitration is at present limited to disputes extending beyond the limits of
any one State; and secondly in regard to the matter of "preference
to unionists."

This question of preference to unionists is one which has been
an important feature of the Labour policy. Its justification is that
it encourages the formation of unions for the purpose of bringing
about industrial peace, as it is considered that the existence of men
outside such organizations makes the securing of peace by a Court
more difficult. Further, in the view of many, the man who pays for
the cost of conducting a case before the Court has a right to receive
the benefits of the award in preference to the individual who does
not pay for it. The history of the question is as follows:

In the first Commonwealth Conciliation and Arbitration Act
power was given to the Court to direct that preference of employ-

ment or service should be given to members of registered unions, but this power was hedged round with safeguards which exercised a restraining influence on any tyranny of union control. The first Labour Government came into power in April, 1904, but being defeated in a proposal to give unconditional preference to unionists, resigned in the following August.

In 1909 the second Labour Ministry introduced an amending bill by which it was proposed to tie the hands of the judge, by making it mandatory that preference should be given to unionists; it was pointed out, however, that such a provision would be unconstitutional, and a new clause was therefore inserted partly restoring the discretionary power to be exercised "whenever, in the opinion of the Court, it was necessary for the prevention or settlement of the industrial dispute, or for the maintenance of industrial peace, or for the welfare of society."[8] An interesting development of the Labour policy of preference to unionists occurred in September, 1911, when the Minister for Home Affairs[9] issued directions that preference should be given to unionists in connexion which Federal public works. This will apply, of course, to such works as the building of the Federal capital, the construction of the trans-continental railway, and public works for the purpose of military and naval defence.

In connexion with this question of preference to unionists the Trades Mark Act passed by the Coalition Ministry of 1905 and inspired by the Labour party is interesting. This Act did not merely co-ordinate and amend the various State Acts on the subject, but also sought to give preference to unionists by introducing the "union label" for all goods wholly manufactured by members of trade unions. If followed up, as the Labour Councils apparently intended it should be, by all members of trade unions refusing to deal at any shops except those which kept union-label goods, the effect of this provision would probably have been to lead employers into compelling their men to join unions, or accept dismissal. After a period of two years, during which the "union label" clause was a source of trouble and contention, a test case was brought to decide the constitutionality of the clause, which was declared invalid, not only because the label was not a trade mark in the proper sense, but because the clause was an attempt to regulate the internal trade of the States.

The subject-matter of plank number 7 (navigation laws) has now been before Parliament for nine years. It has been considered by a Royal Commission, carried to London and discussed by the Imperial Conference, and sifted through many processes in Australia. Last year it went through the Senate and in response to eager requests from the seamen's union it was taken to its second reading stage in the House of Representatives. The caucus has now agreed that it is time that it was passed and it will be taken early in the forthcoming session, of which it will form one of the principal features. Labour members hold that any such calamity as the "Titanic" disaster could not have happened in Australian waters under the provisions of the Bill. Various resolutions relating to the Bill were passed at the Hobart Conference, and it is understood that its provisions are to be made more stringent in view of the recent disaster in the Atlantic.

Restriction of public borrowing is one of the main features of the Federal Labour Government's financial policy, and in accordance with that principle all expenditure, including the cost of the Australian fleet unit amounting to upwards of £4,000,000, is being paid for out of revenue (with the exception of certain items which are being paid for out of an advance from the Notes Trust Fund referred to below).

The Australian Notes Act, 1910, providing for the issue of paper money by the Commonwealth, was claimed by the Labour party to be the first step towards the inauguration of a Commonwealth Bank. Mr Fisher had promised such an issue in March, 1909, and had told his hearers that it would add £100,000 to the revenue at the expense of the banks. Under the Act there is no limitation as to the amount which may be issued, but the Treasurer has to hold in gold not less than 25 per cent of the total issue. The Bank Note Tax Act was simply the corollary of the Notes Act; it levied a tax of 10 per cent on all bank notes in circulation after a stated time, and thus practically prohibited their issue.

The general principles of a scheme for the establishment of a National Bank were adopted at the Inter-state Labour Conference of 1908. No sound business reason appears to have been advanced for the establishment of such a bank, the Commonwealth being already amply provided with banking facilities, prudently managed; its advocates apparently content themselves with declaring that the project is a step in furtherance of the policy of the nationalization of all means of distribution, exchange and production of wealth. The Act providing for the establishment of the Bank was passed in December last, and a Governor has recently been appointed at a salary of £4,000 per annum.[10] The bank is to be incorporated as the Commonwealth Bank of Australia, and is to have the general powers of an incorporated bank, but it may not issue bank notes. The capital will be £1,000,000, raised by the issue of debentures, and the expenses of establishment will be provided out of the consolidated revenue fund, and subsequently repaid. The Governor is now engaged in organizing work. Arrangements are being made for officers of the Postmaster-General's Department to act as savings banks officials, and it is understood that operations will commence in Victoria at an early date. One of the objects of establishing the Commonwealth bank is stated to be to facilitate the transfer of the State debts by affording suitable administrative machinery for the consolidation of the stock; no definite policy in regard to this matter has, however, been formulated by the Labour party. In December last an Act was passed providing for the issue of Commonwealth inscribed stock in any case where authority to borrow is granted by any Act, and in the same month another Act was passed authorizing the advance from the Australian Notes Trust fund of a sum of nearly £2,500,000, to be applied towards the construction of the transcontinental railways and to other purposes.

In regard to the tenth plank (general insurance department) no declaration as to the policy to be pursued by the Federal Government has been disclosed. The plank relates to a general insurance department with non-political control, and though the need for such a department is by no means obvious, it is probable that the Labour party, if successful at the next general elections, will introduce a measure to provide for such a department. This plank does not refer in any way to what is known as social insurance, and a resolution favouring a system of compulsory and contributory insurance against sickness, accident, motherhood, and old age only found three supporters when put to the vote at the Hobart Conference.

In addition to the matters indicated in the platform, a number of resolutions dealing with other matters were passed by the Hobart Conference. The delegates declared against elective ministries, and a proposal for preferential voting at Federal elections was lost on the voices. Nationalization of inventions was negatived, but government rewards for inventions of public utilities were generally recommended. Various proposals for a Federal executive of the political labour leagues were lost; the organization was left as before the Conference, except that, with the object of avoiding some of the ridiculous proposals on the Conference Agenda Papers, it was directed that only such items as have been passed by State conferences, State executives, or the Federal Labour part are to be put before inter-State conferences. The Conference affirmed the principles of (*a*) international arbitration as opposed to war, and (*b*) universal decrease of armaments, and resolved that the abolition of the several State Upper Houses was desirable. Another resolution directs that the portfolios in the Federal ministry be re-allotted by exhaustive ballot after each general election. Should the party return to power next year, ministers must therefore resign and submit themselves for re-election at the hands of the caucus.

Some of the matters in regard to which resolutions were passed by the Conference are small enough to be embodied in amending legislation during the forthcoming session without submission to the public as issues of a general election. In addition to the Navigation Bill the Government will probably introduce measures dealing with electoral redistribution (consequent on the results of last year's census), banking law, Northern Territory constitution and public service, bankruptcy law, copyright, and amendment of the compulsory training provisions of the Defence Act, and of the Public Service and Land Tax Acts. The Prime Minister has also announced his intention to introduce a bill providing for a maternity allowance (probably of £5) to the mothers of all children born and registered in Australia. Should negotiations with Canada, New Zealand, and South Africa produce the desired results, it is probable that bills providing for reciprocal trade with these Dominions will be introduced. It is stated that the bills for the proposed laws for the alteration of the constitution will be held back till late in the session.

The realization of the Hobart platform will mainly depend upon the results of the next general elections and upon the fate of the proposals which are to be submitted by the referendum at the same time. What these results will be it appears at the present stage impossible to forecast. One thing is certain, that the opponents of the Labour party have not a set of proposals so well defined, so clear cut, as those which appear in the Labour platform given above. It seems impossible to bring the non-Labour bodies into line one with another. Those who attempt to do so make the mistake of ignoring the fact that the lines of party cleavage are not clearly drawn only between the Labour and non-Labour parties. Though nominally only two, there are in reality three parties, each with distinct aims and each animated by a different spirit. These three are Labour, Liberal, and Conservative. The failure of the two coalitions between Liberal and Conservative, which have been formed since federation, and the inefficacy of the attempts of party leaders to arrange the differences between the non-Labour leagues at present are due to the underlying diveristy of aim and spirit in the two non-Labour parties. The great need of the present moment, from the anti-labour standpoint, is a constructive Liberal policy, similiar to that with which the first Liberal Ministry faced the first Federal Parliament.

The full significance of the Labour policy can hardly be gathered from its formal statement on the party's fighting platform, which is intended to indicate the practical proposals for which public opinion is considered ripe. The objective and the general platform must be studied to get an adequate idea of the propagandist side of the movement. The first part of the federal objective declares for: The cultivation of an Australian sentiment, based upon the maintenance of racial purity, and the development in Australia of an enlightened and self-reliant community. The second runs: The securing of the full results of their industry to all producers by the collective ownership of monopolies, and the extension of the industrial and economic functions of the State and Municipality. It cannot be doubted that in general the platform has won the party popular support. Containing definite proposals, it counts more with the masses than the doctrinaire proposals and hazy policies of the older parties, and though there is little social idealism among the rank and file of the party, the working men generally are Socialistic in their beliefs, most of them as yet unconsciously so. The rank and file of the party hardly look beyond their own day and generation— nor do they theorize about the functions of government. They support the party in order to obtain more favourable wages and hours of labour and other economic reforms. On the other hand, Labour leaders are fully conscious of their Socialistic purpose. They are perfectly candid in stating it to their supporters, but as they are practical politicians, and have experienced the responsibility of office, they are so much the more conservative in their policy put forward in their "fighting platform." They are endeavouring, gradually and without unduly disturbing existing conditions, to abolish private employment, and thereby to solve the economic problem of securing to the worker a fair share of the profits of his industry. Unfortunately there are not sufficient data available to determine to what extent, if any, the worker has benefited by the efforts of the Labour party. Few of those prominent in the Labour movement are communists; most of them are sceptical as to the possibility of establishing economic equality, and none of them look forward to making a grand division of the country's wealth among all citizens. But they have faith that the Government can in some way eventually succeed in securing to every man a larger share of the results of his labour. It is towards this end that the policy of the Labour party is directed.

c. May 1912

PART TWO
1915–1919

AUSTRALIA AND THE WAR

March 1915, vol. 5, pp. 447–57

IT is safe to say that the feeling of national consciousness has never been so profoundly stirred in Australia as it has during the last four months. Nations, like men, have often to face a great crisis before the secret of their being becomes revealed to the world and to themselves, and it was not until the outbreak of the war, which has jeopardized the very existence of the British Empire, that Australia began fully to realize that Empire's meaning, and the high and responsible part she has been called to play in it. During the last few years her sense of Imperial responsibility has been deepened and quickened by two things—the creation of her national Navy, and the *imperium in imperio* established by her possessions in the Pacific. It is certain that even apart from these factors her offers of assistance in the present crisis would have been wholehearted and substantial, but it is also certain that the possession of ships and colonies of her own has kindled her imagination and enthusiasm with unprecedented vividness and has enabled her to appreciate as never before the larger issues of Empire. Moreover, she is coming to realize that the present war is totally unlike anything that has ever yet befallen England or herself, and that on its issue depends her very existence as a nation. The instinct of self-interest and self-preservation may therefore be taken as a strong factor in her present attitude: that it is the sole, or even the main, factor will be credited by no one who is acquainted with her national temper and has reflected on the fact that thrice already—in Egypt, in China and in Africa—her soldiers have fought on behalf of the Empire in situations where her own safety was in no sense imperilled.[1]

From the beginning of the negotiations preceding the war there has never been a moment's doubt or hesitation in any responsible quarter in Australia as to the necessity of England's taking part in it, nor as to the essential righteousness of her cause. Indeed, during the momentous days when the decision still hung in the balance, Australia, with a brief and misleading account of the negotiations before her, showed considerable perplexity and impatience at the hesitation, as it then seemed to her, of England to fulfil her obligations to France. This keen solicitude for British honour was intensified

39

by the indignation consequent on Germany's invasion of Belgium, and despite the extreme gravity of the issue, the declaration of war was hailed with feelings of positive relief. The British Association was at this period visiting Melbourne, and some of its members caused Australia considerable amusement by their naive expressions of surprise at her "loyalty" and "keenness."[2] If anyone had come here expecting the opposite of these thing , he must have been considerably surprised. At first, indeed, Australia, anxious though she had been for the assertion of the Empire's honour, was dazed by what had happened and by the difficulty of focussing her social, political, and economic outlook to meet the new conditions. One in every five hundred of her own population were born in Germany, and many of these have taken an important part in her commercial, agricultural and artistic life.[3] It was impossible for her to adjust her attitude immediately towards this element in her midst, although disclosures in England, Canada, and elsewhere, showed the great danger of espionage and treachery which might be expected in certain alien quarters. It was impossible, too, that Australia, unvisited as she has hitherto been by war, should at once realize the immensity and full gravity of the issue. Yet her reaction from the shock was swift and practical.

The declaration of war reached her in the interval between the double dissolution of the Federal Parliament and the ensuing General Election. Nearly the whole of the Liberal Ministry were canvassing in their constituencies; yet within two days of the outbreak the Prime Minister, Mr Joseph Cook,[4] had offered a first contingent of 20,000 men to the Imperial Government and this had been gratefully accepted. The Australian Navy was at once put at the disposal of the Admiralty. Mr Fisher, Leader of the Labour Opposition, assured Mr Cook of his party's hearty co-operation in everything relating to the war. Enemy shipping in Australian ports was promptly seized. At the suggestion of the Federal Ministry, the State Ministries took steps to fix the price of foodstuffs, and to prevent the hoarding of wheat and other commodities by persons interested in making capital out of the country's necessity. The Federal Government itself prohibited the export of meat and wheat to any country other than the United Kingdom, and conferred with the Banks concerning the best means of relieving the financial situation. The general result of these precautions has been that never since the war began has there been any symptom of financial panic throughout Australia. One or two industries, notably the mining industry, have suffered severely, and there has been a definite increase of unemployment. But apart from these facts, and as far as the vast majority of Australians are concerned, the conditions and cost of living have been practically normal since the beginning of the war.

After the Federal General Election the conduct of affairs devolved upon the victorious Labour Party.[5] It is worth noting that until a few years ago this Party had been strongly anti-militarist throughout Australia. The earnest efforts of a few of its members, notably the present Attorney-General and the Minister of Defence, Messrs Hughes[6] and Pearce,[7] succeeded in awakening it to the vital importance of a strong defence policy, which, indeed, was easily perceived to be of the first importance if the Party intended to adhere to its cherished doctrine of a "White Australia." The result was its adoption of compulsory training and the elaborate and expensive defence scheme recommended by Lord Kitchener.[8] The latest stage in the Party's evolution has been reached in the preparation and dispatch of what is by far the largest expeditionary force ever sent forth from Australia. This course was greatly facilitated by the War Loan of £18,000,000 requested by the Federal Authorities from the Imperial Government and promptly granted by them. The fact that Australia has undertaken the responsibility and expense of this obligation is a further token of her anxiety to play her part worthily in this supreme crisis, while she is keenly grateful to England for having supplied her with the means of doing this without delay. The Government at once appropriated the sum of £9,800,000 towards covering all expenses connected with the expeditionary force up till June 30 next. Two months ago, after several weeks' preliminary training, the first contingent of 22,373 men was dispatched, and on December 3 the Prime Minister announced that these had been disembarked in Egypt to assist in the defence of that country and to complete their training there. He added that, when this was finished they would go direct to Europe, to fight beside the other British troops. This course was adopted by the special recommendation of Lord Kitchener, who recognized the danger of housing Australian troops in tents throughout the European winter after a long voyage through the tropics and subtropics.

Besides the above force, 16,500 men of all ranks are now in training for service abroad; 13,000 of these will leave Australia shortly, and an additional 3,000 will be dispatched at the end of every succeeding two months. There are also 6,800 men in training for home defence. In answer to a question put to him in the House during November, Mr Fisher replied that as many additional troops would be forwarded as were needed. He had previously declared that Australia would support the cause of the Empire in this war to the last man and the last shilling. At present every man who has offered for enlistment and been found physically fit is being trained and equipped.

The Liberal Opposition are at present attempting to ensure reinforcements being sent on a very much larger scale, and Sir William Irvine[9] recently indicated that 100,000 men was the least number which Australia might reasonably be expected to supply considering the extreme gravity of the issue. Public feeling in the Commonwealth is quite in favour of the increase, and there is no need to think that the Government is blind to the fact that before the war is over Australia may have to make a very much larger contribution than she has made hitherto.

As far as the sea is concerned, the operations in the Pacific since the beginning of the war have triumphantly vindicated the existence of the newly created Australian Navy. Experience had shown that the people of Australia had no heart for a hired fleet, even if the lessor were England. Her own contribution of £200,000 per annum—one which she firmly declined to increase—was indeed no adequate contribution to Imperial Naval Defence; but as soon as Rear-Admiral Henderson's scheme for the formation of an Australian Navy[10] had been adopted, it became clear that her former reluctance had been due neither to parsimony nor to any selfish or provincial regard for her own safety. The policy of Athens with regard to the Confederacy of Delos had been reversed, and with the happiest results. At a vastly increased cost, Australia set about equipping and manning the new ships. During the year 1913–14 her defence estimates amounted to £4,752,735, which represents a larger proportional expenditure than Germany's estimate of £70,785,000 in the preceding year. Of this sum over £2,000,000 was allotted to the Navy, so that it is an understatement of fact to say that Australia's naval expenditure has increased tenfold under the new regime. The result is that the Royal Australian Navy to-day possesses the most powerful war vessels of any belligerent in the Pacific, save Japan. The fleet consists of the battle-cruiser "Australia" (19,200 tons), and the light cruisers "Sydney," "Melbourne," "Encounter," "Pioneer," together with fifteen destroyers, gun boats and submarines.

It had, moreover, been provided that in case of war the new fleet should be immediately placed under the undivided control of the Admiralty, and, as has been above indicated, this was done almost automatically, as soon as war broke out. Directly this happened, the Navy left Sydney and has since then been co-operating in the Pacific with the British China Squadron, the French and Japanese fleets and the New Zealand forces. It covered the expedition sent by New Zealand to Samoa and thus made possible the capture of that possession. Throughout the war it has guarded the coast of Australasia from attack by the enemy's cruisers. It has harried Germany's battleships and destroyed her wireless stations. But for its presence it is practically certain that Sydney would have been shelled by the "Scharnhorst" and the "Gneisenau," and it is probable that these ships, with their comrade vessels, would have remained in the Pacific instead of having been driven to their destruction in the South Atlantic. Australia's Navy has indeed done considerably more than protect her own coasts; its work has had definite Imperial value. It has kept open all the trade routes to Colombo, Singapore, the Pacific Islands and America; and, owing to its presence, not a single British merchant vessel has hitherto been captured by the enemy in Australian waters.

Perhaps the most definite achievement of the Australian Navy and the expeditionary force accompanying it has been the capture of German New Guinea. On September 12 the Australian Naval Reserve took possession of the wireless station at Herbertshöhe after eighteen hours' bush fighting extending over six miles. Rabaul, the seat of government in German New Guinea, was subsequently occupied and a base was established at Simpsonshafen. The casualty lists unfortunately included the deaths of Commander Elwell, Capt. Pockley, of the Army Medical Corps, and four seamen.[11] Still more serious was the loss of Submarine AE1, with her complement of thirty-five officers and men. This vessel was last seen on September 14, and no trace of her has hitherto been found. The Australian Navy has followed up its success in New Guinea by the capture of Kaiser Wilhelmsland (September 24) and other German possessions in the Pacific.

A more sensational and hardly less important achievement was the sinking of the "Emden" by H.M.A.S. "Sydney." On November 9 the Navy Office at Melbourne received a telegram from Cocos Island to the effect that a German warship, immediately identified as the raiding cruiser, had arrived off the island, and was landing men in boats. Immediately an urgent coded wireless message was sent to the "Sydney," which was believed to be in the vicinity. A message urgently requesting help was also sent from the island immediately before the wireless station there was broken up by the German landing party. Soon afterwards the "Sydney" hove in sight. The "Emden" put out to sea, deserting her boats, and attempted to make good her escape. The "Sydney," however, engaged her, and after an hour's accurate and deadly fire set her in flames and reduced her to a sinking condition, in which state her captain ran her aground on the north of Keeling Island. The "Sydney's" casualties list numbered only three killed and fifteen wounded.

Besides equipping the armaments just mentioned, Australia has also taken prompt and drastic steps to prevent the possibility of danger within her own borders. Soon after the present session began, the Government passed legislation enabling them to deal summarily with individuals who might be found guilty of espionage or sedition, and to enter any house or office in search for incriminating documents. Such results as have hitherto been published, though they have not been particularly sensational, have been quite sufficient to show that Australia has not escaped Germany's far-flung net of espionage, and that she has had good cause for fearing the stranger within her gates.[12] Her internal activities have not, however, been confined to the seductive practice of spy hunting. One of the first acts of the present Ministry was to vote £100,000 as a free gift to Belgium, while during the four months of the war over £1,000,000 has been privately contributed to various patriotic funds. This is all the more creditable when it is remembered that owing to the widespread prevalence of drought Australia is at present suffering to an unwonted extent from financial depression.

The war itself has directly and gravely affected Australia's greatest mining centre. The output of the Broken Hill Mines consists of lead, silver and zinc; and of these the last is in the main shipped for treatment to Belgium, the North of France and Germany. Operations in these countries are necessarily suspended by the war, and the commencement of operations elsewhere is a matter involving time, and requiring the provision of a very large amount of capital. This capital would only be forthcoming upon an assurance that permanent supplies of metal could be relied on, and a difficulty at once arises from the fact that mines, at the outbreak of war, were bound by agreements which in most cases have several years to run. What is the effect of war on the legal obligations of these agreements is a matter on which no lawyer speaks with confidence, and litigation insituted in England does not seem to have led, or to be likely to lead, to an authoritative decision. Meantime, the cessation of operations in some of the mines, and the restriction of output in others, is affecting many thousands of people, and may produce a serious industrial situation on the Barrier. The Government is tempted to cut the knot by legislation definitely releasing the contractors from their obligations after the war, so as to open the road for new smelting arrangements.

On the other hand, the agreement appears to be part of an international arrangement respecting output and prices, which is stated by its defenders to be vital to the prosperity of the Australian industry. The case is one more of the many illustrations furnished by this war that the "private relations" of business in modern conditions readily assume a national importance, which makes Government indifference and inaction impossible.[13]

As far as her national sentiment is concerned, it was not till some weeks after the declaration of war that Australia began to understand the crucial significance of the issue, and it may safely be said that she has not fully understood it even yet. Remote as she is from the main scene of action, she at first found it somewhat difficult to realize that, being a belligerent, she was liable to all the responsibilities and rigours of war. Moreover, like the rest of the Empire, she was ignorant of the full measure of Germany's unscrupulous ambition, and did not then believe, as she believes to-day, that that country deliberately manufactured the present war as a preliminary to the enslavement of Europe and the downfall of the British Empire. Her eyes were startlingly opened to this aspect of the matter by the British White Book, and the certainty therein supplied that Germany could by a word have prevented hostilities at any stage of the negotiations.[14] During the last few months all thinking Australians have been educating themselves in the causes of the war by reference to the writings of Cramb, Bülow, Bernhardi, Ussher, Sarolea and others.[15] They have realized that for a generation Germany has been industriously schooled by her professors and dragooned by her militarists into the belief that her national destiny demands that she should become the suzerain of a vanquished Europe and the regent of a vast colonial empire which can only be obtained by England's downfall. They have further realized that by a deliberate application, or misapplication, of the Nietzschean "ethic" she has deliberately "trans-valued all values" in pursuit of this end, and has counted no means common or unclean which would lead to her own maniacal aggrandizement. And the certainty of these facts has been kindled into passionate indignation by the wanton invasion of Belgium, the destruction of Louvain and Rheims Cathedral and the infliction, the inevitable result of the official policy of "frightfulness," of the most revolting atrocities upon innocent women and children.

Moreover, since the beginning of the war, Australia has realized, as never before, the material and spiritual significance of the British Empire and the part she has been called to play therein. She has understood the essential unity of thought and feeling and interest which underlies its superficial diversity. She has contrasted that service which is perfect freedom with the condition of enslavement represented by the blood-tax in Alsace-Lorraine and the Colonization Commission in Posen.[16] Herself in constitution and legislation perhaps the most socialistic community in existence, she has further contrasted the freedom reposed in her of working out her own

45

destiny after her own will, with the implacable hostility and contempt displayed towards organized labour in such a semi-official German publication as Bülow's *Imperial Germany*. These contrasts and the lessons they supply have forced themselves on all thinking men and women in Australia. It would be too much to say that they have yet come fully home to the great masses of the country. In certain quarters, moreover, there has been a not unamiable exultation in the help which Australia has been able to render to England, together with an imperfect recognition of the far greater help which is being at present rendered by England to Australia. Young, light-hearted and unscathed as she is by war, Australia as a whole has hardly even yet been able to grasp the tremendousness of the issue, to feel that it is one of life and death for herself no less than for England; and that in Flanders and the North Sea is being decided the fate of her tiniest back-block township as surely as that of London. She has still to learn, or still to feel acutely, that she has even more at stake in the present war than has England, since, should the unlikely happen and Germany be victorious, it is inconceivable that England should ever become a German province, while it is well-nigh certain that sooner or later Australia would undergo that unspeakable fate. It must be admitted that with very rare exceptions neither her Press nor her public men have given her much light or leading in this regard, nor have striven to create that intensity of feeling without which nations cannot be expected to make the last sacrifice. But whatever Australia's deficiencies may be in this respect they cannot for one moment be attributed to any lack of loyalty or of keenness to play her part worthily, to the best of her understanding, in the defence of the Empire. Once her imagination has been fully kindled regarding the immensity of the peril she will certainly make even greater contributions and sacrifices than she has made to-day. Her will is sound and ready: and it would take but little to make her learn and practise the great lesson preached by Meredith to France after 1870:

> "The lesson writ in red since first Time ran,
> A hunter hunting down the beast in man,
> That till the chasing out of its last vice
> The flesh was fashioned but for sacrifice."[17]

December 1914

THE DARDANELLES

March 1916, vol. 6, pp. 333–7

DESPITE the serious and unexpected developments of the last few months, there has never been the slightest failure of Australia's confidence in the Empire's ultimate success. Her chief danger, indeed, has been a certain tendency to take victory for granted, and to assume that the Russian retreats have been triumphs in disguise, that Germany's recent Balkan *coup* is her dying convulsion, and that she is bound to succumb within the next few months before that convenient, if mythical, commander, Famine. This pernicious variety of "optimism," which stifles effort by disguising the need for it, has been recklessly fomented by a certain section of Australia's Press and public men, and, as might be expected, it exercised for some time a very prejudicial effect upon recruiting. But it has been steadily combated by those who realise the dangers and difficulties which the Empire has yet to face, and a more earnest and sensible tone has latterly prevailed. This has been increased by the warnings recently issued to Australia by men like her returned leader, Brigadier-General McCay,[18] and, above all things, by the accession to power of her new Prime Minister, Mr. W. M. Hughes. There is no man in the Empire who takes the war in more deadly earnest, and, possessing as he does all the force and fire of leadership, he is doing his best to communicate his own spirit to a country which is quite ready to receive it.

Australia's determination to do her utmost in the war has also been sustained and hardened by the unflagging heroism of her troops upon Gallipoli. The habitable portion of the little corner of earth originally occupied by her at Anzac was some 300 acres—roughly the size of an Australian "selection," or small grant of land made to an enterprising settler. None of the settlers at Anzac, is, or can be, more than 1,200 yards from the enemy's trenches; and the whole Australian Army, as long as it remains on land, must be continuously under the enemy's fire—a fire which has cast 1,400 shells upon Anzac within the hour. There is no nightly or weekly conveyance of the weary troops by motor-bus into a zone of safety and comfort and pleasure. The only "safety" enjoyed by the Australian is his shrapnel-spattered dugout, his only diversion from shooting or

47

bayoneting the Turk lies in shooting for sport at the dummy periscopes which the Turk sometimes exposes derisively in his trenches. *Plus ça change, plus c'est la même chose.* The men who took what Sir Ian Hamilton[19] calls the "almost impregnable" trenches of Lonesome Pine[20] had been sixteen continuous weeks in the trenches and were weary unto death. This little corner on which her troops are now entrenched by tens and tens of thousands Australia regards as her own earth. It is this which, as one of her own leaders recently remarked, has given her tradition.

It was, it is true, in the Southern zone of the Peninsula, at Cape Helles, that one of her finest exploits took place, the great charge in which her Second Brigade (Victorians), led by the Brigadier-General mentioned above, charged through the ranks of the Composite Brigade, and, in spite of the heaviest losses from shrapnel, machine-gun, and rifle fire, dug themselves in four hundred yards ahead of the other Allied forces. But it is in the North, at Anzac, that the battles were fought of which Australia is most proud— Quinn's Post and Courtney's Post, at whose indomitable defenders Liman von Sanders hurled his 30,000 troops in vain; those trenches whence, on the night of June 29—30, the musketry and machine-guns of the 7th and 8th Light Horse crumpled up the hordes commanded by Enver, and instructed to drive the Australians into the sea;[21] Lonesome Pine, where the First Brigade charged across the death-swept heath and its survivors wriggled down feet foremost to victory through the manholes in the Turkish trenches; the bristling ridge attacked by the First and Third Light Horse Brigades when the Australians from August 7 to 10 fought what has been described as "the greatest battle ever waged on Turkish soil" to protect the British landing at Suvla; and the summit of Knoll 60, heroically stormed on August 21 by the 4th Australian Brigade in company with the British, Indians and New Zealanders. It is scenes such as these which have made Anzac very precious to Australians at the front and at home. The spirit in which it has been held by the Australian Army has been exactly indicated in a despatch of Sir Ian Hamilton's:—

"I must begin by explaining that their rôle at this stage of operations was —first, to keep open a door leading to the vitals of the Turkish position; secondly, to hold up as large a body as possible of the enemy in front of them, so as to lessen the strain at Cape Helles. Anzac, in fact, was cast to play second fiddle to Cape Helles, a part out of harmony with the daredevil spirit animating those warriors from the South; and so it has come about that, as your Lordship will now see, the defensive of the Australians and New Zealanders has always tended to take on the character of an attack."[22]

Not only has the holding of Anzac given Australia tradition, but it has given her a far fuller feeling of Imperial fellowship than she has ever yet possessed. There is no truer or stronger comradeship than comradeship in battle, and it is this which Australia has during the last few months been forming with the British, Indian, and New Zealand troops. The great majority of these she now respects as fighters and as men, and a particularly warm alliance has sprung up between her soldiers and the intrepid Gurkhas of Lieutenant-Colonel Bruce's command.[23] This has its picturesque aspect, and may be paralleled by Kipling's famous description of the brotherhood between Gurkha and Highlander. But the bond between the different fighters of our Empire is more than picturesque; it implies a certain revelation:—

> The day's lay-out—the mornin' sun
>   Beneath your 'at-brim as you sight,
> The dinner 'ush from noon till one
>   An' the full roar that lasts till night:
>   .   .   .   .   .
>
> Also Time runnin' into years
>   A thousand places left be'ind,
> And Men from both two 'emispheres
>   Discussin' things of every kind;
> So much more near than I 'ad known,
>   So much more great than I 'ad guessed,
> An' me like all the rest, alone
>   But reachin' out to all the rest.[24]

This revelation may be trusted to bear good fruit in the Imperial readjustment which is certain to follow the present war.

Such being the feelings of Australia with regard to the position at Gallipoli, her interest in the recent British discussion of the Dardanelles Campaign has been, as may be readily imagined, absorbing and intense. She now realises that at the beginning the British authorities were uncertain and divided as to the desirability of attempting the position, and that there is at present an equally marked division regarding the desirability or possibility of permanently holding it. She knows that blunders have been made on a large scale and in detail and that in more than one case keener action on the part of those supporting her attack would have secured, instead of losing, the fruits of victory she had already won. She knows that the main attack has so far failed of its objective, and she understands the risks and difficulties attending that objective's ultimate realisation. Yet in no responsible quarter of Australia has there been the slightest sign of bitterness against those responsible for the operations, or of a feeling that she herself has been treated in any way unworthily. Absorbed as she is both by interest and sentiment in the campaign's success, on hearing that this is far from being assured, she has displayed none of the hysteria which has characterised certain British newspapers and politicians, but has

49

accepted the situation with coolness and confidence, and with the knowledge that she for her part has done her best, and will continue to do it, whatever may happen at Gallipoli or elsewhere. She knows, moreover, that whether Constantinople be reached or not, the efforts of the Allied forces and herself have kept a great Turkish army from doing harm elsewhere, and possibly from conducting a successful invasion of Egypt. She knows, too, that what has been done in Gallipoli has maintained British prestige through all the East. In peace time, during drought and bush-fire and flood, she has too often faced and beaten difficulty and disaster to believe them invincible now that they come on her beneath the form of war. And for all these causes, if she be allowed, she will hold on till victory or death to the little plot of earth which she has purchased with her life-blood.

NOTE.—On the eve of the despatch of the above section to England the news of the evacuation of Anzac and Suvla Bay has reached Australia. As has been indicated above, she had been keenly anxious to hold Anzac if this were in any way possible; but this anxiety was mainly due to her pride in the good work she had done there and to the hope that she would have an opportunity of continuing this were the position considered tenable by the British authorities. Her natural disappointment is qualified by the feeling that her troops have been removed, apparently with small loss, from one of the most dangerous and unhealthy positions in the war—a position, moreover, which, according to her previous belief, could not be evacuated without the most terrible sacrifice of life. It cannot be too strongly emphasised that the resolute temper of Australia has not been in the least degree affected by the news of the evacuation. She has accepted it with coolness, and in no quarter worth a moment's consideration has there been the slightest tendency to blame the Imperial Government for what has happened. Australia, now as previously, is prepared to do her best in whatever area of the war she may be asked to fight.

December 1915

THE CONSCRIPTION REFERENDUM

March 1917, vol. 7, pp. 378–94

ON October 28, under the provisions of the Military Service Referendum Act, passed for the occasion, the people of Australia, men and women enrolled as electors, voted on the following question: "Are you in favour of the Government having in this grave emergency the same compuslory powers over citizens in regard to requiring their military service for the term of this war, outside the Commonwealth, as it now has in regard to military service within the Commonwealth?"

It will be observed that the Referendum was in form merely an appeal for an expression of opinion: the vote had no legal effect—the affirmative would have conferred no new power on the Government, the negative withdrew no power that the Government possessed. In this sense the Referendum was extra-constitutional.

The military problem which the Referendum was intended to solve was discussed in the last Australian contribution to THE ROUND TABLE.[25] The Australian Government, with the enthusiastic approval of the people, had sent certain units to the front, and it was necessary to keep these up to strength by adequate reinforcements. The Government, on the authority of the Army Council in Great Britain, stated that reinforcements at a certain rate were required to discharge the obligation. Voluntary enlistment supplied less than half the number; compulsion was proposed as the only alternative. The Senate was known to be unfavourable to conscription, though how far it would be prepared to go in its opposition was not known. There are those who think that an immediate announcement of the policy of compulsion on Mr. Hughes' return from England,[26] and the submission of a Bill, or the promulgation of a regulation embodying compulsion, would have found the Senate hostile indeed, but unready to take up the challenge. In such circumstances it is probable that the country would have acquiesced in the decision. But whatever Mr. Hughes' own policy may have been, such a course would have been too bold for a Ministry bound by Caucus traditions, even if its members had been in favour of conscription. Later events showed that in the Cabinet itself the policy of compulsion was that of a minority. In these circumstances a Referendum was the compromise between a surrender of the policy of compulsion and an immediate break-up of the Cabinet and the Labour Party.

Those in favour of compulsion relied on the sense of justice which demands an equality of sacrifice. The appeal to Australians not "to scab on their mates" in the trenches was intended to touch the trade unionist in a sensitive spot, and it was confidently hoped that the soldiers at the front on their part, who were undergoing the hardships there, would take very good care that others who were equally competent to serve should not evade their obligations.[27]

The case for the opposition revealed various standpoints in the course of the campaign. Avowed hostility to the British cause found no responsible exponents on the platform. It was not a part of the case of the anti-conscriptionists that Australia should not have entered into the war, and many of them were emphatic in declaring that they did not desire that she should "cut out." The opinion that "Australia has done her share" was probably rather the retort to reproaches than either the spontaneous or considered expression of a feeling or a conviction. But there can be no doubt that with many the assertion that "Voluntaryism will do what is necessary" stood for nothing better than a willingness that other people should make the effort if they cared to, and in the mouths of men who refused to take part in the voluntary recruiting movement lost even the appearance of good faith. The stock arguments of the Labour leaders were that compulsion was undemocratic and that it would be suicidal to bring into Australia the evils of militarism, which to them meant the subordination of industry and of industrial struggles to military rule. The opposition, however, was not a peace movement. Even the Pacifists, who were earnest workers against the Referendum, approached the question more from the standpoint of expediency than of principle.

A sentimental appeal was made to those who had relatives in the trenches not to put other people through the same ordeal against their will. Those who were not liable for service, but voted "Yes," were painted as selfish monsters. These appeals had an immense effect. Thousands of women voted "No" because of their acute sense of the horrors to which they were asked to commit the male folk of their country. The economic effects of conscription were dwelt upon by opponents from the point of view of the worker—the fear of a "conscription of industry" and the supposed design to supplant white by coloured labour. Little was said of the financial losses of the farmer or the employer through a shortage of labour, or of the heavy burden which universal service would throw on the taxpayer, but these exercised a big silent influence. The influence

of organisations was immense. The superior organisation of the
Labour Party and the Unions told very heavily. The ranks of Labour
and the offices of the Union contain so large an Irish Catholic
element that it is difficult to separate the Catholic and Labour
elements and to assign to each its share in the opposition. In
Queensland, at any rate, "Irish wrongs" played a prominent part
in the campaign, and the violence of a member of the Ministry was
such that the Governor was compelled to take notice of it. The
syndicalist association, "The Industrial Workers of the World,"
contributed to the campaign threats of incendiary violence, which
lacked neither the will nor the means for their execution; for a
series of fires in Sydney was traced to a gang of leaders of the
organisation, since convicted of treason-felony.[28] A peculiarly
degrading feature of the campaign was the number of grotesque
canards that were circulated mainly about Mr. Hughes. The chief
of these was that his object in striving for conscription was to fill the
places of the men sent away by cheap imported labour. It is hard
to believe that anyone credited this, but it had great weight. Unfortunately, Mr. Hughes made a false step in the campaign, which,
on the principle *ex uno disce omnes*, was readily used to demonstrate
his slimness and to discredit his policy, his facts, and his arguments.
He had a regulation passed by the Executive Council by which
every man who came to vote was to be questioned as to his liability
to military service, and whether he had reported under the Proclamation calling eligible men into camp. If the answers were
negative, his vote was to be set aside for inquiry. On hearing this,
three Ministers who had been present at a previous meeting of the
Executive Council and negatived the regulations resigned.[29] The
Regulation was withdrawn and the questions were not put, but
there is no doubt that the attempt by executive act to use the ballot
for penal purposes was a culpable error not to be excused even by
the excitement of battle.

The chief point in the discussion, however, and the one on which
the Referendum was perhaps determined, was the question whether
the men the Government proposed to send were necessary. Such a
question, of course, implies an ignorance of the nature of war and
its challenge to the civil life of a community. In war the service of
every man is necessary to his state, all resources should be at the
disposal of the state, and every private interest which conflicts with
the public interest should be sacrificed. Only by such methods can
the danger to the state be rapidly removed and the normal social
life restored. War with a limited liability is nearly always more
costly than a war in which every resource is mobilised and thrown
into the scale. Such an argument has, however, never appealed

to any English-speaking community. Most of England's wars have been wars with a limited liability. A similar hesitation to throw the whole of the resources of the country into the war was shown in the United States during the Wars of Independence and Secession.

The argument which was laid before the country was somewhat as follows: Australia's contribution can have little or no actual effect on the conclusion of the war. Germany is confronted with innumerable enemies far exceeding her in numerical strength and her downfall is certain. The Allies have great resources of men still to be called on; within the Empire there are vast populations which have contributed as yet but an insignificant proportion to the armies. One is ashamed to have to record the use of this last argument. The interest of Australia in the result of the war is so great that her moral obligation to supply troops is at least as strong as that of Russia and France. Her people, as the result of the occupation of a vast, fertile continent, are infinitely better off than these people. Yet the people of Russia and France were to be asked to fight that Australians may retain their superior standard of comfort. That there should be Australians again who, while refusing to allow coloured races to enter Australia, should yet be willing to pass on to the people of India the burden of fighting for Australia was the most humiliating revelation of the campaign. For the honour of Australians it should in fairness be explained that these arguments were not widely accepted, and were rather in the nature of excuses on the part of those who felt the obligation to go but were determined not to honour it. The succeeding stages of the argument were more important.

The anti-conscriptionists suggested that the 32,500 reinforcements which were asked for as the quota for the month of October were not required as such but were intended to form new units. They stated that Australia had 120,000 men in camp to reinforce five divisions, which was ample; and that a further 40,000 men could be expected by voluntary enlistment during the year. Under the circumstances the request for 214,000 men for one year was, they said, excessive, and based on a rate of reinforcement contradicted by all military experience. It cannot be said that this argument was effectively met. It was stated by the Government that if the casualties did not render necessary the reinforcements proposed they would not be sent, and at a late stage in the campaign Mr. Hughes stated that it was quite probable that only 100,000 men would be necessary within the year. But, as a matter of fact, the numbers actually asked for by the Government were clearly needed if Australia was to keep five divisions at the front, which, without any request from England, she had undertaken to do. The anti-conscriptionists seemed to have lost sight of certain vital considerations. In the first place, it was to be expected that the casualties of the Australian troops in France would exceed those they had suffered in Gallipoli. Secondly, the distance of Australia from the front makes it necessary for her to have in training at any time a large number of men. It is nine months between enlistment and the trenches; two months of this time being spent on the transports. It may be said, in fact, that to maintain the five Australian divisions and reinforce them at a rate equal to what experience shows to be their losses, we require to have in camp at any time reinforcements for nine months—that is, 148,500 men. And in putting forward their far lower estimates it is obvious that the anti-conscriptionists failed to appreciate what the effects are of the length of time it takes to train a recruit obtained in distant Australia into a soldier fit for the conditions on the Western Front and of the heavy losses imposed by the conditions existing there.

In the absence of a better explanation of the figures than was given at the hustings, it would have been better if the case had been put on the broad ground that every man was required, and that Australia's share should be at least equivalent to that of Great Britain. One of the statements that influenced the decision was palpably false, namely, that Australia had a larger proportion of men in the firing line than Great Britain. This estimate was obtained by comparing the total of the troops enlisted in Australia with a figure obtained from some newspaper that Great Britain had so many men facing the Germans, ignoring, of course, the British reserves and the men in depôts and elsewhere. The way in which the case for conscription was put was disastrous; for it enabled an answer to be made on the figures, and the numbers asked for were so huge that the married men all knew that they would be required in a very short time. In the result the fundamental fact was obscured, namely, that at the present rate of recruiting we shall not be able to replace anything like the number of casualties.

When the Referendum Bill was introduced, the machinery for calling up the men was at once put into operation under the Defence Act, which enables the Government to call up men for defence, though it does not permit of their being sent outside Australia. This was necessary to keep the supply of men continuous, but seems to have been a tactical error. The whole of the unmarried men between 18 and 35 had to register at once, and go into camp if medically fit. This gave everybody affected a practical example of the difficulties and hardships they would have to undergo under the system, and it did not leave them time to get accustomed to the new life before they gave their vote. It was thought that the process of exemption would reduce the number of persons actually affected, and so reduce the selfish vote. But the exemption Courts were notoriously capricious and the effect was the reverse.[30] In fact, when they were called upon to vote, a very large proportion of the electors of Australia found that the measure affected more or less adversely their immediate personal interests, and they were placed in the position of having to decide between these very obvious interests and the less tangible, though just as real, national interests. This fact illustrates very aptly the difficult position in which citizens who have to decide such a question are placed. The Referendum may be a good way of settling important public questions, where what is wanted is an expression of people's views as to their interests. The case is different, however, where individual interests may plainly come into conflict with national interests. It has never been suggested, for instance, that questions as to taxation could be settled satisfactorily by Referendum. The same objection applies where people are asked to support a constructive policy which requires sustained effort and varying kinds and degrees of sacrifice from different individuals. What is required in such a case is a knowledge of facts, a breadth of outlook, a capacity to separate oneself from personal feeling and interest, and a sense of responsibility for consequences which are not to be found in the average man and woman. Individual opinion is of little value unless it is expressed with full responsibility for the consequences. There can be no collective assumption of responsibility in the process of the ballot box. Responsibility can only be effectively assumed by chosen leaders who will initiate the policy, stake personal and political reputation on both the practicability and the necessity of the proposals, and face the consequences of failure. In the present case, Mr. Hughes refused to state that he would resign if the Referendum were defeated. The problem was a military one, and he could not disclose the full military situation and discuss the chances of winning the war and the exact purpose for which troops were required. That being so, he virtually said to the people: "I have all the information on the subject. I cannot give it to you to enable you to decide the question for yourselves. I tell you conscription is necessary. If you decide it is not necessary, I will still endeavour to carry out the policy of the country and conduct the war by other means." Mr. Hughes simply committed the question to the fog of politics, and the people consulted their own individual interests.

The poll was taken on October 28 and the "No" majority as indicated by the returns published up to December 11, is 71,549. The following are the particulars of the voting:

Referendum, 1916.
Progressive Figures and Outstanding Votes.[31]

State.	Date of Advice.	Yes.	No.	Informal.	Majority. Yes.	Majority. No.
New South Wales ..	December 11th, 1916	356,802	474,523	27,038	—	117,721
Victoria ..	,, ,,	353,930	328,216	14,538	25,714	—
Queensland ..	,, ,,	144,017	157,049	7,596	—	13,032
South Australia ..	,, ,,	87,908	119,119	4,009	—	31,211
Western Australia	,, ,,	94,049	40,875	5,680	53,174	—
Tasmania	,, ,,	48,490	37,830	1,037	10,660	—
Territories	,, ,,	2,136	1,269	63	867	—
Commonwealth ..		1,087,332	1,158,881	59,961	90,415	161,964

Yes	..	..	1,087,332
No	..	..	1,158,881
Majority for No	..	..	71,549

The distribution is curious and unexpected. The "Yes" majority was not anticipated in Victoria, and the majority in Western Australia is surprisingly great. In South Australia the conscriptionists hoped for an easy victory, but were heavily defeated. In New South Wales, while forecasts of the result differed, no one foresaw that the cause of conscription would have suffered such a crushing overthrow. The majority against conscription in Queensland is smaller than was expected. A striking feature of the figures is the way in which the people discarded their political representatives. In Victoria all the Senators are Labour, and all but one opposed to conscription, yet Victoria voted "Yes." In South Australia and New South Wales the Labour leaders worked generally in favour of conscription, and there it suffered its severest defeats. With reference to parties and sections, it is pretty clear that there was not a solid party vote from Labour on the "No" side. In every safe Labour constituency the majority against conscription is less than the majority obtained at the last election by the Labour member. In some City Liberal constituencies the majorities for "Yes" were greater than the majorities obtained by the Liberal member against the Labour candidate at the last election. On the other hand, in the country, the "No" totals are in almost every case far in advance of the Labour totals at the last election. This is especially the case in New South Wales and South Australia. It is fairly clear that an important factor in the "No" victory was a large section, fearful of a shortage of labour, from the farming vote, which at elections usually goes to the Liberals. A considerable number of Labour supporters who were in the first instance inclining to conscription were eventually whipped in by the action of the trade unions and officials of the political Labour Party; but, nevertheless, many men who usually vote for Labour candidates voted "Yes." The parties being pretty evenly balanced in Australia, the large country vote for "No" carried the scale against the proposal. The Roman Catholic vote was very much feared by the conscriptionists, and was, no doubt, in the main hostile, except perhaps in Western Australia, where the Archbishop came out as a strong supporter of conscription.[32]

The effect of the Referendum decision on the political situation has been momentous. Mr. Hughes stated that the decision of the country was not a decision against the continuance of the war, but only against the particular means which the Government sought to employ. He would accept the verdict, and continue to prosecute the war as vigorously as possible with the limited means available. He would endeavour to obtain the necessary reinforcements by voluntary enlistment; and, if this were found impossible, he would again appeal to the country. He did not resign. Before the polling day he had been ejected by the New South Wales Branch of the political Labour League from membership. On November 14 a meeting of the Parliamentary Labour Caucus was held, and a motion of want of confidence in him was moved. After discussion, Mr. Hughes vacated the chair and left the meeting with some twenty-four followers. He resigned as Prime Minister; and, having thus got rid of his former colleagues, he formed a new Ministry from his followers, whom he called the "National Labour Party." The remaining members of the Labour Party have called themselves the "Australian Labour Party," and have elected Mr. F. G. Tudor, the late Minister of Customs, their leader.[33]

By retaining office Mr. Hughes undertakes to face the consequences which will result from a policy not of his own choice. He leads the smallest party in Parliament and his Government can exist only on the sufferance of the Liberals, whose support will tend still further to alienate him from his old party and many of his personal following. The Liberals have not guaranteed their support. He is faced also by a hostile Senate. The feeling against him among his revolted followers is intense, and the "Australian Labour Party" will stop at nothing to humiliate him. His power to carry out an effective policy is therefore small, and as his chance of scoring off his opponents is slender, his position in a general election will not be a favourable one. If Mr. Hughes had declined to continue in office, his opponents in the Labour Party would have considered themselves entitled, on the strength of their victory in the Referendum, to form a Ministry. If the Governor-General[34] had been of that opinion and had sent for Mr. Tudor instead of for the leader of the Opposition, there would have been a great risk in placing the conduct of the war in the hands of a party so defective in leadership and so completely dominated by external organisations. This, no doubt, influenced Mr. Hughes in his determination not to cast off the responsibilities of office. But against this course there are the following weighty considerations: The Australian Labour Party allege that Australia's obligations can be carried out without conscription. The country has agreed with them. The country therefore deserves no better than to be governed by them. They should certainly undertake the responsibility of making good their claims and facing the consequences. They have a majority in the Senate, and can therefore act effectively and have no excuse for inaction. This extreme Labour Party are very distasteful on other than war grounds to a large number of people who voted "No" on the Referendum, and are clearly in a minority in the country. Assuming the issue of the next election to be whether such a party should govern or not, and assuming that they had to bear all responsibility for their policy and the consequences, it is probable that they would suffer a disastrous defeat. The suggestion is undoubtedly a bold one; but it is a logical application of the principle of responsible government, and it is the only means by which the people of Australia can be made to realise the true character of the party which has defeated the Referendum.

In its constitutional aspect the Referendum campaign is the culmination of a conflict which has been developing in the Labour Party for the last few years between the leader and the machine. Hitherto the theatre has been New South Wales, with Mr. Holman[35] and the political Labour Conference in the principal rôles. Now a national question has forced Labour both in Commonwealth and in New South Wales politics to a parting of the ways. Both Mr. Hughes and Mr. Holman claim for the leader freedom of action in all things outside the party platform, the right to frame a policy and to administer affairs without the leave of either the parliamentary caucus or the external organisation of the party. Their opponents would in substance set up the parliamentary caucus in place of the Cabinet and would bind it even closer by instructions to the party "conference." But the cleavage has an importance which goes beyond constitutional or even political forms and methods. On one side stands an ideal of social betterment to be attained through a process which, though it may be slow and gradual, is at any rate educative, and presents the possibility of co-operative effort on the part of all classes. Mr. Hughes' abilities and force of character might have led the country, and not merely a part of it, far on the way towards the realisation of this ideal. On the other side stands the alternative of violence and the class war— the social revolution to be achieved not through education and co-operative effort, not by development of the higher human faculties, not even through the action of the state, but by the brute force of organised unionism with the weapon of the general strike. Tending in this direction are "the industrial unionists" (whose conflicts with the politicals have been described in THE ROUND TABLE),[36] the Syndicalists, and the "Industrial Workers of the World"—the last, open advocates of violence and sabotage. Mr. Hughes has always been at daggers drawn with any section which sought to identify the Labour Party with this outlook. He has pointed out with extraordinary power how destitute of promise a movement is which discards every constructive element and uses only the weapons of destruction. The present campaign has been largely a struggle between Mr. Hughes and these forces.

The rank and file of the Labour Party, who have imbibed the set phrases about militarism, and were always led to believe that the International Socialist movement would abolish war, may be excused for shutting their eyes to the logic of facts and believing when they are told that the governing classes of all countries were responsible for the war. But the Australian democracy has never accepted the Pacifist doctrines or the teaching of the philosophic Liberals. The Referendum campaign was not influenced by these considerations to any appreciable degree. The Australian worker has never objected to use force in his own industrial interest. He believes in compulsory unionism and the methods it involves. He excludes the alien from Australia by force. He has never objected to compulsory military service where the object is to protect him from the industrial competition of the Asiatic. He tolerated the "direct action" of the Syndicalist. For such men to use the watchwords of the Pacifist and the English Radical, even to use the arguments of the International Socialist, was a gigantic hypocrisy.

But, after all, it is no use blaming a section for the result. The real discredit must rest upon the Australian people. It is true that a very large number voted "Yes," but it cannot be denied that this was very largely a non-combatant vote. The people have lacked sincerity and intelligence in their political life. There has been in the community as a whole no true insight into the basis upon which Australian security and freedom rest. Since the war began, with a few notable exceptions, politicians and press have failed to impress upon the people the terrible seriousness of the position and the critical character of the issues involved. Disasters were shrouded in a shallow optimism and the greatest moral crisis the world has ever known was met in the spirit of "Business as usual." These tendencies were present in England at the beginning of the war, but they have been overcome there, and in her concentration on the sublime purpose of the vindication of liberty and justice in international relations England has reached a spiritual plane from which all sorts of great results will be possible in the future. Australia has not shared this discipline; and when the call to a supreme sacrifice came she did not respond. The moral elevation of spirit which might have come as a product of this dreadful conflict will not be hers, and in the future her politics will be, to a greater degree than before, a dismal record of sordid strife.

It is, of course, difficult for a country so far from the scene of action, a people who have never even been face to face with that silent conflict which has been going on through so many years of so-called peace, to realise as a whole the peremptory claims which righteousness, justice, and loyalty make upon her. Few other nations in history have honoured these claims even as well as she has done. But few other nations have been so well-favoured as she has been, and no nation has been so completely and utterly dependent on the protection of another as Australia is on the British nation. Relying on the supremacy of the British fleet, Australia has been free to gather in the riches of a vast continent for the exclusive benefit of a handful of people. She has indulged in economic and social experiments of an unique character. These privileges would have been impossible if she had had to face the world by herself. She has been protected by British arms, by the courage and skill with which they have been wielded, and by the heavy sacrifices out of which they were created. Such guardian effort and sacrifice have piled up a moral debt against Australia which it would be impossible for her ever to discharge. She could, however, do her best, but by this answer to the Referendum she has refused to do it. Relying on conscription in England, whose people are far less favoured, she refuses to make an equivalent sacrifice. It is notoriously difficult "to draw an indictment against a nation," and, conversely, it is difficult for a nation to be collectively grateful. In all processes yet devised for the expression of the national will there is a strong tendency for the nobler elements of the national spirit to be lost. In some respects the attitude of Australia throughout the war has been admirable. The many thousands of her sons who have gone to the war have been well equipped and supported, and millions have been given by the public to carry on the war charities. No Australian soldier has ever complained of the hardships he has endured, none has regretted his sacrifice, or felt that it has been in vain. Australia has never complained of the statesmanship that led to the war, nor the way in which the war has been carried on by British statesmen. This much is extremely creditable. But the national will has not been strong enough to secure support for a policy which would enable it more fully to discharge its moral obligations. It cannot be sufficiently emphasised that the broadening of the basis of citizenship which comes with democracy, and the far-reaching economic and social experiments which are a feature of modern politics, imply for their success a higher level of citizenship, a greater power of co-operative action, a more enlightened attitude to public duty than the states of the past have ever shown. If these conditions are lacking, modern democratic developments can but lead to disaster; and the experience of the Referendum has revealed to us that these conditions are not present in sufficient measure at any rate to enable us to look forward to our future with confidence. Not only have we failed to honour our moral obligations, but we have been callous to the suffering and sacrifice of those to whom we owe everything. We have proved ourselves lacking in that faithfulness which the British masses have always shown to the highest ideals of the race, and without which the "island story" could never have been written.

For our future as an Empire the thing has a deep significance. The governance of the Empire must always be a problem of extreme difficulty and complexity, and can only be solved if a very high level of political capacity is present in all its component parts. Australia has shown herself unable to rise to the level required. No more conspicuous illustration could be given of the evils of the present system in which the Dominions have never been allowed to come face to face with the realities of the position and share the responsibilities of Empire. The "patience of England" can be carried too far; and if, after the war, a clear understanding is not given to the Dominions of their obligations and responsibilities, and of the way in which they can be discharged, no satisfactory basis can be laid for the future of the Empire.

Nor is it only the prospects of the British Empire that have been darkened by the Referendum. It will make it more difficult for democratic leaders all the world over to rely on the steadfastness of their constituents in times of crisis. And, all the world over, military states will be more ready now to flout those states which have adopted democracy as the spirit of their political system.

December 1916

THE GREAT STRIKE

March 1918, vol. 8, pp. 383–96

THE last Australian article included a short account of the great strike which commenced in Sydney on August 2, 1917.[37] As it was still proceeding at the time of writing, any attempt at a complete analysis of its causes and implications had to be deferred. The course of events may be briefly recalled in order to make clearer what follows. The strike began with the Amalgamated Society of Engineers and other ironworkers in the Government tramway and railway workshops in Sydney, ostensibly through the introduction by the Railway Commissioners of a card system of recording processes of work with a view to reducing them to terms of cost.[38] Negotiations were brought to an abrupt end by a 24-hours' "ultimatum" from the men. A few days later the majority of the men in the railway and tramway departments came out, and during the next fortnight one union after another declared a sympathy strike, until most of the important industries were practically at a standstill. Railwaymen, wharf labourers, coal miners, seamen and firemen, gas workers, slaughtermen and butchers, and many minor unions entirely ceased work, while practically all others refused to handle goods declared "black," as having been previously handled by non-union labour or as being destined for Government use. Even transports and other war services came under the ban. Another evidence of the disturbed conditions was the large daily procession of strikers through the city. The public were greatly inconvenienced by very severe restriction of all services and supplies. The stoppage of industries with an inter-State sphere of action, together with existing unrest throughout the Commonwealth and the extension of the "black" doctrine, caused the strike to spread to all States. The Federal authorities, however, left the State Governments unfettered to grapple with the situation.

The Government of New South Wales showed great firmness and capacity in dealing with the strike during the ten weeks of its duration. The men demanded the withdrawal of the card system before resumption of work and immediate inquiry into all their grievances. The Government insisted upon an immediate return to work, promising that after three months an inquiry into the working of the card system would be held, and that if the report were unfavourable it would be abandoned. This being rejected, they treated the strike as an organised rebellion, both in its defiance of constitutional authority and its callous neglect of the pressing needs of war-time. A Volunteer Service bureau was set up in Sydney, at which were enrolled several thousands of men, mainly from the country districts, who were provided with camping grounds in various parts of the city. These volunteers, with the aid of the faithful remnant of the employees, maintained a limited and gradually improving railway and tramway service. Other industries in more or less degree were provided for. Even a limited coal supply was furnished by the efforts of amateur coal miners, Parliament having passed an emergency Act permitting the use of such labour. This prompt and determined action, supported by exceedingly strong public feeling and increasing distress among the families of the workers, forced the Unions Defence Committee to accept the Government's terms. The original strikers returned to work, and after some further negotiation the miners, wharf labourers, and finally the seamen also resumed. But when volunteers desired to remain in the work they had undertaken they were kept on, and consequently many of the strikers found themselves still out of their job.

The Government and the general public look upon the grievance against the card system as a mere excuse, covering a deliberate attempt on the part of the Labour leaders to bring about an industrial defeat of a Government over which they had failed to gain a victory at the polls. It is held that the industrial and political leaders of the Labour movement had long been awaiting an opportunity for an upheaval, and that this petty dispute seemed to them to provide the convenient occasion. It is very difficult to determine exactly the part played by the card system. The Government, like employers generally, were convinced of the existence of a policy of "slowing down" systematically pursued by the men, as well as of a good deal of loafing, and were determined to check it. To the rank and file, on the other hand, the card system appeared not the means for checking "slowing down," but a step towards the general introduction by employers of a pernicious system of "speeding up," facilitated by the presence of war conditions. Ignorant and exaggerated talk about the introduction of Taylorism from America,[39] through the card system as a first instalment, was widely believed, though the Labour Press and many of the leaders must have known perfectly well that similar card systems were already in use in many industries in Australia and elsewhere without injury to the workers. There is, however, little doubt that psychological conditions were favourable to the reception of suspicion by the men. The attitude of the workers towards the social system leads them to attach to particular measures of the employers a significance which is out of all proportion to their actual content if they are considered by themselves. It must be confessed that some of the hostility to the card system was caused by frequent references on the part of the Railway Commissioners to the excellences of railway administration in America; and there were complaints concerning the management of the men in the workshops. The existence of alarms and even of grievances may, however, have furnished the occasion rather than the cause of the strike. Undoubtedly some of the leaders of the men were spoiling for a fight. They believed they could wipe out their political defeat by industrial action through a strike. Yet it seems to be certain that the Unions Defence Committee did not wish the strike to spread indefinitely, and it was due to weak rather than over-bold leadership that the area of dispute was so greatly extended. There were contradictory indications. In some cases strikes were called by leaders without a ballot in defiance of union rules. On the other hand, the general body of railwaymen, the wharf labourers, and the slaughtermen came out against the advice of the Committee. The spread of the strike was due, in fact, much more to the industrial and political solidarity of the rank and file than to energetic leadership. Only a few unions, like the Millers' and the Painters', refused to come out, and even they made levies on behalf of the strikers. To what extent defective or unscrupulous leadership is responsible for this upheaval demands further discussion.

So far as the strike is traceable to the condition of labour organisation and the state of mind of the workers the situation of Australian politics must be held largely responsible. The workers and their leaders were genuinely surprised at their defeat in the New South Wales election, and this was speedily followed by defeat at the Commonwealth election. They themselves estimate that at least 25 per cent. of the Unionists voted for the newly formed National Party led by Messrs. Holman and Hughes, who had been recently expelled from the Labour Party for supporting Conscription. This political motive of the strike was frankly confessed by some of the leaders in New South Wales. It also influenced, in varying degrees, the minds of the most class conscious of the rank and file. Desire for revenge and recovery of power in the community was accompanied by an over-weening confidence in the minds of industrial extremists due to their belief in industrial as against political action and to finding themselves in control of the unions in place of the "political" leaders whom they had expelled. They found ready material in the irritated and suspicious minds of the Trade Unionists.

At the same time, it is very easy to exaggerate the extent to which deliberate policy and systematic preparation were responsible for the strike. One fact that points to the conclusion that there was very little deliberate preparation is the exposure of the inefficiency of the leaders in the management of the strike. There were various factors in the situation unfavourable to such an enterprise. The volume of employment tended to shrink. Owing to the lack of shipping, large stocks of wool, wheat and meat had accumulated. Increased cost and scarcity of materials was affecting every industry. The financial position of the unions was very weak, owing to unemployment, loss of members, expenditure on the anti-Conscription campaign. The time of year was favourable for drawing workers from the country. The correct conclusion seems to be that the workers were quite ready for a strike, as were the leaders also, but nobody had thought out any plan of organisation; all trusted to solidarity, and for the rest the movement was allowed to progress by its own momentum. Evidence of the lack of control by the leaders is furnished by the contradictory applications of the "black" doctrine. Some ridiculous incidents occurred, the same commodity often changing from "black" to "white," and *vice versa*, several times in its precarious journey.

Another aggravation of the conditions which led to the strike was the award by Mr. Justice Edmunds, twelve months ago, under emergency legislation, of the demands of the coalminers after a big strike.[40] It is widely felt that such an easy surrender gave the men an exaggerated sense of power, which largely accounts for the abounding confidence with which they entered upon the struggle. Another contributing cause was the rise in the cost of living, resulting, of course, in increased stringency in working-class homes. Moreover, the knowledge that while prices were high foodstuffs in abundance were available in Australia and large quantities of wheat had been destroyed by plagues of mice was a source of grave irritation amongst the workers. The fact that all the stores were under contract to the Imperial Government was no satisfaction to the less thoughtful. Whether enemy influence was stimulating trouble cannot be said with certainty. The increase in strikes in essential industries has certainly had a most serious effect upon Australia's share in the conduct of the war. Enemy agents could, of course, do effective propaganda without the workers being conscious of their presence. At the same time, it is regrettable that allegations of disloyalty and susceptibility to German bribery were brought against the strikers without qualification. No doubt a small percentage of them were actually disloyal. But it is just as certain that the vast majority, though careless and wanting in a sense of responsibility regarding the war, were quite innocent of any disloyalty or corruption. At the Commonwealth elections the combination of Liberals and of Labour men following Mr. Hughes adopted the term "Nationalist" for their designation, and came to be known as the "Win-the-War Party" among their supporters. The assumption of this title by one party, with its obvious implication, was in itself a source of irritation, though the Labour Press subsequently found some satisfaction in applying it derisively to the Ministry and its supporters. But the frequent claims to a monopoly of loyalty tended, naturally and most unfortunately, to give to professions of loyalty some party colour and to provoke counter professions. This tendency was aggravated intensely by the strike, the constant reference to the volunteers as loyalists and to the strikers as rebels and disloyalists being a gravely irritating factor in the situation. While any division of the political parties by such titles as Win-the-War and Pacifist respectively is false and misleading, it is true that to the present Labour Party naturally gravitate all the elements of disloyalty and pacifism, and the whole Party is lamentably wanting in a realisation of the injury done to the cause of the Allies by their irresponsible stoppages of industry. On the other hand, the public and the employers are far too apt to be impatient of all industrial unrest in war time, whatever the cause. There are two sides to the wage bargain. The worker's legitimate grievances must not be neglected. The employer does not need to strike to secure his redress. On the other hand, Australian institutions offer peculiar facilities for the investigation of grievances, and it is difficult to find any excuse for the men's deliberate breach of agreements entered into in the Arbitration Courts, or the thoughtless neglect of the higher interests of the country and humanity which such action implies.

In the system of Industrial Arbitration the conflict and overlapping of Commonwealth and State awards has been the cause of a great deal of unrest for some years. The ill-defined spheres of the two jurisdictions have made inevitable a great number of inequalities in the awards. Such conditions inevitably encourage strikes, as the workers in a particular trade find it extremely galling to be earning less under one award, while their fellow-workers are much more favourably situated under another award. The tendency of the Commonwealth Court to give higher awards than State Courts has caused a multiplication of industrial disputes, inter-State in scope, so as to provide the technical condition under which the workers may secure an adjudication by the Commonwealth Court. Further, many people contend that it is the general tendency of Industrial Courts to unsettle the mind of the worker by offering him a constant inducement to agitate for increases in wages. War-time conditions have, of course, aggravated this general tendency to unrest.

The Australian Labour movement suffers from a very inferior newspaper Press. The tone and outlook of its principal periodicals are intensely prejudiced, while their actual misrepresentations in making out a case exceed those familiar enough in party journalism. The Labour Press generally wielded but little influence before the Conscription Referendum. With that came its opportunity, and it used it very successfully. The same bitter and aggressive spirit which marked its conduct of that campaign is still at work fomenting all causes of industrial unrest and political agitation. It seldom contains any articles marked by deep thought or of an educational character. It is devoted almost exclusively to operating upon the minds of the workers as an irritant, so as to intensify bitter class consciousness. The tone of its personal allusions is generally vindictive.

Another serious disadvantage of the working class is that all their important decisions and movements are conditioned by a state of mind which suffers from all the defects of mass action. Whereas all groups and associations in other ranks of society enjoy a better education and more opportunities for deliberation, and therefore are much more likely to arrive at well-considered decisions, the workers are practically always exposed to the ignorance, prejudice and hastiness of crowd psychology. In ordinary times they suffer from the apathy of the mass, and in times of excitement from its irresponsibility and fanaticism. Thus the organised workers are generally at the mercy of the agitator and the junta.

Though the immediate causes of the outbreak reveal much that is fundamental to the analysis of industrial and political conditions in Australia, there are still more important factors of a general character, an understanding of which is essential to the student of Australian sociology. In a previous article in THE ROUND TABLE (December 1916, p. 165) occurs this passage:[41]

> The continued existence and violence of industrial disputes has proved puzzling to many observers, even when resident in the Commonwealth. They point to the evident fact that the conditions of labour, including wages, are far more favourable to the worker in Australia than to his fellows in any other part of the world. The standard of comfort is admittedly high, the power of Unionism very great, all of which advantages are enhanced by excellent climatic conditions. Why, then, it is asked, should the workers be unsatisfied?

It was further pointed out that periods of prosperity and power are more marked by unrest than periods of stringency and unemployment. The Australian workers have enjoyed a long period of political power. The lavish expenditure of public money by Labour Governments, the want of understanding of large interests and public policies and of social responsibility, natural in the circumstances of their class, have caused a feeling amongst the workers that government is easy, and that the most sweeping changes can be effected with little thought. To these causes also may be attributed that excessive belief in equality common to advanced democracies. The Australian worker is as firm in his belief that the social millennium is easy of accomplishment as in his belief in his own worth and in his right to the economic benefits enjoyed by the more fortunate or more able of his fellow-citizens.

This also accounts in part for the intense class hostility which so keen an observer as Lord Bryce remarked as being possibly more acute in Australia than in any other place in the world.[42] Comparatively good conditions have not prevented the Labour movement from adopting the Marxian theory of the class war. There is within the movement a large and growing minority of irreconcilables whose influence has recently increased to an extraordinary degree. Large quantities of syndicalist literature have been imported from America. A well-known trade union secretary sent to America some time ago for literature. He received a ton of I.W.W. pamphlets, and declares that they completely destroyed his authority with his union.[43] The war has greatly increased the influence of this revolutionary school of thought, for it provides numerous apparent proofs of the truth of the doctrine of the class war. The trial and conviction of twelve members of the I.W.W. in Sydney for sedition and arson aroused a remarkable degree of sympathy amongst unionists entirely opposed to the methods of the I.W.W.;[44] it was enough for them that "these men suffered for their class," a significant indication of the strength of the idea of class solidarity. It is not enough to say that there is no room for the philosophy of violence in a country like Australia, where the worker enjoys good conditions and frequently holds the reins of government. His more fortunate situation whets his appetite, without providing him with the new social system on which he believes. What the ordinary member of the middle class fails to understand is that the doctrine of the class war is sufficiently close to the facts of modern industrialism to offer a plausible explanation of all its abuses in one simple generalisation—capitalism. The Australian worker's class consciousness is deep enough to lead him to see the force of the Marxian call to world-wide labour solidarity. Certainly it is grotesque for the imported revolutionary to preach the same *jehad* in Australia as in America or England; but once the worker has become fully class conscious nothing is easier than to persuade him that the capitalist system is the same all the world over, and that in spite of all the boasted reforms of Australia he is still a wage-slave; there are degrees of slavery, but it is slavery still. Thus Marxianism appeals to the ordinary worker through its simple theory of exploitation, and to the more intellectual through its internationalism and its abstract economic reasoning. It is curious that this growth of a class-consciousness, based on internationalism, exists together with an extraordinary ignorance of the world outside Australia. And yet the one assists the other. In Australia there are few of those many influences which modify extremes and exaggerations of opinion in England. There is no cultured and leisured contribution to the stream of thought and art. There is no complex system of civilisation to give variety and distraction to our society. Issues are too clear cut. The position and outlook of Australia are exceedingly insular and her domestic life very parochial. Everybody's material interests are so obviously involved with those of everybody else; we live too close together. Again, there is no recognition of such striking distinctions between the ability of the best intellects and that of the average worker to give pause to the assumption of equality. Especially is this true in the political sphere, where the continued lack of men of great distinction is remarkable in all parties. The Labour Party has suffered in particular by the fact that the split took away its ablest men in State and Federal politics and among the leaders of official Labour to-day in Australia there are none who can approach in capacity of mind and force of personality the leaders of the British Labour Party. Further, the Australian worker has an even narrower conception of the State than the average Marxian. Not only is his outlook narrowly industrial, but he uses political action as merely another form of industrial action. He neither knows nor cares that politics is wider than economics. It is to him but one part of the great fight against capitalism. If high ability coupled with the statesman's breadth of view is absent from Labour counsels, there has grown up in the last few years a chicane that will seize every tactical advantage and opportunity in a way that the most astute politician of the old parties might envy. This tendency has been fostered by the arbitration system, which turns Union officials and men into special pleaders, keenly on the look-out for the smallest chance to make a point in their favour.

The social and economic theory of the Australian Liberal has all the defects of a commercial and individualist tradition. His natural tendency to repudiate responsibility for the condition of life of the workers has been intensified rather than mitigated by the paternal intervention of the State on the worker's behalf. If the employer admits generally the right of the worker to good conditions, he so frequently opposes any particular efforts to maintain or better those conditions as to induce the belief that he still regards the worker merely as an item in the cost of production and not as a citizen exercising his social function. The striker is a rebel, to be dealt with by the strong hand. Of the worker's psychology the majority of employers know practically nothing. Such employers fail entirely to understand that the most deep-seated cause of industrial unrest throughout the world is the feeling of the worker that his personality has no opportunity in the present industrial system of expressing itself, and his self-respect is deeply injured by his being treated as an inanimate tool. This feeling is even stronger than the sense of economic insecurity. Though such insecurity is by no means so prevalent in Australia as elsewhere, it is within the experience of practically all Australian workers. But far more powerful is the determination of the worker to be satisfied with nothing less than a full human share in the control of industry as in the control of government, and the growing belief that this will not be realised without fundamental social changes—a belief that is greatly reinforced by the worker's exaggerated interpretation of equality. Always opposed to profit-making in any form, he is able to point to the increased prosperity of many capitalists as a direct result of the war. Though he generalises with gross unfairness over the whole field of capitalist enterprise, it is not surprising that he exhibits intense impatience when talk of loyalty and sacrifice differentiates against his class, which has suffered like others in the war. A further aggravation of class division during the war is due to resentment in Labour circles at the number of prosecutions of workers for industrial offences in the last few months, which to them have a decided colouring of political bias. Under the Unlawful Associations Act,[45] many members of the I.W.W. have been imprisoned for six months; three of the strike leaders were prosecuted for conspiracy, though they were not convicted owing to a disagreement of the jury. However divided may be the rank and file upon economic doctrine, they are absolutely at one in regarding these cases as demonstrations of class bias. Furthermore, the use of the censorship to examine the correspondence of the Trades Hall during the strike greatly increased the belief in a political and capitalist conspiracy against Unionism.

Australian Governments are alive to some of the dangers exposed by recent events. At the moment of writing a Conference is being held of representatives of the various States and the Commonwealth for the purpose of dealing with the overlapping of industrial awards.[46] Another measure of amelioration foreshadowed by the Government of New South Wales is a scheme of Unemployment Insurance. It is unlikely, however, that for reasons already indicated, any mere improvement in governmental machinery or in wages and conditions is likely to go to the root of the industrial trouble. Even the system of industrial arbitration, though its potentialities are by no means exhausted, tends to stereotype the cleavage between employers and workers. The workers are certain to go on organising towards the One Big Union.[47] The employers show an equal propensity towards closer union. Many employers have suffered so grievously in recent years from the operations of the Unions that there may be some temptation in the recent success over the workers to use the occasion for breaking the power of Unionism. But there could be no greater curse to Australia than any such deliberate fomentation of the already bitter antagonism between the two sides. There could be no other result than a large increase of I.W.W. influence, to be followed by something in the nature of a social revolution. The prevailing narrowness of outlook and want of social responsibility can be reformed, partly by such movements as the Workers' Educational Association, but chiefly by means designed to carry the worker through his apprenticeship in playing his part in the control of industry. There are so many State enterprises in Australia that the Governments are offered an excellent opportunity for experimenting with some of the measures proposed by the Reconstruction Committee appointed by the Prime Minister in England.[48] It would be comparatively easy to draw the workers into a share of the control of the purely Labour side of Government enterprises, delaying their introduction to any purely business aspect of industry until such an extension should be proved to be safe and practicable. It might be possible also to base upon the Arbitration Courts a similar system of co-operation between employers, workers and the State for the management of industry. The greatest barrier to any such constructive scheme as that of industrial parliaments outlined in the Whitley Report is the hostility between the two classes.[49] But unless some positive effort is to be made to set up a workable scheme of co-operation more extensive than the experiments hitherto made the outlook for Australia is dark indeed. Some words written in THE ROUND TABLE of June, 1916, are even more true of the Australian than of the English worker:

> The unrest in the industrial world to-day has not its roots solely in poverty and want. There is something deeper still at work. The wage-earners are filled with a vague but profound sentiment that the industrial system, as it is now, denies to them the liberties, opportunities and responsibilities of free men.[50]

The problem of industry is to satisfy the demands of human liberty, while inculcating the spirit of true social discipline.

December 1917

THE SECOND REJECTION OF CONSCRIPTION

June 1918, vol. 8, pp. 627–39

TO understand the position in Australian public affairs to-day it is necessary to look back over a considerable stretch of events. The student will find THE ROUND TABLE article in No. 26 (March, 1917) on the first Conscription Referendum[51] helpful in estimating the present situation.

The first Referendum was possibly almost inevitable in the political circumstances which gave rise to it. The divergence between the political parties in Australia was so great, their class-antagonism so pronounced, and the Labour machine was so exclusively adapted to serve the interests of Labour only that the formation of a truly national Government was practically impossible. Further, the Labour party—then in power—was by no means at one with itself on questions of fundamental importance, such as patriotic duty and Australia's national obligations in the war. A deep rift was widening between the older school of Labour leaders, who had raised the Labour movement to its remarkable pitch of success in Australia, and the newer school of industrial extremists, who were gradually capturing the Labour leagues and getting control of the party political machine. Mr. Andrew Fisher, of "last man and last shilling" fame, had handed over the reins of government to his former second-in-command, Mr. W. M. Hughes, the last hope of the older school; and the new Prime Minister, after delivering his soul, with characteristic vigour, upon the wrecking tactics of the extreme section of Labour, had followed Mr. Fisher to England. He went there to transact very important national business, relating to the sale and transportation of Australia's products and the financing of war measures, but also, no doubt, to fortify himself by accurate information and personal knowledge for the war policy he had to carry through in Australia against strong and bitter opposition within his own party.

Returning full of zeal for the principle of universal service, the Prime Minister found himself faced with the most stubborn obstacles in his Cabinet and in the Parliamentary party—especially in the Senate. The Referendum proposal (1916) was the utmost to which he could screw up the party, after the most strenuous efforts. The alternative—a direct appeal to the country—was blocked by the constitutional difficulties of obtaining a double dissolution, which was absolutely essential because of the strongly adverse attitude of the Senate to the Prime Minister's proposals. In a matter of such great national urgency it would, perhaps, have been too much to expect a political leader to see that the longer, constitutional process would prove in fact much shorter and more effective than the apparently swift and sudden method of a quite unconstitutional Referendum (technically described as "extra-constitutional"). And this first Referendum might indeed have given Australia an effective war policy had it not been for the series of blunders in the campaign (see ROUND TABLE article referred to above). On October 28, 1916, Australia came within an ace of giving the most striking vindication of democracy—by making, as a democratic nation, that supreme sacrifice which has ennobled so many individual lives in these years of war. It may justly be claimed that she would have done so under wiser leadership; but, then, the raising up of strong and wise leaders is just the kind of vindication that our Australian type of "advanced democracy" seems chiefly to need.

The main positive effect of the first Referendum campaign was the split in the Labour party which gave the Prime Minister the independence he so courageously asserted at that time, and left him with a remnant of the party—which assumed the name "National Labour" though it had, in fact, only a fraction of the organised Labour of Australia behind it. This merely served to keep Mr. Hughes in power for the time being, by favour of the Liberal Party, which gave ungrudging support so long as the business was confined to the prosecution of war measures.

The position was one of extremely unstable equilibrium, which was bound to be upset by the first wind of circumstance. Just when the life of Parliament was nearing an end the invitation from the British Government to Australia to take part in the Imperial Conference was received. A National Labour and Liberal coalition was formed after some delay and a good deal of bargaining, with the object of obtaining a postponement of the General Election until after the Conference, so that such a deputation might be sent to it as would represent at least the majority of the Australian people. This object was defeated by the "Official Labour" majority in the Senate, which thus forced the General Election upon the country; and the Coalition Government took the momentous step of foregoing all representation at the Conference.[52]

The General Election of May, 1917, has proved to be the turning-point of Australia's fate. The Coalition Government went to the polls on a "win the war" cry, but without a policy adequate to that ambitious phrase. Practically the whole body of "win-the-war" politicians had been supporters of the conscription proposals of the first Referendum, and neither then nor since has the party been able to put forward any effective substitute for that policy. Yet the party decided to put conscription definitely on one side, as having been made impossible, at any rate for the time being, by the Referendum decision and the exceedingly useful political designation, "Win-the-War," came simply to mean that the Government would undoubtedly keep things going as well as it possibly could under an absolutely stultifying restriction.

One leading politician (Sir William Irvine) stood out for the more heroic course, and maintained his independent right to advocate compulsory service as the only effective means for the winning of the war.[53] The other leaders and practically all the rest of the Coalition party sacrificed their personal convictions to the decision which the people had given, and to what they conceived to be the political interests of the party. It was not possible, however, merely to put the conscription issue aside as an irrelevant issue: the Coalition had either to go to the polls with conscription explicitly in its programme—in which case the election would, of course, have been fought upon that issue—or it had as definitely to exclude conscription from the programme upon which it asked for election. Its opponents, knowing the conviction of the Win-the-War candidates, naturally took good care to exact specific declarations on this specific issue, and most of the candidates pledged themselves definitely on the point. The representative pledge is that given by the Prime Minister as follows:—

The Government will not enforce or attempt to enforce conscription, either by regulation or statute, during the life of the forthcoming Parliament. If, however, national safety demands it, the question will again be referred to the people. That is the policy of the Government on this great question. (Bendigo, March 27.)[54]

In his numerous election speeches he gave the same promise again and again in characteristically vehement and picturesque forms. Moreover, he himself and most of his followers made it perfectly clear that they meant by the contingent reference to the people not another election, but another Referendum.

The present most deplorable humiliation of Australia is a direct consequence of the fundamental insincerity of a "win-the-war policy" which did not demand power to put into effect the one method by which the party believed that such a policy could be made effective. The sweeping victory of the party at the polls made it certain that it could at least have put up a splendid fight for a free hand to carry on Australia's part in the war; even had it lost, it could have done much more in opposition for the welfare of Australia than it has actually been able to do in office. This statement is made with the fullest appreciation of all the strong arguments put forward as to the dangers of putting the industrial extremists of Labour into power during war time. Sound democratic theory and ordinary adherence to principle pointed one way; but faith in principle yielded to fear of the consequences, and the moral advantage of position began definitely to shift to the other side. A bid was made for the votes of that section of the community which neither wants revolutionary internal changes nor cares much about Australia doing her part in the war; and the dead weight of this ignoble section of public opinion which ought to have been forced by a bold Government policy to make its choice between Official Labour without conscription and the Coalition with conscription—has made progress impossible ever since.

A period of stagnation followed upon the establishment of the present Government in place if not in power. There has never been any question about the Coalition party's will to prosecute war measures to the best of its ability; but it could do little more than barely "carry on," hampered at every turn by embittered opponents and by the limitations it had accepted. The patriotism of the community was semi-paralysed by the impotence of the Government. The demoralising processes of voluntary recruiting (in its secondary stages) went on, with all their futility of threadbare impassioned appeals, glorified circus tricks, vulgarising advertisements, and lamentable waste of energy, only redeemed by the untiring persistence of the Commonwealth Director of Recruiting[55] and his able staff of workers. There developed in those families which had gladly done their duty and had in many cases suffered irreparable loss a deep-rooted feeling of bitterness towards those other families which refused to do their part; and both among the families which had made the sacrifice and among others as yet untried but equally willing, a strong aversion to supporting voluntarism further at the cost of the flower of the nation's youth.

The Government had gambled on one or other of two events: an early victory for the Allies or a disaster which would make it possible to raise the question of conscription again. Meanwhile its attitude had to be practically to "wait and see" which of these events would happen. Its opponents offered an anticipation of what would occur by affirming that the Prime Minister would seize the first opportunity to bring in conscription. By this means, when the grave emergency eventually did arise, they actually succeeded in discounting much of the Prime Minister's passionate appeal to the nation.

Sir William Irvine, after waiting long enough for the Government to formulate a strong policy, launched a special campaign of his own; and, though he stood politically alone and was looked upon with much disfavour by both political parties, he met with such success in several States that the Government was forced to listen to his voice. He strongly opposed the taking of another Referendum on conscription, believing that course to be contrary to the principles of responsible government as applied to such a question. He urged the Government to take full responsibility, to put a measure through Parliament giving it the power of compulsory enlistment, and then to go to the country on that issue.

When the demoralisation of Russia's armies reached a disastrous climax and the facts of the Italian defeat became known the Prime Minister stated that the time for action had come; and he hastened to forestall any counter-proposal by announcing that the Government had decided to take another Referendum. The speech with which he opened the campaign (Bendigo, November 12) shows, on rereading, with what clearness he grasped the significance of the war situation;[56] but he gave neither Parliament nor the people an opportunity to discuss the situation on its merits, so as to arrive at the best way for Australia to meet it. Apparently he expected the whole country to see the facts as he saw them, or at least to see them through his eyes, and hoped to carry it with him on a wave of anxiety and patriotic revival. He did not reckon with loss of confidence both in himself and in his Government; and with a certain growing coldness to his impassioned appeals. The terms of the proposal for this "Reinforcements Referendum" were as follow:

1. Voluntary enlistment is to continue.

2. The number of reinforcements required is 7,000 per month.

3. Compulsory reinforcements will be called up by ballot to the extent to which voluntary enlistment fails to supply this number.

4. The ballot will be from among single men only, between the ages of 20 and 44 years (including widowers and divorcees without children dependent upon them).

5. The following will be exempt: (*a*) Persons who are physically unfit for service; (*b*) Judges of Federal and State courts, and police, special and stipendiary magistrates; (*c*) Ministers of religion; (*d*) Persons whose employment in any particular industry is declared by the prescribed authority to be necessary for the supply of food and material essential for the war; (*e*) Persons whose religious belief does not allow them to bear arms; but this objection will only exempt them from combatant service; (*f*) Persons, the calling up of whom for military service would, because of their domestic circumstances, cause undue hardship to those dependent upon them.

6. The Government will prescribe the industries essential to the prosecution of the war and the national welfare of Australia, and a special tribunal will determine the amount of labour necessary for their effective operation.

77

7. Where a family is or has been represented in the Australian Imperial Force by the father or a son, or by a brother, one eligible son, or brother (as the case may be), shall be exempt.

8. Eligible males of families which now are or have been represented at the front shall not be balloted for until after eligible males of families not so represented have been called up.

9. All ballots shall be so conducted that families will contribute as nearly as practicable *pro rata*, and that in no case shall the sole remaining eligible member of a family which is or has been so represented be called up for service. Males under the age of 20 will be exempt, in addition to the one eligible male over that age.

10. In determining the *pro rata* contribution regard shall be had to all members of the family who have joined the Australian Imperial Force, irrespective of age.

11. Ballots will be taken by States, on the basis of the proportional number of eligible persons in each State.

12. The tribunals for deciding exemptions will be constituted by magistrates specially appointed; and an appeal will lie to a Supreme Court judge.[57]

The following were disqualified from voting:

(*a*) Every naturalised British subject who was born in a country which forms part of the territory of any country with which the British Empire is now at war, except a natural-born citizen of France, Italy, or Denmark, arrived in Australia before the date upon which the territory in which he was born became part of Germany or Austria; and (*b*) Every person whose father was born in any enemy country.[58]

The question put to the people was:

Are you in favour of the proposal of the Commonwealth Government for reinforcing the Australian Imperial Force oversea?

It was at first exceedingly doubtful whether the Government intended to accept full responsibility for its proposals and to stake its existence upon them. It was strongly urged to do so by those most in earnest about the prosecution of the war, while, on the other hand, certain powerful newspapers—anxious at whatever cost of principle to keep the present Government in office—described any disposition in that direction as sheer quixotism. The point was apparently settled at a Cabinet meeting on the train journey to Bendigo on the day of the above-mentioned speech, and the decision arrived at was stated by the Prime minister in his peroration thus:

We who were elected on a Win-the-War policy tell you plainly that the situation in Russia and Italy is such that without the power to ensure reinforcements we cannot give effect to the policy which you approved with such enthusiasm last May. I tell you plainly that the Government must have this power. It cannot govern the country without it, and will not attempt to do so.[59]

This statement is to be specially noted in view of subsequent developments.

The Referendum campaign proved for a second time the folly of submitting such an issue to a direct vote of the people. It is true that the worst blunders of the previous campaign were not repeated, but others took their place. The Government agreed that no more than the usual military censorship should be exercised upon the Press; but, as a matter of fact, one of the most telling features of the "No" propaganda was the production (on platforms) of galley-proofs of matter censored on its way through the Labour printing press. The official substitute for censoring was to be drastic action against the publication of statements calculated to mislead the voter, but this again operated most adversely to the Government's own case. It gave rise to a number of somewhat farcical legal proceedings in which the Government failed to secure a conviction. The Prime Minister conducted the campaign characteristically, with quite unnecessary bitterness, using the offensive epithets Disloyalist, Sinn Fein, I.W.W. indiscriminately against his opponents. His misdirected zeal reached a climax in Queensland, where he prohibited the publication of certain statements about military statistics by the Premier and the Treasurer of that State,[60] and afterwards, when these statements were given publicity through the State Parliament in a special "Hansard," first had the copies of "Hansard" seized by the military authorities and then prosecuted the Premier of Queensland (by no means to the disadvantage of the latter) for having made the statements. Further, in connection with this episode and some rough treatment at the hands of a Queensland crowd, the Prime Minister instituted offhand a Commonwealth Police Force to protect Federal interests where these might be in danger of suffering under the existing police systems of the States.[61] It is not necessary to deny the seriousness of some of the matters attacked by the Prime Minister; the point to be observed is the recurrence in new forms of the bad tactical methods which marred his conduct of the first Referendum campaign.

All the cross-currents of personal interests and prejudices again revealed themselves. The feelings of women-voters especially, but also to a considerable extent of men, were worked upon by appeals to their now much fuller knowledge of the horrors of modern war. They were asked whether they would condemn any man to such horrors against his will; and to the question thus put, those at whom the appeal was specially directed—whether thinking of their own men or of others—had only one answer. Many alleged, as sufficient reason for voting "No," advice received from their sons or brothers or husbands at the Front.

Very active opposition was organised in several of the States by the authorities of the Roman Catholic Church. The new Archbishop of Melbourne, Dr. Mannix, formerly Coadjutor,[62] was the head and front of this activity. He was specifically recognised by the Prime Minister as the leader of the "No" forces, and he now takes credit for having turned Victoria at least from "Yes" to "No." The fact of his thinly veiled utterances and the complete failure of the Government to deal with them as seditious and treasonous have been a most sinister feature of the situation. He is an Irish Sinn Fein zealot, with a deep hatred of the British Commonwealth and especially of England. His deliberate policy, in which he has had disquieting success, is the inculcation of an Australian Sinn Fein attitude of mind among the more ignorant or gullible of the community, for whose support he angles with a certain crude demagogic cleverness. His method is cynically indirect. He exhorts his following to "put Australia first, the Empire second," but succeeds in making it quite clear that he actually means *the Empire nowhere*. Any references he makes to German militarism and German methods of warfare always carry the innuendo that Great Britain is nearly, if not quite, as bad. His most notorious phrase is "a sordid trade war," in description of the British cause. He pays lip-homage to the principle of voluntary enlistment—if only because the people of his Church have their representation of brave Irish blood in the A.I.F.—but he makes it perfectly plain that there is, in his view, no obligation on the part of any man to offer himself for service; he hints that it is mere quixotic chivalry for any young Australian to go upon what loyal citizens regard as the path of supreme duty in these times. The reason why it is considered important to state his attitude at such considerable length is that the influences of which he is spokesman have in fact effectually succeeded in stopping the flow of Irish Roman Catholic recruits, and were largely responsible for the great "No" majority in December. It is essential to add, however, that some of the most prominent and distinguished Roman Catholic citizens have come out unequivocally on the side of allegiance to the Allied cause.

As in the first Referendum campaign, the most damaging opposition to the Government's proposals was based upon criticism of the statistics adduced in support of these proposals, and of the number of men asked for per month. The Ministry had made no careful study of the figures they used, and even the tables produced by their military advisers would not bear close investigation and analysis. These facts were publicly demonstrated in the above-mentioned legal proceedings against the Queensland Premier during the campaign. To the mere politician it may be a small matter that Australia's contribution to date was estimated at figures varying from 300,000 to 400,000 men, according to the audience and the particular object in view; but it happened to be a point of supreme importance to serious voters endeavouring to answer responsibly the question put to them by the Government. Again, the 16,500 per month—so desperately needed in 1916 that twice that number was demanded for October of that year, and men rushed into camp to anticipate the country's mandate—had given place to 7,000 in 1917, although the war-situation was stated to be so very grave. Might there not be something, after all, in the anti-conscriptionist contention that the 4,000 per month actually obtained by voluntary enlistment in 1917 was sufficient to meet the need? No incontrovertible statistical evidence was forthcoming; and not nearly enough was made of the fact that the 48,000 men obtained in 1917 had mostly come forward in the earlier part of the year. The clause to the effect that "in any month only the number actually required (if less than 7,000) will be called up or enlisted," was not given sufficient prominence; yet it involved the really fundamental principle that effective warfare cannot be carried on with a definite liability specified beforehand, and was at least one step back to the solid ground of responsible representative government.

It is a disconcerting fact that the anti-conscriptionists, who did not succeed in producing a single argument of weight upon the principles involved (the arguments as to "freedom" and "the sacredness of human life" were typically unreal in view of the Prussian menace staved off by conscript France, England, Italy, and America), should have won by so large a majority, even without the German vote. The final figures were: *Yes*, 1,015,159; *No*, 1,181,747; majority for *No*, 166,588.

The figures for the several States were:—

						Yes.	No.
New South Wales	..	..	..	..	..	341,256	487,774
Victoria	..	..	..	..	..	329,772	332,490
Queensland	..	..	..	..	..	132,771	168,875
South Australia	..	..	..	..	..	86,663	106,364
Western Australia	..	..	..	..	..	84,116	46,522
Tasmania	..	..	..	..	..	38,881	38,502
Territories	..	..	..	..	..	1,700	1,220

The honourable position of Western Australia cannot be passed by without a word of appreciation.

The fact must not be overlooked that the overseas soldiers returned a small *yes* majority (*Yes*, 91,642; *No*, 89,859; majority, 1,783),[63] and when it is remembered that many of them voted *No* for reasons which, however mistaken we may consider them, command our respect and admiration, it becomes all the more tragically significant that the soldiers asked for adequate reinforcements and the stay-at-homes "turned down" their appeal. This makes December 20, 1918, a black day indeed in the annals of Australia;[64] and though Labour leaders exulted over it and are insistent that "the conscription issue is dead" and must be buried out of sight and mind if there is to be any getting on with Australia's business, it must remain the darkest blot upon our national character till somehow we shall expiate it in days to come.

March 1918

THE POLITICAL SEQUEL

June 1918, vol. 8, pp. 639–46

THERE was, however something even worse to come in the political sphere. Behind everything in the anti-conscription case was a fundamental distrust of the Government. Large numbers of Labour men, whose loyalty and patriotism cannot be questioned, affirmed that nothing would reconcile them to trusting this Government with the powers conferred by a compulsory system. They were convinced that their political opponents would use the powers of conscription in the interests of "the master-class" and to the detriment of the worker. They believed, and stated, that the restrictions specified in the Referendum proposals were temporary expedients; and, in particular, they warned the married men that their turn would surely come, not realising that thousands of clear-sighted, patriotic married men supported conscription in order that they might rightly know when their turn had come. They ridiculed the assumption that the Prime Minister and his colleagues would keep their Referendum pledge and go out of office in the event of a "No" majority; and the facts in connection with this most crucial test lend great force to the general distrust and suspicion which constitute the one valid excuse for the "No" vote. These facts throw back upon the Government and its National Party the greater burden of responsibility for the present discredit of Australia in the eyes of the world.

The Government was, according to vehement asseverations made during the Referendum campaign, to be out of office within twenty-four hours of an adverse result; but in the actual event the decision was first delayed for as long as possible after the adverse result was seen to be beyond any possibility of doubt, and even then resolved itself into one in favour of a most lamentable process of political manoeuvring. Organs of the Press identified in interest with the Government began to canvass a variety of alternatives to the straight and narrow course of honesty. Gradually it emerged that neither Government nor party meant to relinquish office if this could by any plausible means be avoided; and their supporters began to persuade themselves—with just enough justification to make it certainly a sore temptation—that the paramount patriotic duty was to keep the

Official Labour Party out of power.

The Government, having first decided to refer the decision of its fate to the party—though, indeed, much was made throughout the affair of the fact that it was the Government and not the party which had brought about the whole situation—the Prime Minister, with his unenviable skill in handling political difficulties, succeeded in obtaining as the one tangible result of a first long meeting of the caucus, a vote of confidence in himself as leader of the party, "carried by an overwhelming majority." This effectively ensured that he would not be made the scapegoat.

When the caucus resumed on the second day (January 4) there were perceptible signs of stiffening on the part of a minority, partly, no doubt, due to pressure of public opinion applied in the interim. The proceedings at this second meeting, of which a good report appeared in the Press, are of special importance to this review of the position. The following resolution was first carried, again "by an overwhelming majority":—

That this party, in view of the recent declared attitude of the Official Labour Party on the vital questions of the conduct of war and peace, declares that in the interests of the country and the Empire it will not support any course of action that will hand the government of the country . . . to the Official Labour Party.[65]

Sir William Irvine who, by implication, must have voted against this resolution, stated the case very plainly as it appeared to him. He described the Government's Referendum pledge as "a clear, definite and welcome assertion of the principle of government responsibility," and stated his conviction that "in an issue vital to the national honour and safety of the Commonwealth no other course was possible." In his judgment the Government had said in effect to the electors, "You must choose between our party with conscription and the Official Labour Party without conscription." He said that he considered all members of the party to be bound in honour by the pledge, and that, therefore, no ministry could be formed from the Nationalist side of the House. He stated as the only two possible alternatives: "Either the government must be handed over to Mr. Tudor's party (Official Labour), or the National Party in Parliament must take full responsibility for its policy, even if that should necessitate an appeal to the constituencies." In the end he moved a motion to that effect, but "received little support."[66]

The caucus had by this stage arrived at the view that the Government was acting unfairly in attempting to fasten on to the party full responsibility for the pledge, seeing that the party had in fact neither been consulted as to the taking of the Referendum nor as to the giving of the Referendum pledge; and the following resolution was passed:

That the matter be left in the hands of the Government to take whatever steps it deems advisable with a view to giving honourable effect to the pledge given by it to the people of Australia. (Carried with seven dissentients.)[67]

Sir William Irvine was not slow to point out a possible, or even a probable, conflict between this resolution and the previous one (defining the attitude of the Nationalists to the Official Labour Party). His view was that to give honourable effect to the Referendum pledge, a dissolution was practically necessary so as to give the Official Labour Party its opportunity to formulate a policy and see whether that policy actually had the support of a majority of the people.[68]

The next stage can be most succinctly stated in quotations from official statements emanating from Federal Government House:

(January 8.) Mr. Hughes waited upon His Excellency the Governor-General this morning, and tendered his unconditional resignation as Prime Minister. At the request of His Excellency, Mr. Hughes will continue the administration pending the issue of a new commission. During the course of the day the Governor-General sent for and discussed the political situation with Mr. Tudor, Sir John Forrest, Mr. Cook, Mr. Watt, Mr. Higgs, Mr. Poynton, and Mr. Wise."[69]

(January 11.) "On January 8 the Prime Minister waited on the Governor-General and tendered to him his resignation. In doing so, Mr. Hughes offered no advice as to who should be asked to form an Administration. The Governor-General considered that it was his paramount duty—(*a*) To make provision for carrying on the business of the country in accordance with the principles of Parliamentary government; (*b*) to avoid a situation arising which must lead to a further appeal to the country within twelve months of an election resulting in the return of two Houses of similar political complexion, which are still working in unison. The Governor-General was also of the opinion that in granting a commission for the formation of a new Administration, his choice must be determined solely by the Parliamentary situation. Any other course would be a departure from constitutional practice and an infringement of the rights of Parliament. In the absence of such Parliamentary indications as are given by a defeat of the Government in Parliament, the Governor-General endeavoured to ascertain what the situation was by seeking information from representatives of all sections of the House with a view to determining where the majority lay, and what prospects there were of forming an alternative Government.

As a result of these interviews, in which the knowledge and views of all those he consulted were most freely and generously placed at his service, the Governor-General was of opinion that the majority of the National party was likely to retain its cohesion, and that therefore a Government having the promise of stability could only be formed from that section of the House. Investigations failed to elicit proof of sufficient strength in any other quarter. It also became clear to him that the leader in the National party who had the best prospect of securing unity among his followers, and of therefore being able to form a Government having those elements of permanence so essential to the conduct of affairs during war, was the Right Honourable W. M. Hughes, whom the Governor-General therefore commissioned to form an Administration."[70]

There are two points to be particularly noted in this latter memorandum: (i.) The fact that "Mr. Hughes offered no advice," taken in conjunction with the fact that "the Governor-General sent for and discussed the situation with" half a dozen others. This point was much discussed at the time, and it was ridiculed in Parliament by the Opposition. The point is an important one, as bearing upon Mr. Hughes's direct responsibility for what followed, and on his practical interpretation of the Referendum pledge. But in the absence of knowledge which has not been revealed it cannot be discussed here. (ii.) The other point to note is the astuteness with which the Prime Minister had succeeded in predetermining the Governor-General's decision by means of the first two resolutions passed by the caucus of his party. This was the indirect way in which the Prime Minister became responsible for what transpired.

The fact is that "honourable effect" could only be given to the Government's pledge by Mr. Hughes himself interpreting the Referendum result as a defeat of the Government upon the issue most vital to its policy, only to be redeemed by a constitutional appeal to the country upon that policy and that issue as one indivisible whole.

In any case the final responsibility definitely rested with Mr. Hughes. In explaining the precise constitutional position, a correspondent, "Lawyer," of the *Age* newspaper stated:

There is no doubt whatever that the Governor-General was right when he requested Mr. Hughes to form a Ministry. It is quite another question, however, as to whether Mr. Hughes was right in accepting the invitation to form a Ministry.[71]

It is an obstinate fact, against which all waves of excuse must break themselves in vain, that Mr. Hughes and all his Cabinet colleagues without exception returned to office after having explicitly stated that they must have the power of compulsion to ensure reinforcements, that they could not govern the country without it, and would not attempt to do so. Any attempt to excuse or justify must necessarily resolve itself into the veriest quibbling.

When Parliament met in the middle of January, the Government was challenged by the following motion of No Confidence, moved by Mr. Tudor:

That the House protests against: (*a*) the repudiation of the pledges of the Prime Minister and of other Ministers; (*b*) the political persecution of public men and other citizens and the press under the War Precautions Regulations during the recent referendum campaign; (*c*) the deprivation

of statutory electoral rights of Australian-born citizens by regulation behind
the back of Parliament; (*d*) the general administration of public affairs;
and wishes . . . [72]

To have been effective this motion should have been confined to
its clause (*a*). The fact that it was not indicates either unpardonable
blundering on the part of the Opposition or else more political
finessing—this time on the other side, to manoeuvre members of
the coalition party into the position of voting against the prime
charge (*a*). This motion was, of course, lost on a division entirely
on party lines.

A whole article might well be written on the reasons which
influence those who believe (as one writer has extremely expressed it)
that "the entry of the extreme Labour Party into power at present
would be a national disaster as tragic as the Bolshevik ascendancy
in Russia." But the proper venue for argument on this question is a
public contest before the electorate. In a democratic system there
is no alternative to the community itself deciding such questions; any
other course leads inevitably, as we in this country have had ample
opportunity of realising, to a last state much worse than the first.
If the conviction of the Coalition was that the Official Labour Party
must be kept out of power at whatever cost, there should certainly
have been no pledge given at the Referendum, or rather no Referendum should have been taken in 1917, since the pledge was in fact
implicit, by all the principles of responsible government, in the
taking of it. But once it was taken, the issue was of such supreme
importance that the popular decision upon it should have brought
into power a Government in consonance with the declared will of the
people. That is what links the present position so closely with
the last General Election, and makes it certain that only a General
Election, contested upon basic convictions, could clear up the ugly
situation.

The people of Australia, by means of the two Referenda with
an emasculated General Election sandwiched between, have
succeeded so far in evading the necessity to accept the political
consequences of their decisions upon the supreme issue. The present
Government has been driven to the repudiation of its pledges on the
plea of necessity. The position of moral advantage has been quite
gratuitously conceded to the Official Labour Party, which gives no
promise whatsoever of being able to provide good government,
especially in time of war. All this means a political outlook which
is dark indeed.

But there is hope in the absolute dimensions of the "Yes" vote,
which would in itself be a thing to be proud of, if so much did not
depend on the fact that, however large, it is still only a minority.

This million of voters is the raw material of a real Australian Win-the-War party. It is practically compact upon the war issue, while the "No" voters include many who really belong to its ranks. The problem—and there is no use in shutting one's eyes to its desperate difficulty—is how this great body of "Yes" opinion is to find for itself adequate representation and effective practical expression. And the problem is not only desperately difficult; it is also desperately urgent.

March 1918

THE PEACE CONFERENCE

June 1919, vol. 9, pp. 601–11

DISCUSSION of the Peace Conference in Australia has been confined almost entirely to two matters—the fate of the Pacific possessions of Germany and the League of Nations. We have read in the press of elaborate claims made in Australia's name—"reimbursement of war costs and losses, the annexation of former German possessions in the Pacific over a wide zone, and her free autonomous development within a paramount British Empire, behind her own fleet, under Australian control."[73] Smaller items, we gather, are the increase in the Australian navy and mercantile marine from German sources, the transfer of German private possessions in New Guinea, the distribution of money obtained from the sale of enemy-owned stock, and the punishment of German officials who cruelly treated Australian soldiers. The bill of costs so presented seems to have been framed on the basis that, while you are in no case likely to get all you claim, the more you claim the more will be allowed by the taxing-master, in this case the Peace Conference. Australian opinion would probably be willing enough to make Germany pay. But it is not impressed by the suggestion that Australia has peculiar grounds for consideration which should make her a preferential creditor among the Allies, either on the ground of "dislocation of her trade and shipping" or the advantage which Canada has enjoyed from the profits of munition contracts.

Before entering on a consideration of the Peace Conference itself, a word is called for on the question raised by Mr. Hughes on the acceptance of President Wilson's fourteen points by the War Council of the Allies in November last. Australia certainly expected, on the repeated assurances by the British Government, that her Government would be consulted before peace terms were accepted. Both the Government and the people no doubt considered that this assurance imported consultation at a stage when the question of acceptance or rejection of actual terms had to be determined. If then the only answer to Mr. Hughes's complaints was that in 1917, or even at meetings of the War Cabinet in the earlier months of 1918, there had been discussions on the conditions of peace at which the Dominions had the opportunity of presenting their views, this would not be regarded as a substantial fulfilment of the assurance given; and the further explanation offered on behalf of the British Government—that all that was agreed upon was armistice terms and not peace terms—was wholly unconvincing. A temperate protest, confined to the actual matter, would probably have won the united support of the country. But the Australian Prime Minister took a course which effectively drew off public attention from a great matter to the trivial personal matter of Mr. Hughes's manners and tactics. The facts are still too obscure at any rate in Australia to warrant a confident judgment on the main question; but it is significant at any rate that the Australian Government was so far informed and alive to the importance of President Wilson's fourteen points as possible terms of peace preliminaries as to cable to Mr. Hughes their objections to certain of them several days before the acceptance of the terms was notified. If, then, there was a lack of consideration to the Dominion representatives in not summoning them to a Council at which the momentous decision was to be taken, it would appear that Mr. Hughes might have made use of his rights as Prime Minister of a Dominion and as a member of the War Cabinet to see that the views of the Commonwealth Government were laid before the Prime Minister of Great Britain.

"So far as we know the facts" must be an implied qualification of most Australian impressions on the Conference. We have a generous cable service, picturesque enough in its incidents and in its attributions to Australia's Prime Minister. But we have to guess at how much is gossip, how much is inspiration, and how much is sober truth. The Government have maintained silence, and beyond stating that Mr. Hughes has their confidence and support, they have done nothing to inform the public mind either as to the claims which have actually been made in Australia's name and the manner in which they have been met, or as to the effect of the determinations which have been provisionally arrived at upon matters vital to Australia's interests. If one thing is more clear than another in this time of confusion and doubt it is that decisions of Governments if they are to be more than scraps of paper must have behind them the knowledge and understanding of the peoples concerned. Attempts to mobilise national opinion upon partial statements in delicate international matters are no improvement upon the "secret diplomacy" of the past.

In regard to the Pacific colonies of Germany the growth of an informed and settled opinion in Australia has been hindered by a censorship which during the years of the war vetoed the discussion of Pacific questions affecting Australia and her relations with the

Allies. This may well have been wise or even necessary, but it is a principal cause of a lack of knowledge or even of interest in Australia outside Sydney. Upon one point indeed there was unity of feeling, and this was expressed in the resolutions of the Commonwealth Parliament at the close of 1918—the the German colonies should not be returned to her and that Australia should be consulted as to their disposition. And all the discussion of the two months that have elapsed since the assembly of the Peace Conference indicates that the Government correctly interpreted Australian opinion in not asking for more. The Labour Press denounces the claim for annexation as immoral, and treats it as a further proof that the war for right and justice was after all merely a phase in the sordid endeavours of capitalistic exploitation. But the "capitalistic Press" (as the Labour papers call their opponents), represented by such organs as the Sydney *Daily Telegraph* and the Melbourne *Age*, are not behindhand in repudiation of annexation as an Australian policy. The standpoint of both these papers is that Australia with her vast continental territory and her small population has not the resources either in men or wealth which would enable her to undertake new responsibilities; and this opinion is strongly held in the official and business world. Both the *Telegraph* and the *Age* consider that the simplest and most satisfactory solution of the problem would have been annexation by Great Britain. The view that the islands are a burden to be assumed as part of the cost of Australian defence, and not an asset which can be accepted as an economic offset against war losses, is almost universal.

If annexation would have been preferred to the mandatory system, the reason is because of the novelty and obscurity of the latter, and the fear that it indicates merely a temporary settlement. There is also the tradition of failure which attaches to attempts to solve the problem of national rivalries by international government, and the Condominium in the New Hebrides, the *mêlée* in Samoa, and the mixed *régime* in Egypt have been rather glibly cited as illustrations, without a clear appreciation of the distinction between international administration and national administration under international supervision and control. The failures cited belong to the former kind, the proposed system to the latter.

How far the distinction is real must of course depend a good deal upon the character of the mandate and the amount of freedom that is allowed to the mandatory. It is understood that Australia's mandate is to be a wide one, as befits the recognition that she among the nations has the primary interest in the Southern Pacific islands—an interest which, by the way, the United States acknowledged at the time of her own annexation of Hawaii. It would obviously create great administrative inconvenience if Papua were governed under one set of conditions expressive of Australian policy and German New Guinea were administered by Australia under conditions which expressed some other policy. What exactly will be permitted and what forbidden by the mandate is still a matter of some conjecture, and there is a good deal of difference of opinion on the subject. It is assumed that "it will not be possible either to 'ring-fence' the resources and markets, or even to provide for a moderate amount of discrimination" (Sydney *Evening News*).[74] But save for some such restriction, it is considered that the mandate may enable Australia to apply to the islands the trade and economic policy of the mainland, including the Navigation Act policy and the exclusion of Asiatics.

The "White Australian" policy views with hostility the immigration of Asiatic races into the islands for more than one reason. First of all, just as it demands that Australia shall be inhabited by a people capable of forming one community, unembarrassed by the presence of unassimilable elements—whether better or worse than the Australian matters not—so it believes that in the case of the islands under its control, justice to the natives requires that they shall be given the opportunity of rising to higher things by a development of their own social life. This is the policy which has been pursued in the Papuan administration. It is believed that this policy is impossible if free immigration is permitted; and the menace to the social development of the natives is greatest from those who are best fitted to increase and multiply and who could best turn the peculiar conditions of soil and climate to account. In the second place, the security of the White Australian policy is deemed to require that those lands in proximity to Australia shall be subject to the same restrictions on immigration as are applied to the Continent itself—that safety requires a "buffer state" or "neutral zone."

In all this it is not to be expected that there should be general acquiescence outside Australia; and a warning note is from time to time sounded within Australia itself. It is pointed out that in Australia a vast extent of tropical country is kept out of productive occupation by dedication to the White Australia ideal. If this policy requires further that tropical lands outside Australia shall similarly be left unproductive, and placed out of reach of those who desire access to them, it may incite critical and perhaps unfriendly attention to the policy itself even as respects the mainland.

There was undoubtedly a good deal of impatience in Australia at what appeared the waste of time in discussing a League of Nations, while the peace itself was still unaccomplished, and there was not a little in the cables to suggest that all this discussion was no more than the practical statesmen's tactful indulgence towards the academic theories of President Wilson, whom fortune had placed in a position where he had to be humoured. But Mr. Hughes's belittling of the League and his statement that Australia regarded it as utopian met with little sympathetic response. The Labour Press was loud in protest. Mr. Hughes's statement might truly represent the opinion of "Australian profiteerism of the commercial brand," but it was a monstrous misrepresentation to call it Australian opinion. A typical Labour view is contained in the following extract from the Brisbane *Daily Standard* (December 28, 1918):—

> The thorough organisation of the world's workers on the economic principle of co-operation will eventually remove the causes of wars between the nations; but in the meantime the proposed League of Nations is the only solution of the problem while the classes control the production and distribution of the world's wealth.[75]

There is perhaps less reason in Australia than anywhere in the world to identify "the classes" with warlike preparation—we have no great armaments companies, and we have no social class with a tradition of service in the army and navy or in civil administration. There is, in fact, nothing to separate the interest of one class from another in the supreme interest of all in peace and security. From the first, when the League of Nations seemed little more than an idea, the Sydney *Daily Telegraph* gave it a welcome as hearty as did any Labour paper, and has vigorously, almost passionately, urged that the present was an opportunity which, if lost, might never recur. The Sydney *Morning Herald*, if less vehement, hailed the proposal as one full of good hope. Other National or Liberal organs were courteous, full of good will to the notion in its right place, but some of the most important among them were rather sceptical and disposed to wait-and-see. As the idea became a plan, elaborated in detail, and backed by statesmen to whom it would be presumptuous to refuse the title of practical, as it became clear that these men were not merely playing a diplomatic game but were very much in earnest, there came a recognition that while the League might not guarantee the world against war, it did at any rate contain many things which were not utopian dreams but practical necessities if there was to be an international organisation corresponding with the actual facts of international relations.

For a country which has been peculiarly sensitive on constitutional matters in their bearing upon the relations of Colonial or Dominion Governments to the British Government, Australia has been singularly without interest in the significance of the change which marks her entry into the Peace Conference and her projected membership of the League of Nations. It may be possible to show that upon some isolated occasion, or for some special purpose, or with some particular country, a Dominion has had direct relations with foreign States. But now we have the full, formal and complete admission of the Dominions to the family of independent nations.

The British Empire has existed in the legal sense mainly in the fact that the King was the head of each colony or Dominion as well as of the Government of the United Kingdom; that there was at any rate this community of citizenship, that allegiance throughout the Empire was a duty owed to the Crown; and that the whole of the British Dominions were subject to the sovereignty of the Imperial Parliament. But all these things were made to serve or to conform to the internal self-government of a Dominion—the prerogatives of the Crown are in the main the instruments through which the Dominion Government carries on its functions; the privileges of British nationality in a Dominion are precisely those which the Dominion law permits, and no more; while the sovereignty of the Imperial Parliament in the case of a Dominion is usually exerted upon the invocation of the Dominion itself. If there was an appeal from the Courts of the Dominion to the King in Council, the Commonwealth and South African Constitutions furnished precedents sufficient to establish the principle that this link of connection remained only so long as the Dominions desired to maintain it. But the political substance of the matter—the thing which prevented the ties of legal subjection from a gradual decay into legal fictions—was the unity of the whole in foreign relations. In the world of states, the British Commonwealth was one state, with one Government answerable for the whole. We may recall the terms used by Mr. Asquith at the Imperial Conference in 1911, when he declared that authority could not be shared "in such grave matters as the conduct of foreign policy, the conclusion of treaties, the declaration and maintenance of peace, and all those relations with Foreign Powers, necessarily of the most delicate character," then in the hands of the Imperial Government. This *articulus stantis aut cadentis Imperii* is now apparently abandoned.

Here, as in other matters connected with the Peace Conference, our information is incomplete. The cables published in the Australian Press vaguely suggest some basis of understanding between the British and the Dominion Governments as to the place of the latter in the League of Nations. Also, we must not overlook the fact that the Dominions are also represented in the Peace Conference, and presumably in the League of Nations, in the British delegation, so that a position is created which is without parallel in modern international arrangements, though it has some analogies in the German Confederation, 1820–1866.[76] *Prima facie*, the international status accorded to the Dominions would involve the right of each of them to pursue and voice its own policy in the Conference and in the League, a policy which need not be in accord with that of the British Government and may be in accord with that of other Governments, and the right to pursue that policy in association with other Governments against Great Britain. Indeed, it is clear from the reports which reach us from the Peace Conference that the Australian and British Governments have been at odds in some matters, at any rate, which the Conference has dealt with, while we learn that more than one of the Dominions have associated themselves with the small nations' remonstrance against the predominance of the Great Powers, including the British Empire. President Wilson, indeed, seeking to reconcile his countrymen to the *quantum* of British representation in the League of Nations, calls attention to the improbability that in practice the British nations will be found in agreement.

Each member of the League of Nations will presumably be separately answerable to the League for its conduct and policy, and the League is entitled to call on every one of its members for support against a recalcitrant member. It appears to follow that in case one of the members of the Empire became embroiled, each one of the others would be placed in a state of hostility towards it. Moreover, as before the League of Nations the nations of the British Commonwealth are fellow-members of the League, differences arising between them would be cognizable by the League, and the constitutional control of an Imperial Government would pass to the League. It is difficult to see how the British and Dominion Governments will stand towards each other in anything but the relation of separate sovereign states, unless the formal admission of the Dominions into the family of nations is qualified by some understanding—to which in the circumstances it is hardly possible that the British and Dominion Governments can be the only parties.

If that is what we really intend, there is no more to be said; but it is vital that we should know where we are going. In present conditions, any tendency to extreme assertions of independence in policy is checked by the knowledge that ultimately the defence of the Commonwealth depends upon the support of the forces of the Empire, or at any rate of Great Britain, while at the same time many points in Australia's actual legislative policy are possible only because of the knowledge that that support is behind her. With the League of Nations a reality, these considerations would be weakened, and there would be little or nothing left to check the disintegration in substance which the new status of the Dominions presents in form. How far mature reflection in Australia will accept the new model as satisfactory remains to be seen. Anyone who reflected at all realised that after the war the relations of Great Britain and the Dominions would be profoundly altered. But it was at least expected that the Parliaments and peoples of these countries would have had the opportunity of deciding what these relations were to be, before their Governments presented a *fait accompli* to foreign countries for their recognition. Australia certainly expected consultation in the peace terms and the association of her Ministers with the British Ministers at the Conference. But representation as a separate nation formed no part of her expectation, and she has as yet no conception of its implications or the responsibilities it imports. Current opinion accepts the fact of separate representation, but scouts the notion that it is really significant of a breach in the unity of the Empire, for this reason if for no other that Australia cannot as yet go alone. The British are not a logical people in their political arrangements; but to be and not to be, is a question which to answer will tax all our political acumen. Whether the League of Nations becomes a reality or not, a step has been taken which will be found to involve serious permanent changes. The most obvious of these is the precedent for the establishment of direct relations between the Dominions and foreign countries. The summoning of an Imperial Conference at the earliest practicable moment to consider the Constitution of the British Commonwealth has become a matter of urgent necessity. Only after such a Conference shall we be able to know whether the changes into which we have been hustled are the work of statesmen planning with foresight for the future, or are a hasty device for avoiding difficulties and responsibilities.

March 1919

THE RETURN OF MR HUGHES

December 1919, vol. 10, pp. 179–85

DURING the last few weeks Mr. W. M. Hughes, the Prime Minister, has made a triumphant reappearance on Australian soil. He has been away sixteen months, and during that time he has attended a meeting of the Imperial Conference, sat in constant consultation with British statesmen as a member of the Imperial War Cabinet and the British Empire Delegation in Paris, and, lastly, attended the Peace Conference at Paris and Versailles as Australian delegate. The welcome he has received has been unsurpassed in the history of Australia. Landing at Perth on August 22, he has made a progress through the States of Western Australia, South Australia, and Victoria amid acclamations comparable only with those given to a Roman victor. These demonstrations have been quite spontaneous and have a deep significance. The welcome has been entirely a personal one. It has not been given to Mr. Hughes as the representative of any party or section of the community. The public of the three States has, apparently, whether in a sudden mood of excitement or on more solid grounds, selected Mr. Hughes as the personality most fitted to lead the country through the next few years of reconstruction and reparation. His reception in New South Wales and Queensland may be colder, but similar influences will work there in his favour, and the strength of his position will not be affected.

It cannot be gainsaid that the remarkable character of the welcome given to Mr. Hughes has profoundly affected the political situation. Mr. Hughes occupied a peculiar situation in politics comparable with that of Mr. Lloyd George on the signing of the Armistice. His qualities as a war leader brought him to the front during the war in spite of party difficulties. His own following is almost negligible. The two other parties in the House dislike him intensely. He became leader of the Nationalist Party through combination with one of these parties, but the war was the sole bond of union and the coalition is most precarious. The problem is whether Mr. Hughes will be able to convert into cash the credit which he obviously possesses in the community and by a stroke of political virtuosity provide himself with the followers and party organisation which he now lacks. Whether he will succeed depends a good deal on the true character of the welcome which has been given him, whether it is hysterical and ephemeral or whether it is permanent. To estimate this it is desirable to analyse somewhat more in detail the causes which have led to the late outpouring of emotion.

The element in Mr. Hughes's record which has attracted to him the admiration of the majority is undoubtedly that he stands as a symbol of Australian nationalism. Before the war the Australian was assertive with the assertiveness of a man who had to prove his case. The record of the Australian soldiers in the war has proved that case, and Mr. Hughes has returned as the leader of the country through the crisis of the war and the man who secured in Paris the fruits of victory. This accounts for the conversion to his cause of many who were his political opponents.

Another factor of great importance is undoubtedly the support of the returned soldiers. When Mr. Hughes arrived in England in 1918 he quickly realised that there was a considerable amount of incipient discontent amongst the soldiers, some of which was justified. He set to work, in ways that were not at all acceptable to military authority, to allay this feeling. He was at once able to secure the return to Australia of men who had left in 1914. In every way he made himself personally accessible to the soldiers. This enabled him to realise the conditions under which they lived; and, by inviting complaints to be addressed personally to himself, he got an insight into their psychology and was in some cases able to help them. This would probably not have carried him very far, for the administration of the A.I.F. was humane and many petitioners had to be disappointed. But Mr. Hughes was in temperament well fitted to appeal to the Australian soldiers. He has that combination of pugnacity, impulse and brains which made them the wonderful fighters they were. Mr. Hughes is himself a Digger, and understands their mentality better than anyone. They approve of and delight in public acts which from the point of view of the old diplomacy would be regarded as highly dangerous. The more Mr. Hughes brandishes his fist in the face of other nations the more the Digger approves. The combative element in Mr. Hughes's character has entirely won them, and he can rely upon them for a very large measure of support in anything he undertakes.

Another factor in his success is the complete lack of an outstanding personality amongst the other members of the Australian Parliament. Never were the Councils of Australia so bankrupt of men capable of leadership. Mr. W. A. Watt, the Acting Prime Minister, has shown many elements of statesmanship during Mr. Hughes's absence, but the state of his health is precarious and early retirement has been predicted. There is no other figure capable of formulating the great schemes of policy needed for reconstruction or even of compelling loyalty or support from the somewhat diverse elements of which the National Party is made up. Mr. Hughes is, moreover, obviously superior as a politician to the leader of the extreme Labour Party, Mr. Tudor.

But the most important element in his present prestige is his record at the Peace Conference. Australia suffers very much compared with the rest of the world in the means it possesses to follow the events in the world's centre. The cable service is most inefficient, and there is little attempt to secure continuous correspondence devoted to matters of international politics which is essential to supplement the scrappy and sensational cabled news. The result is that only very rough impressions as to the course of international affairs can be gathered in Australia.

At the present time the general public in Australia believes that Mr. Hughes, in order to protect the White Australia policy and to secure for Australia the islands in the Pacific which were the indispensable ramparts for her defence, had to fight the opposition or indifference of the British Government and European nations and the implacable hostility of President Wilson. This impression has been created by the way in which Mr. Hughes fought his case in Paris. But it does not accord with the facts or with opinion in Europe, and as truth will out even from a Peace Conference, the unsoundness of these claims may ultimately affect Mr. Hughes's position in Australia. It is not possible within the limits of this article to deal with the Australian interest in the Peace Treaty, and to analyse its effects on the future of Australia. Nor is it possible, with the information at present in the hands of the public, to definitely assess the credit due to the persons representing Australia for their record at the Congress.

Two principal matters were involved in which Australia played a leading part—the question of racial equality, and the disposal of the German islands in the Pacific. As to the latter, the policy of annexation advocated by Mr. Hughes would, if adopted, have had to be applied to the islands assigned to Japan as well as to those assigned to Australia: that would have implied the right to use them in full sovereignty, including the right to fortify. From this danger Australia was saved by the British and American foresight which secured the substitution of the mandate. The Japanese proposal for the express recognition of racial equality was met apparently by Mr. Hughes with an offer of compromise—he would accept the recognition of the principle coupled with an admission that it did not extend to a right of immigration. This compromise was not acceptable to Japan, and thereupon Mr. Hughes offered relentless opposition to the proposal as a menace to the White Australia ideal. The issue, in reality one in which several countries were concerned, came in appearance to be one between Australia and Japan. The courage which forced such a situation readily commands the admiration of Australia. But splendid isolation has its perils, which might have been avoided by more skill and experience in the ways of diplomacy. Actually, Japan secured a majority in the League of Nations Commission for her proposal, but President Wilson held that it could not go through in view of the powerful dissent from it. In the circumstances, Japan is not likely to accept the decision as final and will probably use the League as a means of reopening the matter.

Here we are brought to the new status of Australia, which is implied in the separate representation of the Dominions at the Conference and their membership of the League of Nations. The Prime Minister applauds this achievement of his diplomacy, and the nation accepts with satisfaction the place of honour which she regards as a testimony to the brave deeds of her sons. But it is not a fortunate conjunction of events that the time when Australia's political situation in relation to Japan has become more acute should be also the time which suggests an impairment of Imperial responsibility for Australia's security. What the separate representation of the Dominions in the Peace Congress and on the League of Nations really involves is a difficult problem to determine. Those responsible hardly seem to have worked out its implications. They do not appear to have realised that, while anomalies in the old Imperial system were practically harmless, ambiguity in a written constitution like the League of Nations may be full of peril. But whatever the result may be it is quite clear that the responsibility of Britain for the policy and security of the Dominions, which the small nations of the world would have regarded as a priceless boon, is less than it was, and the Dominions are now placed in that position of apparent independence which small nations of the world have found so dangerous during the war. These things, however, do not appeal to the public mind, which is at present in no mood for criticism.

The enthusiasm of the moment, however, has only half concealed the difficulties of Mr. Hughes. The chief of these is the lack of personal loyalty of the major half of the National Party—the old Liberal element—to him. In the absence of any party organisation or following of his own it is difficult to see what other course he can adopt than to retain the present National Party organisation. At the same time few men in the history of Australia have had a more wonderful opportunity than has Mr. Hughes at the present time.

He could impose on any party to which he lent his name almost any terms, and he alone can command the support not only of thousands of party voters but of the great unattached voting strength which really decides elections in Australia.

Since he returned his speeches and his general attitude have been moderate. He has made two claims—that he has protected the White Australia policy, and that he has secured for Australia the islands which are the ramparts of Australia's security. He proceeds to denounce on the one hand the profiteer who is securing unfair advantages from the community by means of monopolies and combines, and, on the other hand, the Bolsheviks who are attempting to secure power for a minority by methods of force. So far he has not assumed to lay down any definite programme. He states that he does not know to which party he belongs, but he still retains the labour ideals which have dominated his whole political life. This absence of definition makes his speeches read thin from the political point of view. The antithesis between the profiteers and the Bolsheviks is somewhat cheap. The Bolshevik is not a live force in Australia at the present. He might become so if the problems of reconstruction are not properly handled and vested interests and monopolies reap the benefit. On the other hand, profiteering is a complex problem which can only be solved by constructive legislation, including the amendment of the Constitution. Continuous constructive effort is essential if the needs of the situation are to be met. Mr. Hughes's past career does not afford any indication of such capacity. He is only too likely to be lured into hostile relations with bitter enemies and expend the whole of his force and ability on provocation and vituperation. Nevertheless he is undoubtedly the most prominent personality in Australian politics at the present day. He is superior in brain and force to any other figure, and those who are sincerely desirous of forwarding the truest interest of the Commonwealth have a great responsibility to discharge in deciding whether to give or withhold support. The public are in the grip of the strong man theory. Mr. Hughes is acclaimed because he is expected to "do things." But strong men may lead in the wrong direction. Strong autocratic personalities frequently bar the way for the more modest and intelligent workers on whom the real work of politics depends. For the present, however, Mr. Hughes's authority is a *fait accompli*. He now wields the sceptre, and for the next year he will lead the country. Responsible persons will not impede the exercise of his power, but will see how his leadership can be turned to the greatest good of Australia.

September 1919

PART THREE

1920–1929

THE COUNTRY PARTY

March 1922, vol. 12, pp. 405–8

FOR some time prior to the outbreak of war the Commonwealth Parliament and the Parliaments of the States were divided into two parties, called respectively Liberal and Labour. The Labour Party was the direct descendant of the group which, after for some time holding the balance of power, had gained strength until, in the Commonwealth and in all the States except Victoria, it had had more than an equal share of office and of power. The Liberal Party was composed of representatives of the more conservative section of the community, which had previously been divided between the advocates of Protection and Free Trade, and had afterwards come together in opposition to the more collectivist programme of Labour. During the war a readjustment took place. Many prominent members of the Labour Party were expelled for their advocacy of conscription. They formed a new party in coalition with the Liberals which took the name of Nationalist, their opponents retaining the attractive name of Labour, and with it the support and control of the Labour Leagues.[1] Since the end of the war a third party has emerged composed for the most part of representatives of country constituencies, and variously described as the Country Party, the Farmers' Party and the Progressives. The new party has exercised a great influence on political events throughout Australia, and its origin and policy deserve attention.

As the names Country Party and Farmers' Party suggest, the original object of the new party was to protect rural as opposed to urban interests. Years ago the annual Conferences of the Farmers' and Settlers' Associations were disturbed by proposals that the Associations should take part in politics as bodies distinct from either of the recognised parties. But in former days it was generally held that the time was not opportune to divert the movement from purely educational and co-operative activities.[2] Expressions of distrust of the recognised political parties were frequent, but as a rule they had no more decisive result than the formation of intra-party groups. These groups were always vigilant against what they claimed to be excessive expenditure in the cities, or over-representation of city constituencies in the ministries; but as a rule their members obeyed one or other of the party whips. During the war, however, various causes of dissatisfaction arose which brought about a decision to act independently for the future. These causes were in some cases personal, and varied in the different states. But generally it may be said that the growth in numbers and independence of the country parties was a protest against the manner in which primary products, such as wheat, butter and wool, had been controlled during the war, against attempts to fix the price of meat, butter and other products for domestic consumption, and against a tariff designed to foster Australian manufactures. In addition to these particular grievances there was a widespread, if less clearly defined, sense of dissatisfaction with the growth of public expenditure and the consequent increase in taxation, and a feeling that, at all events in New South Wales and the Commonwealth, the executive had become all-powerful, allowing members no real control over expenditure, and always able to prevent criticism from becoming effective by the threat of dissolution. Again, in New South Wales at least, there was widespread dissatisfaction with the methods of the party organisations, and in particular with the method of preselection, which deterred many eligible citizens from coming forward and was thought to give too much power to the old parliamentary hands.

Undoubtedly the candidates of the new party attracted some votes that would have been given to Labour, either because of the prevailing sense of grievance against war-time administration or because of the hostility of the small farmer to the large landowners which is traditional in New South Wales and, in districts not yet divided into small holdings, is still a powerful factor in elections. But on the whole representatives of the new party were of a conservative type, and their position and tactics varied according to whether the Nationalists were in or out of office. In the Federal Parliament the Country Party, if at full strength, could, in conjunction with Labour, threaten the existence of the Government, and a few months ago, on an economy motion, very nearly defeated it. In Victoria it did actually drive the Government to the country on a motion for a wheat guarantee which the Labour Party supported for purely tactical purposes. In Queensland it forms the larger section of an opposition which is still in a slight minority. In New South Wales it has recently combined with the Nationalists to defeat the Labour Government by one vote. But there the Progressives differ slightly in their composition from the Country or Farmers' Parties. Distaste for the administrative weakness of the Holman Government and for the methods of the Nationalist machine drove into their ranks a number of members from suburban constituencies, and they in consequence have given the party a degree of experience and of debating ability which is not possessed by country parties in other states. There can be little doubt that the formation of these parties has, on the whole, been beneficial to politics in Australia. It has brought into politics a number of men of independent views and character; many of them are extremely well informed in the subjects of interest to their constituents. The weakness of these parties is inexperience and a tendency to forget their denunciation of extravagance and of Socialism whenever a farmer constituency feels the need of Government assistance. The test of the new movement will come when its representatives are asked to take part in the formation of a Government. In Australia, where population has become concentrated to so great an extent in two or three cities, it is unlikely that a Country Party will command a majority in any Parliament, or that it can for long remain a third party when the Labour programme is so definite and so relentlessly pursued. In New South Wales the test has come already, for a majority of the Progressives have been forced by the social and financial measures of the Dooley Government to join with the National leader in forming a ministry. Whether their decision will be approved in the electorates is yet to be seen; but the Progressives in Parliament realised, though with great reluctance, that they could do nothing else.[3]

It should be added that in furtherance of the protest against centralisation and against excessive expenditure in the cities, proposals to form new states, one in the north and another in the south of New South Wales, and a third in the north of Queensland, have been made. But these proposals are as yet very nebulous, and cannot become effective except in connection with the reform of the Federal Constitution. Had the proposed Constitutional Convention been held it would have been necessary for the Country leaders to bring forward their plans and to expound them in greater detail than they have done hitherto. But the Convention has now been abandoned,[4] and for the present no arrangement has been made as to the steps which are to be taken to bring about the division, although the Country leaders still consider them to be vital to the development of their districts and to the progress of rural industries.

December 1921

IMMIGRATION

March 1922, vol. 12, pp. 416–22

IT is frequently stated that Europe, and especially Great Britain, is over-populated. Australia is certainly under-populated. The too crowded state of European countries may lead to very severe economic difficulties. The under-population of Australia results in economic and other evils due to causes of the reverse nature. Her strategic isolation is made more dangerous because of the scanty numbers and resources available for her defence. She cannot find sufficient labour or capital to develop her vast territory to the fullest extent. Railways and public works become a heavy burden and big undertakings fail for want of population. Land settlement is difficult for want of adequate markets. The five million people now in Australia would probably possess more stable prosperity if they were concentrated on the east coast of New South Wales or in Victoria. The scattering of a small population over so large an area creates not a few social difficulties. The loneliness of the settler on the large farms is unnatural, especially to the newcomer from England, where less than 20 per cent. of the population is rural. Capital also has to be dispersed over too wide an area, and in this way it is less efficient and a good deal is wasted. The need for greater numbers is thus paramount—not only would the extra population in itself bring a large addition to our wealth, but by remedying the evil of under-population it would render prosperous areas and undertakings which are now languishing for want of producers and consumers.

The spectacle of 5,500,000 people occupying such a huge territory and utilising it as they do is one of the most remarkable incidents in social and economic history. It indicates much virility and enterprise. The skill with which the pastoral industry has been built up has been remarkable, and the advantage of unstinted doses of British capital has been all-important. But to the individual there are advantages in such a spacious existence. It gives him large ideas and a sense of freedom. It has permitted him also a variety of social experiment. Hardly understanding the basis on which his well-being rests, the Australian settler loves his extensive methods of development, and despises the methods of the petty cultivator and peasant of Europe. The worker, on the other hand, sees a considerable advantage in the scanty nature of the labour supply, quite insensible of the fact that the cost of living then becomes so high that his high wages are of little extra value to him.

Thus at a period when the need for a greater population is most apparent, we find in Australia a positive opposition to immigration by the worker, and an unreadiness in other sections of the community to adopt methods which are necessary if immigration is to succeed. Such an attitude, if shortsighted, has one merit. It induces a feeling of caution in the advocate of immigration, and prevents him from making blunders which would defeat his object.

Wholesale attempts at immigration into Australia would probably fail and justify all the hostile criticism which is made of it. Countries in which population is arriving generally show great prosperity. Wages are high. The new immigrant immediately demands labour for his house and furniture, implements and food. He generally brings some money with him to pay for it. But there is a distinct limit to the absorptive capacity of a country. Its economic machinery cannot be indefinitely extended on a sudden. Wholesale immigration may easily create unemployment and the breaking down of industrial standards. Besides, the influx of new residents puts up rents and land values, and their money causes inflation and rises in prices. There is a tendency to boom and reaction which often causes harm to the whole movement. And the difficulty applies particularly to Australia. In the United States and Canada settlement developed more slowly from the ancient starting points in the east of that continent. There remained at the period of maximum immigration huge areas of unoccupied land in the hands of the Government. In parts of the Middle West of the States and Canada this was of good, even quality, admirably suitable for wheat. A crop could be produced in the first season. The State could thus easily settle vast numbers on the land, and they could be producing in a very short time. In Australia a very large proportion of our Crown lands were taken up by pastoral occupants in the early days. Though they were not intended to get the freehold, they obtained a great deal of it by various devices, so that before the end of last century a very considerable proportion of the land fit for agriculture had been obtained in fee. And to-day, though there are vast areas of Crown lands in Australia, there is not very much of it in areas where the climate is suitable for agriculture. Land settlement in Australia is thus complicated by the problem of land values. In order to settle immigrants it would be necessary to expropriate the present holders and pay them current prices. Now strictly speaking, the value of land is based upon what it will produce. But one or two other factors creep in. In the first place land is desirable for other purposes than production. It makes a home. It confers distinction on the owner. It is unique as a pledge for money. It cannot be destroyed, and, as it tends to rise in price, one does not stand to lose by investing in it. This all tends to bring the price of land above its productive value. Lastly, a skilled farmer can produce more than an amateur from the land he works. The price of land thus tends to be above what an amateur or an immigrant can pay for it and succeed. Where Governments are demanding land for settlement purposes, the price soars and the result is often that men are settled on land at too high a price and a considerable proportion of them fail. These considerations are mentioned to show that the difficulties in the way of immigration cannot be ignored and that public schemes of immigration on a large scale often lead to disaster unless great care is exercised.

These objections have induced a feeling of timidity on the part of politicians. The Labour Party is inordinately suspicious and sees in every step in favour of immigration some attempt to break down Labour standards. The general body of healthy opinion on the subject does not become sufficiently vocal. There are signs, however, that this is changing. Sir Joseph Carruthers, with his scheme for a million farms for a million farmers on unalienated Crown lands has caused a great deal of interest, while the Lord Mayor of Melbourne has received an immense amount of support all over Australia for a New Settlers' League, the object of which is to welcome immigrants and facilitate their placing in employment.[5] Lord Northcliffe also stimulated public feeling by a startling presentation of our danger.[6] But the progress of the work depends upon a thoughtful, systematic and enterprising handling of the principal and minor problems involved in the whole policy of immigration. Uncontrolled immigration would probably do less damage in the long run than the Labour politicians profess to fear. But methods are available by which large numbers of immigrants can be secured without any disturbance of social and economic conditions. For instance, boys can rapidly adapt themselves to new conditions. Apprenticed or adopted into families they soon merge into the life of the community fully equipped for its struggles. Women also are in constant demand for domestic service. Immigrants of this type rarely remain unemployed for more than a few hours after the boat arrives. Subsequently they marry and take a valuable part in the life of the community.

The practice of nominated immigration also affords a means of introducing new settlers without any disturbance of existing conditions. Both those who have been born in Australia and recent arrivals have friends and relations in Britain. Seeing opportunities here and knowing the capabilities of their friends they can nominate them as immigrants and get specially favourable terms for passage money. The nominator in these cases has a special responsibility for the nominee. He will not make the nomination unless he is sure of the vacancy and the suitability of the nominee, and when he arrives he takes a special interest in him. Before the war the practice of nomination was reaching great proportions and it is now being restored. It is expected that we will have had nearly 13,000 immigrants from Great Britain during the year 1921.

One world movement which is showing itself will greatly assist industrial immigration. This is the movement of world-famous firms to inaugurate manufacturing establishments near the source of the raw material. The proximity of vast markets in the East and the advantages of cheap sources of power in Australia, such as the vast field of brown coal in Victoria and the water power in Tasmania, are inducing British firms to start branch factories here. Lysaghts have started a factory for galvanised iron in Newcastle. The famous confectionery firms of Cadbury and Pascall have started a joint enterprise at Hobart and the Swiss firm of Nestlé have started a milk product factory in the western district of Victoria. Big developments are hoped for, and Australians desire to turn into finished cloth a much larger proportion of our raw wool. The immigration of workers qualified for particular industries which it is intended to start should be organised. Skilled men would tend to educate the industrialists. The most important type of immigration of all—that directed to settle and develop an empty country-side—needs deep consideration. To some extent we are suffering from difficulties pointed out by Gibbon Wakefield, from neglect of his advice. It might not be out of the way to start a Land Settlement Association in imitation of his Colonisation Society to study the problem on scientific lines. In California modern community settlements have been established on the basis of an experience covering half a century. They are, it is understood, highly successful. A capitalist will acquire a large area of land at its prairie value. He will have it surveyed by land surveyors, water and mining engineers, soil experts, road and bridge constructors. Upon their data months will be spent in planning the estate out on suitable lines. The farms will be laid out, fenced and planted before a single acre is sold. This is done on a comprehensive scale by team work and at a moderate cost. Provision is made for common utilities and administration, and also for a residential section because the place is attractive. Industries are inaugurated on a co-operative basis for handling the products. The whole is built up as a complete economic unit and the staff maintained for the purpose of advising settlers. The farms are sold just before they come into bearing. It will be seen that not only does such a scheme solve many of the social difficulties involved in new settlements such as the loneliness, the ignorance of the new settler in the selection of and working his block, but it solves the difficult question of land values. The block is almost immediately reproductive, and the original unimproved value is unimportant compared with the valuable improvements which give the land the ability to produce immediately. Such schemes are well justified from the capitalist point of view, each additional development which brings the whole nearer completion being represented by other greater increases in the value of the whole as a going concern. In Australia there are Government settlements which have proceeded a good way on the American lines.[7] They appear likely to succeed very well, but in their lack of some of the most characteristic features of the American system, the co-operative industries, the systematic and economical development, there are elements of weakness. The completeness of the American system is a great factor in its success. Government policy also lacks continuity and is subject to strains and influences which prevent the systematic application principles. Though Australia is loath to allow private enterprise to indulge in these schemes it would probably be better for her to do so and the opportunity for capitalists is a very good one. From the point of view of the immigrant such schemes, whether governmental or private, are excellent. He can select a block before he leaves England. When he arrives he will find a going concern in which he will find his place and where he can be tutored for the first few years.

Our vast spaces, our vast responsibilities and scanty population have tended to make the Australian people shy of big schemes. Many have failed which might have succeeded with more determination. The need now is so urgent, that we must see that there is more enterprise shown in the future.

December 1921

FEDERAL POLITICS

June 1923, vol. 13, pp. 634–40

THE General Election for the ninth Parliament of the Commonwealth, which was held on December 16 last, had most important and interesting consequences. It resulted in the defeat and downfall of one of the greatest and certainly the most picturesque of all Australia's Prime Ministers—Mr. Hughes. It resulted further in the emergence into political power, for the first time in the national government of a British Dominion, of a Country or Farmer's party.

The parallel frequently drawn between the fall of the Coalition Government led by Mr. Lloyd George and of the Nationalist Government led by Mr. Hughes is not without some justification. In both instances there was a popular revolt against the attempt of "the man who won the war" to carry on far into the peace "a one-man government" having most of the characteristics of a war government. In Australia, as in England, the change was more one of persons than of parties and policies. In the late Parliament the Nationalist Administration held a majority over the other two parties of one in the House of Representatives—38 members as against Labour's 23 and the Country party's 14. In the new Parliament the Nationalists have fallen back to 29, whilst Labour has risen to 29. The Country party remains at 14, and there are two Liberals and one Independent. Most significant of all was the fact that more than half the Nationalist casualties were in the Ministry itself, which lost five of its twelve members. Whilst the Nationalists lost more heavily than was expected, the gains of Labour were unexpectedly large, not merely in the House of Representatives, but also in the Senate, where Labour carried a majority of seats in five out of the six States. The Country party did not increase its numbers to the extent anticipated, but the mere maintenance of its position was sufficient to give it the balance of power. In the leadership, the policy and the outlook of this new factor in Australian politics lay the centre of interest, not only of the elections, but also of the formation of the new Government.

Where and how would the Country party throw its weight? On the answer to this question hung the fate of the Hughes Government. The Country party gave the decisive answer without hesitation.

It refused to "support or co-operate with" any Government containing Mr. Hughes. Since the gulf between the policies of Labour and the Country part was too deep to be bridged by any alliance, the only alternative to a new election (which might not give any party a majority but would certainly increase the strength of Labour) was a coalition or alliance between the Nationalists and the Country party. Mr. Hughes was the chief barrier to such a solution. The objections of the Country party to him were based on three grounds. (1) The electors had passed a vote of censure on his administration. (2) His policy was objected to because of its tendency towards autocracy, its disregard to economy, and above all its predilection for State Socialism "of the fig-leaf disguised variety," to quote the phrase of Dr. Earle Page, the leader of the Country party.[8] (3) The third ground was the personal factor. Many months before the elections Mr. Hughes had seen the Country party as the chief threat to his power, and on every possible occasion had attacked it and its leaders ruthlessly.[9] After being pilloried for months by one who does not let his talent for vituperation go rusty for want of use, the Country party was not inclined to stay its hand. Through several weeks of tangled and obscure negotiations between the two parties, Mr. Hughes stove hard to maintain his power. Neither his own effort nor the support of his party—given partly out of loyalty to their leader, and partly because of resentment at the bluntness and pertinacity of the demand for his retirement—could avail against the fixed resolve of the Country party. The complete breakdown of the negotiations on February 1 was followed the next day by Mr. Hughes's dramatic resignation, and his advice to the Governor-General to send for Mr. Bruce, the Federal Treasurer.[10] A week later Mr. Bruce announced the formation of the Bruce-Page Ministry.

No estimate of the nature and possibilities of this Ministry can be made without a clear understanding of the problems Mr. Bruce and Dr. Page had to solve. There were the difficulties inherent in the formation of any coalition—the problem of a common policy; the nature of the coalition; the strength of the respective parties in the Cabinet and their relationships in the House. Besides the ordinary difficulties of personnel—the expectations of members and the vested interests of past Ministers—there were difficulties peculiar to a federal constitution. The practice of having each State represented in the Ministry, and the traditional balance of the Ministry between the House of Representatives and the Senate, had to be considered. In solving this jig-saw puzzle it was inevitable that some individuals, some States, some sections of the respective parties, and the Senate itself, would be disappointed and dissatisfied. This indicates some of the weakness in the Ministry. It is not regarded as a particularly strong Ministry, nor even as the strongest which could have been formed under these conditions.

The most striking feature of the negotiations was the strength of will and decision of purpose shown by Dr. Earle Page; and it is generally agreed that these qualities have greatly strengthened the position of his party. He placed great emphasis upon the preservation of the identity of his party, believing that this was essential to the realisation of the programme of the party and especially of one of its main planks, the creation of new States. Rather than risk the absorption of his party in the larger Nationalist party he would have preferred to support a purely Nationalist Ministry of whose programme his party approved. The second alternative being ruled out by Mr. Bruce, the Country party was prepared to enter a Coalition, but only upon most stringent conditions. In the earlier stages of the negotiations they demanded a predominant voice in the Cabinet, which they considered to be necessary in order to preserve their identity. These demands were described by prominent Nationalists as "arrogant and outrageous." Rather than risk a breakdown of negotiations Dr. Earle Page was prepared in the end to accept a compromise which in fact gave equality in the Cabinet to the Country party, though nominaly the Nationalists maintained a majority. To effect this compromise the members of the Cabinet were reduced from twelve to eleven, the Nationalists receiving six places to the Country party's five. But it was provided that if any matter before the Cabinet were decided on a strict party vote of six to five the decision was regarded as being in the negative. The compromise was not very favourably received by the Nationalists, the official party publication complaining that it invented a new conundrum, namely, "When is a Cabinet resolution defeated?" Answer: "When it is passed by six votes to five." It was agreed that the identity of the two parties should be preserved, each continuing to meet in a separate party room, but acting together in the House. At the opening of Parliament Mr. Bruce set a precedent by speaking for the combined parties on the floor of the House. Further, the positions of Mr. Bruce and Dr. Earle Page were made, as far as possible, equal in the Cabinet. Dr. Page is to act as deputy Prime Minister should the occasion arise; and the Ministry is to be known as the "Bruce-Page" Ministry. In justifying to his constituents the formation of the "composite Ministry," Dr. Earle Page claimed that he had preserved the identity of the party "so that if the policy they advocated could not be secured they would be able to pull out, just like an army corps, with their lines of communication and all their forces intact, to put their case before the public again as an independent political organisation." In view of the tendency throughout the Empire for the rise of Farmers' parties to replace the two-party system by a three-party system,[11] the working of this novel agreement will be watched with widespread interest. It might, as Dr. Earle Page has suggested, "come to be regarded as historic."

With regard to the policy of the new Government, little that is definite can be said at this stage. The Ministry has secured the adjournment of Parliament for several months, after the short preliminary session, in order to work out its policy. Although inspired statements of policy have been made by the Press, the Prime Minister has discounted them as "unauthorised and incorrect." In his speech in the House in reply to the Labour censure motion, which was directed primarily against the failure of the Government to produce their policy immediately, the Prime Minister contented himself with indicating some of the problems which the Ministry would have to face and their general attitude towards these problems.[12] Both Mr. Bruce and Dr. Earle Page, in speeches outside the House, have indicated the general principles upon which the Ministry is based and have set its tone. That every member of the Ministry is Australian born has possibly some small significance, since in his first public utterances as Prime Minister Mr. Bruce has emphasised that the Government stands for a vigorous national policy. "We will endeavour," he said, "to think nationally, see nationally, and act nationally."[13]

But there are indications that the new Ministry will show a deeper insight than any previous Ministry into Australia's most vital problem, that of harmonising her nationhood with the two great complementary aspects of her external relations, namely, her fellowship in the British Commonwealth and her membership of the League of Nations. The League of Nations has a strong friend in Mr. Bruce, who ably represented Australia at the second meeting of the Assembly. Both Mr. Bruce and Dr. Earle Page have placed strong emphasis upon the development of the foreign policy, the defence policy and the trade relations of the British Commonwealth. In his opening speech in the House the Prime Minister placed these matters in the forefront of the Government's policy.

In view of the emphasis which he has laid upon the importance of holding an Imperial Conference at an early date to consider these questions, his statement in the House should be quoted:—

The Government believe that to-day, for the discussion of the question of an Empire naval defence scheme, consultation between the Dominions and the Motherland is essential; and if an Imperial Conference is not summoned, Australia will press for one at the earliest possible moment, believing, as we do, that it is vital to our safety and our whole future welfare, wrapped up in the question of Empire foreign affairs . . . . We have to try to ensure that there shall be an Empire foreign policy which, if we are to be in any way responsible for it, must be one to which we agree and have assented.[14] With full appreciation of the responsibility for what I am saying I suggest that this question to-day is not in a satisfactory position, and that, unless some better arrangements can be made, the position of an outlying Dominion like Australia will become intolerable. If we are to take any responsibility for the Empire's foreign policy, there must be a better system, so that we may be consulted and have a better opportunity to express the view of the people of this country. This is a matter that will have to be considered at the Imperial Conference.

If this strong statement is any true indication, Australia is likely to play an unusually important part at the Conference. What its policy will be the Ministry has not yet indicated. But it should be noted that Dr. Earle Page has repeatedly drawn attention to the necessity of more effective consultation between the Commonwealth and the British Government, and has urged that Australia should be represented in London for this purpose by a Cabinet Minister.

As regards domestic policy an important conference between the Commonwealth and the States will be held in the near future to consider, *inter alia,* the following matters: (1) the whole question of immigration; (2) the duplication of tax-collecting bodies, and the allotment of spheres of taxation as between the Commonwealth and the States; (3) amendment of the present dual control of industrial relations.[15]

The Government is committed to an early consideration of the question of creating New States, and this will probably involve the summoning of a Constitutional Convention. Although the Ministry is in no sense a free trade Ministry, the Country party is pledged to ease the tariff somewhat in favour of the primary producer. Further, the strong anti-socialistic tendency of both sections of the "composite" Government, and their belief that trade and industry are not legitimate functions of Governments, will find vent in a rigid scrutiny of all government enterprises.

March 1923

AUSTRALIAN ADMINISTRATION IN PAPUA

June 1925, vol. 15, pp. 573–82

NEARLY twenty years have passed since the Commonwealth assumed the administration of Papua—twenty very varied years of changing markets and falling prices, of peace and of war—a period long enough and eventful enough to test fairly the capability of the Commonwealth to carry out the responsibilities that it had undertaken. There were many gloomy forebodings twenty years ago, and many prognostications that the Australian government of Papua would be a fiasco, for it was said that there were certain qualities in which Australians were lacking. Consequently, it was argued, the Australian administration was doomed to failure.

Now that the twenty years are nearly over, a convenient time has arrived to take stock and to review what has been done in Papua since it became an Australian territory in 1906.

Papua was but little known in those days, for the interior had hardly been touched except for the explorations of Sir William MacGregor,[16] and it was almost entirely undeveloped; the fertility of the soil had been questioned both by Sir William MacGregor and Sir George Le Hunte;[17] and the natives had been described as "a fierce and intractable race of savages," so lost to all sense of decorum that "when attacked they did not scruple to retailiate." There had been practically no agricultural development in 1906, for the total area under cultivation amounted to less than 1,500 acres; there was a fair amount of gold mining, chiefly alluvial, but other industries hardly existed.

Elsewhere it has been found that those who come looking for gold have stayed on to cultivate the soil, but this has not been the case in Papua. The searcher for alluvial gold is generally of a roving and adventurous disposition, and the humdrum life of a cocoanut plantation offers few attractions to men of this type. Many attempts had been made both by Sir William and Sir George to settle planters on the land, but without success. The soil of Papua is generally patchy and not particularly rich, the climate has but few attractions for those who have lived in the temperate zone, and in those days money could perhaps be made quicker in Australia; in any case, whatever the reason may have been, planters refused to come when they were called, however wisely the Lieutenant-Governors sought to charm them. The assumption of control by the Commonwealth[18] was probably the best advertisement that the Territory could have had, and with the beginning of 1907 a mild land boom had set in. Most of the usual mistakes were made that are inseparable from pioneer enterprise, and no doubt much money was wasted and many anticipations formed which were quite impossible of realisation, but on the whole the settlement was a success—a far greater success than could have been anticipated from the history of previous attempts.

And indeed, there was no reason *a priori* why it should not be a success. The soil, it is true, has been described as "not rich" and "patchy," and the description is doubtless correct, but the best plantations in Papua are probably as good as the best elsewhere in the Pacific, and the average yield per acre is about the same, though it may be more difficult in Papua to find a large area of uniform fertility. Then there has never been a real shortage of labour, although with a wise determination to avoid so far as possible the racial problems that have arisen in other parts of the Empire the Imperial Administration had never allowed the introduction of labour from over seas into Papua, and although this policy was continued with even greater strictness by the Commonwealth Government after 1906, had the importation of Asiatic labour been allowed, Papuan development would have been enormously accelerated, but only at a price of racial discord which the Government was not prepared to pay. Thus the only labour available in Papua has been that which could be recruited from among the native Papuans. The population of Papua is small—the native inhabitants are estimated at 275,000—but the labour supply has always responded to the demand, though there has never been anything to spare, and in quality the Papuan labour is probably as good as elsewhere in the Pacific. The opinions expressed by employers are varied in the extreme—some will tell you that it is the best labour in the world, and others that it is absolutely the worst—but it is interesting to note that the low wage of 5s. a month paid in the Mandated Territory is justified on the ground that a native of that Territory only does about half as much work as a native of Papua; and from this one may conclude that labour in Papua is probably as good as in other parts of the Pacific.

Still the plantations in Papua have so far not been profitable, and it is interesting to consider why this has been so. Originally the tendency was to blame the Government, but of later years a more reasonable view has been taken.

Probably many companies would have been paying dividends

long ago, had they not (very wisely) been putting their money into the extension of their planted area; but what has really affected the Papuan planter has been a succession of extraordinary pieces of ill fortune.

Rubber boomed in price some 15 or 20 years ago, but by the time that the Papuan plantations were producing the market was falling rapidly, and continued to fall until it no longer paid to tap the trees. Now the price is struggling back, and planters in Papua are beginning to tap again, but only after years of very heavy loss. So with copra. When Papuan cocoanuts were first coming into bearing the Great War burst upon the world with its general disorganisation and disruption of commerce, and after the war came the Navigation Act,[19] so that Papuan copra, like Papuan rubber, has hardly had a decent market yet. If planters had enjoyed a few years of prosperity before this accumulation of disasters befell them, they might have amassed sufficient reserves to pull them through, but they had had no extended period of prosperity and they had to stand the full brunt of the war, the falling market, and finally the crowning horror of the Navigation Act, with no reserves at all. It is only their pluck and tenacity that has enabled them to survive; and it may be hoped with some confidence that this pluck and tenacity will eventually be rewarded by the removal of the Navigation Act and the establishment of a stable market at reasonable prices.

The Annual Reports show the total area planted as 1,467 acres in 1907, nearly 43,000 in 1914, over 58,000 in 1919, and over 60,000 in 1923. Exports show £63,000 for 1906–7; £123,000 for 1913–14; £270,000 for 1919–20; £239,000 for 1923–4. Imports for the same years are £87,000; £212,000; £422,000; £354,000. These figures would be satisfactory but that they disclose the fact that development has practically been stationary since 1919.

This is the result, partly of unsatisfactory prices, but chiefly of the Navigation Act. This is an Act which was originally passed by the Commonwealth Parliament in 1912, and which was not extended to Papua and the Mandated Territory until 1922, although its threatened extension had cast a shadow over Papuan development for some time previously. The effect of extending this legislation to the Territories is to make the ports of those Territories Australian ports within the meaning of the Act, so that no vessels, except those which comply with Australian conditions, can carry passengers or cargo between Australia and any port of Papua or the Mandated Territory. The practical result is that all Papuan overseas trade is confined to one shipping company trading between the Territory and Sydney;[20] and it will remain so confined until Papuan exports are sufficient to provide regular cargoes to Europe. No fresh investment of capital for agricultural development can be expected while that Act is in force, for investors will naturally seek fields where they are assured of commercial freedom; but existing plantations may do well, with such assistance as the Commonwealth may give to make up for the handicap which it has imposed. Even if the Act is removed, the effects of the removal will not be immediate, for there will be a fear (although almost certainly a groundless fear) that it may be reimposed; but by degrees this anxiety will disappear, and the prosperous days of 1910–14 may return, when Papuan plantations were extending rapidly, and Australian, Dutch and German shipping were competing for Papuan trade.

There can be no doubt that the Navigation Act must eventually be removed, for its continuance and the consequent shipping monopoly seem quite inconsistent with Australian ideas, but immediate relief may come from the growth of the mining industry. A good mine will carry a handicap which would crush a cocoanut plantation, and the development of Papua may be in the future, as it was originally, in the direction of mining rather than agriculture. There is a vast copper field in the neighbourhood of Port Moresby, and the adequate development of this field or the discovery of petroleum in commercial quantities might revolutionise the conditions of the Territory completely. It is certainly to be hoped that some new industry may soon arise to make up for the complete stoppage of agricultural development. It is possible that this new industry may take the shape of plantations owned and managed by natives, on lines somewhat similar to those on which the native plantations of West Africa are conducted. Such plantations have been established in Papua, and have been as successful as could be anticipated with so primitive and conservative a people. Last year about 180 tons of rice (unhusked) were produced by natives of the Gulf of Papua, and other cultures which have been encouraged are cocoa, oil palms, cotton, and of course cocoanuts. The policy should be persevered with in spite of difficulties and disappointments, but it will not be for some years that the native plantations can be expected to make any noticeable addition to the volume of Papuan exports.

It has been said that the greatest asset in Papua is the native population, and doubtless this is true, for without the natives there would be no labour, and without labour there could be no industry. But the Papuan Government, with the full approval of the Commonwealth, has consistently taken the higher view, and has realised that the natives are something very much more than an asset—that they are a very grave responsibility.

The native policy of Papua has been entirely original. Questions of purely native policy, such as native taxation, native education, native agriculture, and so on, had not arisen in the time of the Imperial administration. Of course, anything like ill-treatment and oppression of natives had been sternly discouraged by both the Imperial Lieutenant-Governors, but this did not carry one very far towards the discharge of the "sacred trust" which has since been discovered to exist between Governments and their primitive subjects. Nor were precedents from other countries of much assistance, on account of the difference in the character of the native populations.

So the Australian Administration had to formulate a policy for itself, and fortunately it seems to have hit upon the right one. It is a commonplace nowadays that a wise native administration should endeavour so far as possible to retain native customs; this has become a commonplace through the writings of Dr. Rivers and others, but it was not a commonplace in 1907.[21] So it is perhaps fortunate that the Papuan Government acted from the very first upon those lines. There are of course certain customs which clearly should not be retained. It is said that some anthropologists would contend that cannibalism and head-hunting should not be put down, because, they argue, the harm you do to the native community by suppressing these practices (which are often closely interwoven with the whole social fabric) more than counterbalances the suffering and loss of life which they involve. But torture, for instance, no one would defend, nor would any sane administration tolerate cannibalism and head-hunting whatever disaster their cessation might cause to the social organism.

However, there are many native customs which are either harmless or even beneficial, and the policy has been to preserve those, and also other customs which, though in some ways objectionable, are not wholly evil. Feasts and dances, for instance, do much harm by creating an artificial famine in the village during the time immediately preceding the feast—for all food must be preserved for the great ceremony—and a very real famine afterwards when all the food has been consumed, and they also lead to feuds and loss of life. But they are not wholly evil and are therefore not interfered with, and are even encouraged.

It is of course quite impossible to keep native customs alive indefinitely in a stone age community like that of Papua, where every European resident acts as a solvent of the old culture, however much he may wish to preserve it. The Papuan Government recognises this, and its policy is to maintain the most useful of these customs as long as possible until the native can adapt himself to the new life which the arrival of the white man has made inevitable.

The idea that the Papuan can go on with his head-hunting and his cannibal dances while the white man is searching for minerals alongside his village, and is preparing to bore for oil in his sacred places, is one which no administrator and no sane anthropologist will admit for a moment. The Papuan must adapt himself; his old culture will leave him more or less rapidly according to circumstances, and the question arises, what is there to put in its place?

Now as regards his religion—his indigenous ritual and his traditional morality—there seems to be no difficulty; when this goes, as it must eventually, there is only one thing which we can put in its place, and that is some form of Christianity. It is not in the least a question whether Christianity is true or false, or whether it is good or bad, though one may conjecture that if it is good enough for Europe it is good enough for Papua; but true or false, good or bad, it is the only substitute, and the Missions deserve well of the Administration in making Christianity available to the native.

So with regard to other customs—head-hunting, for instance, and tribal warfare. If these are suppressed, as of course they must be, something must be provided to take their place. Whatever is provided will be infinitely tame and uninteresting in comparison with what is taken away. The natives in some parts of Papua put a pig in the place of the man who was to be eaten, but a pig must be a very poor substitute for a hereditary enemy, and equally poor as a substitute is the activity which has been offered to the Papuan in place of the delights of battle and bloodshed. Industry is the alternative which has been put before him—certainly a most unsatisfying one, but the best one probably that can be devised—and the object aimed at is to substitute an industrial for a military ideal, and to turn a tribe of disappointed warriors into a more or less industrious race of artisans and agriculturists. Sport, too, cricket, and to a less extent football, and recently hockey, have been valuable in taking the place of the old customs, and in giving the native an interest in life; but unfortunately they are hardly possible except in the neighbourhood of centres of European population. All kinds of sport are encouraged both by the Government and missionaries and also by many employers of labour, with the happiest results, but it is not to be expected that any of our games will extend beyond the direct influence of the Europeans. They would be especially valuable in taking the place of the native dances which are dying out in many parts. It is interesting to note that Christian natives have occasionally given up dancing of their own accord, and even against the advice of the missionary, who has wished the dancing to continue. "We know more about it than you do," say the natives, "we know that the dances are bad, and we do not want to have anything to do with them." It is difficult to make a man dance against his will, but he may be induced to play cricket; and it is hoped that in time he will.

This is being done partly by technical education, with the assistance of the Missions, but principally by the encouragement of native agriculture. This has been made possible by the system of native taxation which was introduced a few years ago. The maximum tax is fixed at £1 a head per adult male, with exceptions in favour of certain classes such as the Native Constabulary, and also of the fathers of four children, and the money collected is paid, not into revenue, but into a certain fund which can only be expended for native education and other purposes which are solely for the benefit of the natives.[22] The costs of the native plantations are borne by this fund, and the earnings of the plantations are divided between the fund and the natives who have worked on the plantations. If the native plantations which are now being established are successful, much will have been done to help the native race in their perilous and rapid passage from the Stone Age to the twentieth century, and something to assist in the development of the Territory. The plantations should certainly succeed if the policy is persevered in. The chief obstacle is the incurable conservatism of the native, and his inability to see any good in anything which was not done by his grandfather. But a few good harvests may overcome this conservative instinct and then all should go easily enough.

Papua is no longer the *terra incognita* that it was twenty years ago. Most of the Territory is now under Government control, and nearly the whole of it has been explored. This has been the work of officers of the Papuan service, who have carried out a very difficult duty with a courage, a tenacity and a restraint for which they get but little credit. Most of them have a fair knowledge of social anthropology, and contributions by them appear not infrequently in anthropological journals.

No review of the period of Australian control in Papua would be complete without reference to the work of the Administrator, Sir Hubert Murray.[23] Sir Hubert has held his present position for some twenty years, and is now able to see the reward of the foresight with which he established his scheme of government and the patience and determination with which he has adhered to it. The most conspicuous feature of his policy has been the fidelity with which he has followed the British ideal of a trusteeship for the native races. Mainly for that reason he has been subjected from time to time to some severe criticism both from residents in Papua and from Australians. To-day, however, the value of his work is universally recognised. His criticis admit that had not the interests of the natives been safeguarded, the maintenance of development in Papua would have been impossible, and all observers bear witness to the energy which he has shown in the exploration of a difficult country. The Administration has been handicapped by scarcity of funds and by the lack of any satisfactory system of recruiting the civil service. These difficulties have been overcome mainly through the personality of the Administrator, whose example has been reflected in the work of his subordinates, and has earned him the gratitude of his fellow-countrymen.

The Papuan is well worth preserving, and it is hoped that the sincere efforts which are being made to prevent his even partial extinction may be crowned with success; and the evidence points to the conclusion that they will.

March 1925

THE FEDERAL ELECTION 1925

March 1926, vol. 16, pp. 387–406

IN the last number of THE ROUND TABLE reference was made to the decision of the Federal Government that Parliament should be dissolved some months before it had completed its normal term of three years.[24] The elections were held on November 14, and resulted in an unquestionable victory for the Government. It secured majorities in all the six States. A number of seats were gained and none were lost. In certain industrial centres, which had hitherto been regarded as impregnable strongholds of Labour, the minorities in its favour were exceptionally large; in other constituencies which had been held with difficulty by the Nationalist or Country party, majorities were greatly increased. Labour retained the greater number of its pledged adherents, and they constitute a large proportion of the voting strength of the Commonwealth, but the unpledged vote on which almost every Australian election turns went unmistakably in favour of the Government, the final result being that in the House of Representatives the Nationalists have 38 supporters, the Country part who support the Government, 14, and Labour 23.

THE CAMPAIGN AND ITS ISSUES

THE election campaign though very short aroused unprecedented interest, and it may be useful to describe the conditions under which it was fought. The reason given by Mr. Bruce for the early dissolution of Parliament and for his claim to support was the failure of several of the State Governments to suppress the growth of Communism as manifested in a series of strikes, or to associate themselves with him in suppressing it, and the consequent need for conferring new powers for that purpose on the Federal Government. For some time prior to the dissolution the Labour party had been in power in five out of the six States, the exception being Victoria. Mr. Bruce, therefore, was in an unusual position as the leader of the party in office, since on the main issue of the election he could concentrate his attack on the failures of his opponents rather than defend his own acts. The chief responsibility for the control of the police and for the enforcement of the law is with the State Government. The Government of New South Wales had refused to allow its police to act on behalf of the Federal Government and serve notices on persons who were required to show cause why they should not be deported under the provisions of the Act passed in the month of July, and briefly referred to in the last number of THE ROUND TABLE.[25] That Act was passed after a number of strikes which had disorganised shipping on the Australian coast, and which were generally ascribed to the instigation of two leaders of the Australian Seamen's Union. It provided that if the Governor-General should be of opinion

that there exists in Australia a serious industrial disturbance prejudicing or threatening the peace, order or good government of the Commonwealth, he may make a proclamation to this effect, which proclamation shall be and remain in force until it is revoked by the Governor-General.[26]

It also provided that when any such proclamation is in force the Minister administering the Act, if he is satisfied

that any person not born in Australia has been concerned in Australia in acts directed towards hindering or obstructing to the prejudice of the public, the transport of goods or the conveyance of passengers in relation to trade or commerce with other countries or among the States . . . and that the presence of that person will be injurious to the peace, order and good government of the Commonwealth in relation to matters with respect to which the Parliament has power to make laws, may summon the person to appear before a Board to show cause why he should not be deported from the Commonwealth.[27]

The necessary proclamation was published shortly after the commencement of the strike of seamen in British ships in Australian ports against the reduction of their wages, which had been agreed upon in England, and summonses were prepared for Messrs. Walsh and Johnson, the two leaders of the seamen already referred to.[28] It was these summonses which the Premier of New South Wales refused to allow his police to serve. Mr. Bruce was able, in spite of strenuous resistance from the Labour members of the Federal Parliament, to pass an Act authorising him to enrol Commonwealth police. The summonses were served, and the enquiry was held. But the refusal of a State to assist in carrying out a Commonwealth law was one of the reasons put forward for the demand for additional powers and for the charge that the New South Wales Government had shown sympathy with Communists.

There were, however, other grounds for the same charge which were urged before and after the dissolution. It was said that Mr. Lang, the State Premier,[29] should have used his influence as a Labour leader to persuade the strikers to return to work, and that although no Communist was a member of his Ministry or even a member of Parliament, some Communist leaders occupied important positions in the trade unions and were able to exert a considerable influence on the Government. In Queensland, where Labour had been in power for a longer period than in any other State, there was convincing evidence of the incapacity of the Government to control the Labour unions even in the State services. There was no disorder on the waterfront in that State until towards the close of the election campaign, but there had been a strike in the railway service which had disorganised traffic throughout the State until the Government had capitulated. And, both before and after the election, ships were held up in the Queensland ports. In Western Australia, however, there had been attacks on ships lying at the wharf at Fremantle, where many were held up, and the Premier had refused to strengthen an inadequate police force on the ground that no one had suffered actual violence.[30] Ships laden with timber for South Africa had also been held up at Bunbury, and it was said that their crews had been intimidated. In South Australia there had been no actual violence, though it is said that at Adelaide crews which had not wished to join in the strike were intimidated. In Tasmania there were no British vessels, and the only complaint that could be made against the Government was that the Premier[31] had expressed his sympathy with a proposed attempt to test the deportation law on behalf of the States. In Victoria, the only non-Labour State, vessels had been held up as elsewhere, but there had been no violence, and the Premier,[32] besides offering to guarantee protection to union seamen who might fill the places of the strikers, had refused to join with his fellow Premiers in testing the Federal law.

In so far as Mr. Bruce's case rested on the conduct of the maritime strike it was strengthened by the continuance of the strike until the end of his electoral campaign. In New South Wales the strike was never welcomed by the unions other than the seamen's, yet it received intermittent help from time to time which made ultimate success appear possible. Some unions gave financial help. The Waterside Workers, although they refused full co-operation, decided not to load vessels worked by other than their original crews, and towards the end of the strike the Australian Seamen's Union refused to take colliers to the ships' sides. But in Sydney, although it was suggested that producers might come in and insist on vessels being loaded, as they had in 1917, there was very little violence. Although most of the British ships worked by white crews were held up, cargo was carried in vessels of the Commonwealth line, in ships worked by coloured crews and in foreign vessels. It was a paradoxical result of the protest against a reduction in wages that lines whose rates were far below those of the British ships should benefit, but the fact was that a large proportion of the cargo available was sent away and, for the time being, no great hardship was suffered by producers.

In Queensland the position was different. In the northern ports of that State there was for a time some danger of a conflict between the producers and the strikers because of a well-grounded fear of the producers of meat and sugar that owing to the strike their produce, if not lost altogether, would seriously deteriorate. The difficulties caused by the Seamen's strike had been accentuated in these northern ports by a demand from the wharf labourers that what was called the rotary system should be enforced and the work of loading be equally distributed among all the labourers available irrespective of merit. It was found that under this system the cost of loading was approximately doubled. The owners, therefore, refused to accept it, and the Queensland Arbitration Court declared the consequent refusal of the wharf labourers to work to be a strike. The immediate cause of the crisis, however, was the inability of a ship lying off Gladstone, the port of a large beef producing district, to obtain sufficient coal for her refrigerating chambers. The farmers, fearing the loss of the cargo, came to Gladstone and threatened to see themselves that sufficient coal was put on board, and no doubt would have carried out their threat had not the strikers offered a satisfactory compromise. In Bowen, the port of a sugar district, the neighbouring farmers demanded that their sugar should be loaded, and the vessel to take the sugar be supplied with coal, and although a strike was threatened by the railway workers and there was much backing and filling by the State Government, they were ultimately successful.

Besides these events in the north, there was a serious outbreak at Brisbane, where a number of British strikers made an attack on a vessel in order to prevent her sailing, and where firearms were used for the first time during the strike. This attack occurred on November 7, so that in Queensland the attention of the electors was directed to the ineffectiveness of the Labour Government up to the date of the election. Since the end of the railway strike the State Premier had resigned, having been appointed to the position of lay judge of the Industrial Court created by his Government.[33] His successor had shown a disposition to exercise control over the Government service and to maintain the law, but he had not restored confidence in the ability of his Administration to deal with strikes, and the impression was general that their produce would have been allowed to perish had not the farmers come together to protect themselves.

Western Australia, too, had suffered from the strike, and had been the scene of more than one outbreak of violence. Some little time after the attacks already mentioned at the wharf at Fremantle, an announcement was made on behalf of the owners that their ships would not call at that port on the voyage to or from Europe or Africa. Fremantle is the first port of call for a great many vessels trading with Australia, and the announcement meant a serious loss of work for the wharf labourers and of trade for the townspeople of Fremantle and Perth. Shortly after this announcement the police force was strengthened, and the strikers having been encouraged by their previous impunity, a riot broke out on November 7, in which many of the participants, both strikers and police, suffered serious injury.[34] Shortly after this the strike in Fremantle was declared at an end, and it was said that in other ports it was continued only because of the hope that a victorious Labour party would be able to secure favourable terms of settlement from the British owners. Whether this is so or not, the continuance of the strike, the occasional outbreaks of violence and the danger to the producers that their exports would suffer, enabled Ministerial candidates to keep the public attention concentrated on what they desired to make the outstanding feature of the elections, the presence in Australia of a number of men determined to attain their ends by violence, the impotence of Labour Governments to control them, and their unwillingness to denounce them.

Mr. Bruce never very clearly defined the new powers for which he would ask if successful at the polls. He did say that he would pass a Federal Crimes Act and would if necessary enrol a Federal police force to carry it into effect. He also announced that he would introduce a Bill declaring strikes illegal unless preceded by a secret ballot among the unions concerned, together with measures of social reform intended to remove legitimate sources of discontent. But the substance of his speeches on this issue was a claim that the influence of Moscow in Australia, as shown by a series of strikes, was increasing, however few its professed adherents might be, and he appealed for a vote in favour of the maintenance of industrial peace and the enforcement of the law. His Government, however, could point to work done and to a programme for the future on which it could have asked for support if the strike issue had never arisen. The record of the Administration included substantial reductions in land and income taxation, and in the Commonwealth debt, the establishment of a higher tariff and the expenditure of large sums both out of loan money and out of revenue on rural development. Following recent American precedent the Government had devoted part of its annual surplus to the improvement of country roads, and had spent 18 millions of loan money on the extension of postal, telegraphic, and telephone services, and on other reproductive works. It had also sought to establish a better system of marketing butter, fruit and other primary products, and had set up a department of the Commonwealth Bank for the benefit of farmers. Dr. Page, as Treasurer and associate Prime Minister, had paid off 22 millions of unproductive war debt, and established a sinking fund in connection with Commonwealth loans, besides bringing the States together in the Loan Council, from which New South Wales under its Labour Government had seceded. This record contained nothing sensational and nothing, with the possible exception of the tariff, calculated to attract any one or more groups of votes, but it was a record which justified the temporary alliance of the country and the Nationlist parties for the life of the Parliament, and had induced them to pledge themselves to a loose form of co-operation during the elections before both made common cause in support of Mr. Bruce's appeal on the strike. The Government claimed to have done much for the cities by its tariff and much for the country by improving means of communication, to have established a sound and economical defence policy, and to have taken practical steps to maintain a place for Australia in the councils of the Empire.

The programme for the next Parliament is extremely ambitious. Mr. Bruce in his policy speech announced an elaborate social policy including schemes of child endowment, of national insurance and of advances to be made through the Commonwealth Bank to enable manual workers and persons of small means to acquire their own homes. He proposed to continue and increase the subsidies for the improvement of country roads and for the development of markets for exports, to spend £100,000 on scientific research and a further sum on an enquiry into the best means of increasing agricultural and pastoral production. Mr. Bruce also announced that Parliament would be called upon to consider the revision of the Constitution, which is now long overdue. Mr. Hughes in his last policy speech had proposed to summon a convention for this purpose.[35] Mr. Bruce maintained that the idea of a convention was impracticable, and that Parliament would be asked to pass Bills to be submitted to the people at a referendum. Recently the two States of Tasmania and Western Australia have complained that they have suffered financially through the Federation. The claims of each of them and also proposals for the formation of new States will be considered at this special constitutional session of the new Parliament. The defence policy of the Government had been initiated in the last Parliament when orders had been given for the building of two 10,000 ton cruisers, and the announcement had been made that a seaplane carrier, a floating dock, and an oil depot in the Northern Territory would also be built. In his policy speech Mr. Bruce also formulated a programme of defence on land and in the air which will include the establishment of factories with nucleus staffs and the co-operation of manufacturing industries. The policy of the Government was summed up in the declaration that

no party should be intrusted with the executive power of government which is not prepared to subscribe to the fullest possible measure of defence, and to declare in detail and without any equivocation what its proposals are on this most vital issue.

Mr. Bruce also laid emphasis in all his important speeches on the position of Australia in the Empire. "It is impossible to imagine Australia outside the Empire. We declare for the British Empire with all the privileges and responsibilities that it involves, but within the Empire we demand freedom, independence and the fullest consultation."[36] These extracts from his policy speech were repeated in all important centres by Mr. Bruce and by his colleagues. Throughout his very extensive electioneering tour he appealed to his countrymen to realise the lofty destiny which Australia might attain within the Empire, if Communist influences were suppressed and Parliament could give its attention to the task of eliminating industrial discontent and developing the resources of the country.[37]

The answer of the Labour party to Mr. Bruce's main charge was a declaration that there was no serious danger of Communism in Australia, and a denial that Labour had any association with the avowed Communists who supported it. It was also claimed by some candidates, including the former Premier of Queensland, Mr. Theodore,[38] that the settlement of strikes could with a greater probability of success be left to the Labour party than to Mr. Bruce. Mr. Charlton[39] also undertook that if he became Prime Minister he would repeal the deportation provisions of the Immigration Act, but as a rule the Labour candidates preferred to divert attention from the subject of Communism and direct it to specific details of the Government record. Indeed very little was heard of the low wages of British seamen, a topic usually calculated to evoke expressions of sympathy, nor was any great effort made to exploit the fairly widespread dislike of deportation as a form of punishment, or of the method of investigation set up under the new Act. The Opposition quite naturally sought to exercise the right of an Opposition at a normal general election to criticise the record and programme of the Government. The two charges most often directed against Mr. Bruce in the cities were that he had not caused the two cruisers ordered in Great Britain to be built in Australia, and that he had not sufficiently protected Australian industry. In the country it was said that Labour would develop the Rural Credits Department of the Commonwealth Bank in the interests of farmers, would establish a more satisfactory method of marketing overseas, and would abolish that much abused person the middleman. Mr. Charlton, the leader of the Federal Opposition, propounded a defence policy which included the abolition of compulsory military training and the substitution of seaplanes and submarines for the cruisers as a protection against invasion. In the country districts Labour candidates sought to warn the farmers and settlers against Nationalists, by playing on the hostility of the country for the town, which had brought about the formation of the Country party. In the last Parliament this party had numbered 14, and although it had supported the Government in which its leader, Dr. Earle Page, had held the Treasury portfolio (as equal with Mr. Bruce) it had maintained its separate organisation. During the election Labour warned the country electors that a bogey had been raised for the purpose of absorbing their representatives among the Nationalists. Whatever success these tactics might have had in normal times, they could have none so long as the farmers were threatened with the loss or deterioration of their exports. The numbers of the Country party will be the same in the new Parliament as they were in the old, and Nationlist majorities in the country in doubtful seats were increased. Unexpected prominence was given to a proposal that Mr. Spahlinger should be brought to Australia to carry out his cure for tuberculosis in this country. Sir Neville Howse, the Minister for Defence, after enquiries made in Switzerland while a delegate to the League of Nations, had declared any such scheme premature and impracticable, but Mr. Charlton without specifying the means undertook that it could be carried out.[40] Another change somewhat vaguely formulated was that the Bruce-Page Government did not represent a truly Australian spirit. The charge was somewhat difficult to analyse, for both Mr. Bruce and Dr. Page were born and have their interests in this country. But the warning was uttered in many articles and on many platforms that Mr. Bruce would place Australia at the mercy of an Empire Council, and that the only safe custodians of the national spirit were the members of the Labour party.

THE RESULTS ANALYSED

THE aggregate vote for Australia was approximately 2,798,634, of which 1,535,795 were for the Government, and 1,262,839 for the Opposition. The Government, therefore, have a decided majority, but not so great as the distribution of seats in the House of Representatives would suggest. The aggregate Labour vote is a clear indication that a great number of electors did not accept the issue as one of Communism or revolution against orderly government and the supremacy of Parliament. Property is so widely held in Australia that the number who would vote for Communism or revolution on a referendum would be ludicrously small, and the conditions of life in Australia make it an exceedingly unpromising soil for propaganda in favour of either of these objects. Great advantages have been obtained for manual labourers through legislation, and as already mentioned, Labour Governments are at present in power in five out of the six States. In the Labour party politics is the career open to talent. Savings Bank deposits have steadily increased until at the end of 1924 their total number is 3,798,662, or considerably more than one for every two men, women and children of the population. The average value of the accounts was £46 11s., the total amount deposited being £176,871,477. A similar inference can be drawn from the statistics of life assurance and friendly societies. At the end of 1923 there were 1,960,000 life or industrial policies in force, or about one policy for every three persons, the average amount of an ordinary life policy being £270, and of an industrial policy £35. Adequate statistics of the ownership of homes are not easy to find, but it appears from the census of 1921 that in that year there were 1,107,000 private dwellings in Australia, of which approximately 56 per cent. were occupied by owners or prospective owners. The Commonwealth loans raised in Australia are widely distributed, and among the largest investors are the insurance companies which hold or guarantee the savings of their very numerous policy holders. From these figures it will be seen that the bias in favour of private property and of parliamentary government in Australia is likely to be very strong. But the term Communist is used in public controversy as loosely as the term Bolshevist. It was strictly applicable to and was accepted by a few trade union officials who, though they were disowned by the Labour party, claimed to exercise a great influence over it. It was used also to describe the Australian leaders of the seamen who from their conduct in a series of strikes had appeared to aim at making the regular transport of goods by Australian or British ships impossible. Political Labour had never identified itself with the strikers, but had never openly denounced them, and there had been continuous strikes on the water-front throughout 1925, and the latter part of 1924 to the detriment of other unions than the seamen's, and of many sections of the producers. It seems clear from the election figures that Labour was identified in the minds of many electors with these strikes, that the Ministerialists were supported as the party which was opposed to strikes and would strive to repress them, that Labour failed because it was thought to have acquiesced in, if it had not actually favoured them. Another circumstance which favoured Nationalism was the conduct of the Lang Government in New South Wales, which had gone to the country on a policy of moderation and in office had proved to be among the least moderate of Labour Ministries. For this reason, amongst others, many of the electors in New South Wales who had voted Labour at the State elections refused to regard the Labour denunciation of Communism as a trustworthy indication of the policy of the movement. All the State electors were strengthened in this attitude by the selection as a candidate for the Senate of a confessedly unrepentant revolutionist.[41] Again, the Roman Catholic vote, which in New South Wales not many months before had been cast almost unanimously in favour of Labour, and was said to have decided the State elections in New South Wales, was at the Federal elections about evenly divided. The Government was free from the embarrassment of sectarian questions, and the Church as a whole was against Communism. Generally it was thought that Labour when faced with a crisis had failed either through lack of courage or because the nature of its following had made decisive action impossible.

The outstanding figure of the campaign was unquestionably Mr. Bruce. His energy was prodigious. In the short election campaign he visited every State of Australia, Western Australia excepted, and spoke in many districts in which the head of the Government had never before been heard. From being one of the least known of Australian Prime Ministers, he became as well known as any of his predecessors. Throughout he kept all controversy on a high level, refusing to descend to personalities, and showing everywhere a grasp of the problems of the country and a high ideal of its destiny. Much was expected of Mr. Theodore, who had retired from the Premiership of Queensland in order to enter Federal politics. But he found his time fully occupied in a widely scattered constituency, and was ultimately defeated. He will be heard of again, for he is generally regarded as one of the ablest of the Labour leaders, and had he been a member of the present Parliament would probably have ultimately succeeded Mr. Charlton.

The election was remarkable for the interest taken in it by young men who outside the Labour movement had previously been inclined to neglect politics. Impressed with the danger of disorder, both from the prevalence of strikes and from the obligation thrust upon the farmers of protecting their own interests where Government had failed, they formed Constitutional Associations in many of the States. In this election they did useful work for the Ministerialists, and it is hoped that in the future they will remove the reproach of indifference often directed against the Australian youth. Another novel feature of the election was compulsory voting, which had been made part of the electoral law on the motion of a private member during the last Parliament. The percentage of votes polled to voters on the roll was over 90 per cent., which is far higher than is usual at Australian elections, and would have been still higher had the electoral roll been up to date. But the expediency of compulsion is doubtful. Though the number of informal voters does not appear to have been higher than at an average election, many came to the poll who were ignorant of politics or indifferent, and it is probable that apart from any compulsion the numbers voting would have been exceptionally high, owing to the universal interest taken in the campaign. The result of the Senate elections has furnished another proof of the absurdity of the method of counting the votes now in use for that Chamber. There were twenty-two vacancies to be filled in a House of thirty-six, four having been caused by death or resignation during the last Parliament. Approximately four votes out of every nine were cast for Labour, yet every one of the vacancies was filled by a Ministerialist. The method of counting is extremely complicated, and may be described as the antithesis of the proportional system. Each State votes as one constituency. The names of candidates are ranged as far as possible in party lists, and the electors must put a number against the name of every candidate indicating the order of preference. At the last Federal election when the present method of counting was in use, men of exceptional prominence were elected in certain of the States, although their party as a whole was not successful. But this can happen only when there is a large amount of cross voting and candidates are supported on personal grounds. When feeling runs high, as it did this year, there is little cross voting, and the party which polls the majority of votes is almost certain to fill all the vacancies from its ranks. It is for some reasons satisfactory that the Government for the time being should have a majority in both Houses. A hostile Senate, though it could not unseat a Government, could make legislation impossible, and ultimately force a double dissolution; but it is unsatisfactory that Labour should be represented only by the Senators who were elected three years ago, or that the Bruce-Page party should, unless it suffers from death or resignations, be able to count on at least half the Chamber for the next six years. The new Parliament should be an exceptionally busy one. Mr. Bruce has a mandate for the preservation of order and the maintenance of industrial peace, and within the somewhat limited powers of the Constitution must look for a means of carrying it into effect. He has pledged himself to a programme of development and of social reform, which is likely to bring some of the contentious questions of the States before the Commonwealth Parliament and to a scheme of constitutional revision which will involve the passage of a number of equally contentious Bills to be submitted to the electors at a referendum.

In the House of Representatives the Nationalists now have a majority over any possible combination between their present allies, the Country party, and Labour. It has been suggested that as the Nationalists have increased in numbers and the Country party remains at its former strength, the Nationalists should have representation in the Cabinet more nearly in proportion to their voting power; but it is improbable that any change will be made. Co-operation between the two parties was at the last election of great value to both. It is quite possible that in many electorates where there were only Nationalist and Labour candidates, farmers would not have voted for the Government had they not been assured that the Country party would retain an independent existence. Labour candiates, at any rate, appeared to hold this belief, for they did their utmost to prove that the strike issues had been raised for the express purpose of submerging the Country party. Again, it was an advantage to the Government that Country candidates could claim to have exercised an influence over its administration. Many concessions had been made to primary producers, and many were promised, which bore witness to the ability of the man on the land to obtain his reasonable demands without compelling his representatives to remain in isolation, as they have done in some of the State Parliaments. Some Country members have expressed decided views on the tariff, detailed consideration of which was held over from the last Parliament; but they cannot look to Labour for any remission of duties, and it is not likely that there will be any secession from the Government on this ground. What effect this defeat will have on the policy or composition of the Labour party it is difficult to forecast. The election was a disappointment to long-cherished and confident hopes. Before the issues raised by the Seamen's strike had become prominent in Federal politics, the opinion was very widely held that Labour, after ten years of opposition, would be returned to power. The record of the Bruce-Page Ministry, though solid, was thought to be colourless. Its programme was not considered likely to contain anything sensational, and its leaders were rather respected than popular figures. Possibly those who held this belief attached too little importance to the absence of outstanding figures in the Opposition, an absence which was afterwards brought into relief by the conduct of the election campaign, and by the importance assigned to Mr. Theodore's contemplated appearance in the Federal

Parliament. Even after the dissolution had been precipitated and the campaign was near its end, confidence was expressed that the election would bring, if not absolute victory, a substantial increase in strength to the Labour party. The immediate outcome of defeat was an expression by several of the Labour leaders in New South Wales and Queensland of their determination to rid the party of its "red" elements. It seemed to be acknowledged that the Australian people had demonstrated that they would always decide in favour of constitutional methods and industrial peace once the issues were put to and accepted by them. But the expulsion contemplated will not be effected without opposition, if at all. The State Labour Governments vary in their shades of opinion, but the industrial element, including unions of which the officials hold extreme views, is in the two States already mentioned influential in the councils of the party, and controls more than one electorate. The political leaders, therefore, have to consider whether they will take a step which may destroy the unity of the movement, or continue to bear the reproach of association with extremists, and it seems likely that as the first shock of defeat loses its vividness the tendency to compromise will become stronger.

Two questions, therefore, will come up for decision during the early days of the new Parliament, both of importance. How will Mr. Bruce carry out his intention of securing industrial peace by the methods advocated in general terms throughout his electoral campaign, the enforcement of the law and the punishment of those who ignore the established means of settling their claims on the one hand, and the removal of sources of discontent by schemes of social amelioration on the other? What means will the Labour party take to apply the teachings of adversity and escape similar disaster in the future?

POSTSCRIPT

Shortly after polling day it was announced that the Board before which the two leaders of the seamen had been called upon to show cause why they should not be deported had made recommendations adverse to both of them. Messrs. Walsh and Johnson were, therefore, taken in custody by the Commonwealth officers to await deportation. A writ of *habeas corpus* was then applied for on their behalf, and the application came on for hearing before the High Court. In the course of an exhaustive argument the powers of the Commonwealth, the deportation provisions of the Immigration Act already referred to,[42] and the method of investigation adopted by the Board were discussed, with the result that the Court unanimously came to the conclusion that both prisoners should be released. The Court consisted of five judges, and they were by no means unanimous as to the reasons for their decision. The majority, however, are of opinion that under the power given it by the Constitution "to make laws for the peace, order and good government of the Commonwealth with respect to immigration," the Federal Parliament cannot treat as an immigrant a man who had come into Australia before Federation, and the balance of the judicial opinions seems to be that it cannot so treat a man who has settled in Australia and acquired an Australian domicile. As Walsh arrived in Australia before 1900, and Johnson from Holland in 1910, and both have since made their homes in Australia, these conclusions operate in favour of both. Some of the judges also found defects in the general terms of the section under which the summonses were issued, and with the summonses themselves, and also in the powers which the section purported to confer on the Minister. Whether the Federal Parliament has power to provide for deportation on the decision of a Minister after enquiry by a specially appointed Board is not quite clear from a perusal of the five judgments, but apparently it is not suggested that the Federal Parliament cannot provide for deportation as a penalty to be inflicted after a trial before one of the ordinary courts for an offence with respect to any matter within the ambit of the powers of the Federal Parliament. One of the judges (J. Starke) quotes from an expression of opinion by Lord Haldane given when announcing the advice of the Privy Council (in the Sugar Company case)[43] that none of the powers conferred by the Federal Constitution relate to that general control over the liberty of the subject which must be shown to be transferred, if it is to be regarded as vested in the Commonwealth. Presumably, however, this does not affect the power to control the liberty of the subject in relation to matters within the sphere of the Commonwealth. It must be added that the decision of the High Court in no way turned on the manner in which the enquiry had been conducted by the Board. The judgments agreed that the enquiry had been carried out impartially and with dignity under difficult conditions.

December 1925

THE SALE OF THE COMMONWEALTH LINE

September 1928, vol. 18, pp. 873–6

THE Federal Government has retired, more or less gracefully, and rather gratefully, from the shipping business. The war-time success and later financial difficulties of the Commonwealth Line have been reviewed in previous numbers of THE ROUND TABLE.[44] The establishment of the line by Mr. W. M. Hughes in war-time has been characterised by the present Prime Minister as a "statesman-like act," but in doleful company with other national shipping enterprises, the line has felt very severely the effects of the general depression in the shipping industry. The Government has accepted the £1,900,000 offered by the White Star Line, and has thereby emerged from the venture with a total loss, it is said, of nearly £8,000,000. There is no doubt that the dominant factor in securing the decision to sell the line has been its financial losses which, apart from depreciation, have exceeded half a million for each of the last two years. The Joint Committee of Public Accounts issued an interim report to reassure those shippers who, expecting the sale of the line, were doing business elsewhere, and recommended that the line should be retained and reorganised. The final report, however, shows that only a minority of the Committee still holds this view.[45] The majority, probably influenced more by the final balance sheet than by the evidence of the single additional witness examined, advocated the immediate disposal of the line, preferably to a specially formed company which, in return for preferential treat-ment, would eschew agreements with the combine. This proposal evoked vociferous protests from the Labour Opposition, while an appreciable section of the press chorused its disapproval. These protests were inspired partly by what the Prime Minister referred to as "Mr. Charlton's fetish for State enterprise," but largely by the belief that the Commonwealth Line stood as Australia's one line of defence against exploitation by the shipping combine.

It is difficult to determine what success the line has had in keeping down freights. While Mr. Bruce asserted that it carried 2·7 per cent. of homeward bound cargo, Mr. Scullin (deputy leader of the Opposition)[46] claimed to be in possession of figures showing that the line bore 18 per cent. of Australia's oversea trade. The best objective measure of changes in freights is the *Economist* index number. This shows that freights to Australia are now as low as in 1913, but that the reduction from the excessive war-time freights has been, in general, slower for Australia than for other parts of the world. This, however, may be not so much an effect of the impotence of the Commonwealth Line in reducing freights as a tribute to the "ever mounting handling costs" in Australia. The Country party, which might be expected to articulate the misgivings of the freight-burdened exporters of primary products, whole-heartedly supported the proposal to sell the line. Little protest was audible from the importers, perhaps through scepticism regarding the power of the line to keep down freights in their interests.

Even the supporters of the Government regretted the passing of Australia's mercantile marine. National defence problems and sentiment have fostered the ideal of a merchant marine, owned by Australia and manned by Australian seamen, bred and trained to the sea. The Government was reminded that the "Bay" liners had been specially strengthened to carry armaments. The Prime Minister thought it unwise to acquaint the House with the armament capacity of the ships, but Mr. Scullin obligingly vouchsafed the information that each could mount eight heavy guns as well as anti-aircraft and other light pieces. One newspaper published a detailed survey of the capacity of the ships, any one of which, the public was informed, could be turned into an auxiliary cruiser at short notice. But ships and guns are only half a mercantile marine, and the report of the Public Accounts Committee gave little encouragement to the belief that Australia is breeding a race of seamen. Less than half the personnel of the line was domiciled in Australia. This consideration tempered the regret of those who mourned the loss of the mercantile marine, but still more consolation was to be found in the Prime Minister's assurance that "if it is to continue, this Parliament will have to vote it a considerable sum of working capital."

Accordingly, tenders were called for under conditions which, it was hoped, would safeguard the exporters and importers and yet be less discouraging to buyers than the unsuccessful offer of the line in 1925, when it comprised 27 vessels. On that occasion it was prescribed that the buyer should conduct certain specified services with those vessels for a period of seven years, and that freights or passenger fares were not to be raised without the approval of a committee to be appointed. This time an equivalent service for passengers and refrigerated and other cargo for ten years was demanded and preference was promised to offers "containing proposals for safeguarding the interests of Australian exporters and importers in regard to freight rates."

Only three tenders were received, of which two were unflattering. The shipping world did not regard the occasion as a bargain sale. The seven vessels were sold to the highest bidder, which incidentally was prepared to pay the largest cash deposit, and it was hardly accurate to state that the line was sold for an old song. As Lord Kylsant[47] has a large interest in the White Star Line, it is generally thought that the line has passed into the hands of the conference lines. The buyers have agreed to maintain a fortnightly service via Suez, if trade justifies it, supplementing the fleet where necessary with additional vessels. This will be an improvement on the present service. Freights are not to be increased without reference to a committee to be appointed, representative of shippers and owners. An equivalent passenger service involves carrying over 20 per cent. of the passenger traffic between Australia and the United Kingdom since the Commonwealth Line had become popular to this extent with travellers. Equivalence of service will not be maintained in respect of inter-state traffic. As the ships are to be placed upon the British register, the Navigation Act will normally prevent their participation in inter-state trade. This local problem will have to be solved by other methods than an Australian marine.

The change of register means a lowering of living conditions for the personnel of the ships, but many have been doubtful whether it was possible to retain both an Australian merchantile marine and Australian sea-faring conditions. This aspect has provoked the disapproval of the seamen, and the White Star Line has been promised a difficult time by trade union leaders. Thus the mercantile marine has been relinquished to the accompaniment of uproar from the radicals, mild regret from many patriots, and threats of boycott from the militant maritime unions.

July 1928

THE CHANGE OF GOVERNMENT

March 1930, vol. 20, pp. 396–408

WITHIN eleven months of its return to power at a general election the Bruce-Page Government was overwhelmingly defeated on a dissolution of the Lower House, the Prime Minister lost his own seat (by 305 votes in a poll of 62,435), and the party which he had led for over six and a half years was reduced from 29 to 14 members.[48] Five of his previous supporters had deserted him, and two of these were defeated by Nationalist candidates. The Country party led by Dr. Page suffered no defections, but lost three of its thirteen members, while the Labour party gained fifteen seats and the largest majority in its history. This remarkable revolution was not anticipated by any party. It can only be explained by the fact that the electors, as last year's results showed, were already growing tired of the old Government, and were shocked and alarmed by what seemed to them a precipitate, reckless, and indeed almost sacrilegious attempt to abandon the Federal control of wages and labour conditions. Mr. Bruce subsequently remarked, "we tested democracy as high as we could," but it is not clear that any democracy could have been expected to agree at short notice to the reversal of an industrial policy which had been the most conspicuous feature of national administration for twenty-five years, and which the Government a few months before had apparently pledged itself to uphold.

Whether the change of policy was itself justified is not here under discussion. For years there has been dissatisfaction on all sides with the operation of the industrial arbitration system, divided as the powers are between the Commonwealth and the States, and during 1928 other causes led to trade union dissatisfaction with the Commonwealth Arbitration Court. The long talked of testing time had come when the Court had to concede more to the employers than to the unions. The incidence of opposition changed, and the Attorney-General, who had entered the Government expressly to devise methods of enforcing the Court's awards, was created Minister of Industry also, with a new department.[49] The story of the timber workers' strike is a story of the failure of this policy.

Meanwhile it was becoming apparent that the increasing and

detailed regulation of industry by both Federal and State tribunals was burdensome to industry and also an obstacle to improved industrial relations. Criticism by such differently constituted bodies as the British Economic Mission and the Tariff Board, and the still more impressive facts of unemployment and industrial depression, brought home the need for reduced costs of production. It was clear that this could be brought about only by throwing the two parties in industry more on their own resources. It was also clear to students that the conflict of jurisdictions allowed neither the Commonwealth nor the States freedom to experiment in this direction. The people had repeatedly refused to confer full power on the Commonwealth, and it was known that the States would not voluntarily give up their powers. After a rather formal invitation to the Premiers to do so, the Prime Minister startled the Commonwealth by stating baldly that his Government would abandon the field.

The ostensible reason was that the duplication of authorities had become a menace to prosperity, and that by its withdrawal the Commonwealth Government would assist towards lower production costs. The Government protested that this did not mean lower wages, but some of its supporters and the organised employers were ambiguous on this point. The electors suspected the motives of the Government and did not accept its protestations. They were told, with arguments they could more readily follow, that the wage-earners' incomes depended upon the Commonwealth standard first laid down by Mr. Justice Higgins in 1907; that without this standard the lowest State standard would prevail, and that either labour conditions would steadily deteriorate or Australia would be thrown back upon the rule of the jungle. Mr. Hughes, for example, told his electors that if costs of production were to be reduced they were sure to be reduced at the expense of the wage-earners, and his gift of imagery found expression somewhat as follows: "Mr. Bruce has been Australia's doctor for nearly seven years; he now tells his patient—'you are in such a bad way that there is no cure; you must be reborn. Therefore I am going to cut your throat.' "

The action of the Government may have been heroic. It did not rush blindly to its doom, nor was it trapped into a choice of the issue by astute political manoeuvring. Nevertheless, its hand was forced, and the background of this political drama must be sketched in. The picturesque William Morris Hughes is of course the villain of the piece. He has bided his time with growing impatience during the long years of eclipse since February 1922, when he was deposed from leadership at the edict of the newly arisen Country party and his young lieutenant S. M. Bruce was appointed in his stead. The Bruce-Page Coalition lasted an intolerable time, but it was reaching the end of its natural span. The Country party, which had grown with, and perhaps because of, the decline of the Labour party, was not increasing in power or influence, and the old stalwart who had led the nation during the war might at any time be needed to lead it again. This was at least a possible hypothesis. But such calls do not come spontaneously outside romantic history; they have to be inspired; the wreck has to happen before the saviour can appear.

The small size of Australian Parliaments, and therefore of normal majorities, gives an often unmerited importance to an individual member or to a small group, and it became evident early in the 1928 Parliament that, for different and largely personal reasons, the Government's reduced majority was susceptible of division. Almost at the outset the Government had been saved on a minor issue only by the Speaker's casting vote, and from then on it was faced with the choice between constantly placating the malcontents or challenging them outright. After some years of power and prestige the Government was not disposed to linger through a miserable existence and eventually to perish from popular contempt. Its forthcoming budget was bound to be unpopular, and it was in an embarrassing position over the coal trouble. In these circumstances, therefore, the Government chose to take a bold line on a major issue and to go out, if necessary, on an appeal to the people to face economic realities. At the worst, the Senate would remain a party stronghold until another election.

It was in this atmosphere of challenge that Parliament reassembled in August, and the Government was met with a no-confidence motion involving the integrity of its administration of the law. Mr. Hughes and another Nationalist voted with the Opposition and were promptly excluded by Mr. Bruce from the party meetings. Eventually the Government was defeated by one vote in committee on a motion by Mr. Hughes to postpone withdrawal from industrial arbitration until after an appeal to the electors. The Speaker, Sir Littleton Groom, who had been Mr. Latham's predecessor as Attorney-General,[50] refrained from voting, and a last minute rebel voiced his objection to the Government's proposal to tax the gross receipts of the cinema interests.

It is interesting to compare the circumstances which led to the downfall of Mr. Hughes in 1922. The same complaints of high-handed and autocratic action were made against both leaders, each of whom had had a remarkably long tenure of office. But in 1929 there was no alternative leader acceptable both to the malcontents and the Country party. Mr. Bruce had his Cabinet solidly with him and the Country party also. When Mr. Hughes fell, he fell ingloriously and alone, and nothing else was materially altered;

but while Mr. Bruce has brought down with him both the Nationalist party and the Coalition, he has also destroyed the hopes of the malcontents.

Mr. Bruce goes abroad on a well-deserved holiday to study economic conditions elsewhere. His mantle has fallen upon Mr. Latham, who would probably be willing to hand it back to his former chief should the occasion arise. At the moment there is some inevitable confusion, but a period in opposition will give time for readjustments, and the new Government's policy will probably force them. It is very doubtful whether the Hughes faction will gain anything out of the wreck or Mr. Hughes himself ever again become a rallying point for the non-Labour forces.

There is, on the other hand, quite a prospect that Mr. Bruce may return with increased personal prestige. His record is one that will wear well. Throughout his period of office, while completely loyal to the pact with the Country party, he consolidated his own position and became more and more the Prime Minister and less the mere partner of the Country party leader. He was perhaps too easily converted to the optimism of Dr. Earle Page in his capacity as Treasurer, and to that of Mr. Latham, the Attorney-General, in his capacity as reorganiser of industrial arbitration. The late Prime Minister cannot be acquitted of such blame as may attach to his Government for extravagant expenditure on roads and for the large deficit that has accumulated in the past few years after a period of abnormal customs revenues. Mr. Bruce will be remembered, however, for his principal achievements, the stimulation of scientific research and of research generally, and the financial agreement with the States.[51] In these, as in the manner of his exit, he was personally and obviously the prime mover. He has been conspicuous for his interest and leadership in Imperial and international affairs. He first came into prominence at a League of Nations Assembly, and his contributions to the discussions at Imperial Conferences and elsewhere have given some distinction to Australian representation.

The circumstances warrant some such recognition of the defeated leader's services and this fact is generally acknowledged throughout Australia. It may be added also that Mr. Bruce is likely to be remembered for the frankness and sincerity of his appeals to people of all classes to face the economic facts, to employers without constructive ideas in the management of labour, and to manufacturers constantly demanding a higher and still higher customs tariff, as much as to the trade unions. If, as seems inevitable, Australia must learn its lesson only from experience, Mr. Bruce may become known as a prophet not without honour in his own country. In nothing has he so touched the instincts of Australians as by the sporting manner of his challenge and his acceptance of defeat. It is possible that Mr. Hughes may find his favourite legend of a strong national statesman attached to Mr. Bruce rather than to himself, and time is on the side of the younger man.

The victory of the Labour party was wholly incidental to the defeat of the Bruce Government. Although it had been recovering from the disasters of the war period, when it split over the conscription issue, there was no indication in 1928 that on its own merits it could gain sufficient support to give it a majority. In the "anti-red" election of 1925 the party lost six members, but in 1928 it had gained only two more than in 1922, and these two gains were lucky ones. It seemed to be carrying too much "dead wood," and its inability or unwillingness to break with extreme elements hampered its progress in the electorates. Nor had Labour any attractive policy to excite the enthusiasm of recruits. It had been in power in each of the States and had been dismissed in every one of them except Western Australia. Its only hope lay in the swing of the pendulum and in the failure of the Bruce Government to save the country from the effects of economic depression. To Australians particularly, with their remarkable faith in political action, a period of depression means incompetent government. The fall in wool prices, and the general reduction in the national income, sounded the knell of the old regime and gave Labour its opportunity.

It was a very different opportunity which the old Labour party was able to grasp in 1910, and the only point of similarity is that it followed the defeat of the Coalition Government. The country was then prosperous, and the Labour party was full of new ideas which were attractive to the young Commonwealth, and which seemed to express more adequately than the old parties the vigour and nationalism of the new nation. It had also increasing revenue from customs duties and from land taxation, which gave scope for its policy. In those days also the party was zealous for the provision of capital expenditure out of revenue rather than from loans, and its self-reliant nationalism found expression in a strong defence policy, which it had shared with Mr. Deakin through the establishment of compulsory training and the creation of an Australian Navy. It had also gained a majority in the Senate. Such opportunities do not often recur and the party now has none of its former advantages.

The new Government can scarcely claim that it was returned on its party platform, which was kept very much in the background by the issue at the election. The party nominated no candidates against any opponent of the Bruce Government, and it received a definite mandate on the single issue—the maintenance of the Commonwealth Arbitration Court. On the other hand, the party leaders have committed themselves to various promises which are likely to give them sufficient occupation for the life of this Parliament. They undertook not to tax the receipts of the amusement interests, as had been proposed by the late Government—to its peril from the cinema interests. Mr. Theodore described this as "a paltry and inglorious attempt to extract money from the children's entertainment."[52] Promises which involve heavy demands on the Treasury were unemployment insurance, financial assistance to any State to meet special disabilities due to Federation, and a steamship service for Tasmania. The only economies forecast were to be made by the non-appointment of Royal Commissions and the limitation or abolition of the Commission for Development and Migration. "The fullest possible protection," was to be afforded "to all industries, primary and secondary," and the tariff was to become more of protective and less of a revenue producing instrument.[53]

The new Ministry assumed office on October 23, having been elected by the Parliamentary party, several of whom were new members. The election was influenced by two rival trade union groups: the Australian Workers' Union and the Australian Council of Trade Unions. Mr. J. H. Scullin became Prime Minister and allotted the portfolios, retaining for himself the new Ministry of Industry. He is without ministerial experience, but is everywhere regarded with respect. The Treasurer, Mr. Theodore, is of course the most experienced member of the Government and probably the ablest also. He is looked upon as the driving force, and has not been averse from making pronouncements of policy on his own account. The other members call for no special mention; they are for the most part old Parliamentarians who have reaped the reward of long service. The only Minister new to Federal politics is the Postmaster-General, Mr. J. A. Lyons, formerly Premier of Tasmania.

The Government almost immediately put into effect one of the newer planks of its platform by suspending the operation of compulsory military training, thus reversing the policy of 1910. In its place it is establishing a voluntary system. It also suspended assistance to immigration except for the dependants of immigrants already here.

On November 20 the new Parliament assembled. The Government lost no time, and within six weeks of the elections it brought down its budget and a comprehensive list of tariff increases, claimed to be the most important tariff revisions since 1921. This, it may be noted, is in flat contradiction to the recommendations of the expert committee on the tariff, whose report was summarised in the last number of THE ROUND TABLE.[54] The income tax was increased by a supertax on individual incomes exceeding £2,000, and the additional income tax is in place of the discarded tax on amusements. Mr. Theodore found it necessary to budget for a greater expenditure and to estimate lower revenues from existing taxes. Customs and excise duties had been increased by Dr. Page to yield £2,750,000 more revenue, and this amount was further increased to about £4,000,000. No provision was made to liquidate the deficiency of £4,987,718 accumulated during the past two years. Dr. Page had budgeted to reduce this by £360,000 from revenue, and to use also a sum of £1,200,000, the profits from expropriated enemy properties. Mr. Theodore has left this fund unallocated, possibly in case his own estimates of revenue prove to have been too optimistic.

The new Government's problems fall into three main groups: the budget (quickly disposed of), the maintenance of employment, and industrial arbitration. The Governor-General's speech described present and impending further depression as seasonal, and the Government reckons on the return of past prosperity to the export industries. It also regards its increased tariff as a permanent contribution to employment, and to its "fiscal faith" is added a belief in the efficacy of credit control. Some members of the party began at once to demand an expansion of the note issue, which is independently controlled by the Commonwealth Bank. The Government resisted these demands, and it has in Mr. Theodore a Treasurer who at least understands the far-reaching economic consequences which would follow inflation. The Parliament, however, has given him power to control the gold reserves of the Commonwealth. The Commonwealth Bank during the later months of 1929 exported gold to the value of £6,000,000, and all export is now to be controlled by the Government. It is interesting to note that the Government is pledged to "assist in the development of existing gold mines." By the restriction of export and the continuance of present production the note issue may be increased without reducing reserves. It was the prohibition of the normal export of gold produced that made possible the inflation of prices during the war.

The temptation to use the note issue for stimulating industry and employment will be all the greater because of the party's pledge to raise loan moneys in Australia. The practice of providing work for the unemployed on what are always optimistically described as development works has been effective in recent years only because of heavy borrowings from abroad. This practice has done much more to maintain wage standards than any legislation or arbitration courts, and the unemployment now prevailing is due in part to a fall in the loan moneys received from overseas.

The revision of industrial arbitration is postponed until 1930, and further conferences are to be called. In his policy speech Mr. Scullin gave a summary of the party's intentions as follows:—

> The Arbitration Act to be revised to provide for a system of sound, business-like arbitration, free from the entangling legalisms of the law court—a system framed on the lines of the Industrial Peace Act to be handled by men of industrial experience, to ensure equitable, expeditious, and less costly methods of dealing with industrial matters.[55]

This declaration is to be read in conjunction with the policy of "unlimited powers for the Commonwealth Parliament," but the Government will need to frame its proposals under the powers that now exist. The Federal Labour party would willingly take over the whole field of industrial regulation, as indeed Mr. Bruce would have done, but it is not likely that the Labour party as a whole or the trade unions will agree to give up the State tribunals, or to withdraw from State Parliaments the power to legislate on these matters.

So far as the mind of the people can be judged on referenda results and the recent election, they desire the retention of both Federal and State activities, however confusing the result may be. Mr. Scullin's aspirations for a system "free from entangling legalisms" seems destined to disappointment.

It is clear also that the supporters of the Government conceive of arbitration not merely as a means of settling disputes but as an instrument for gradually improving the lot of the workers. The support given by the party to the timber workers in their strike against an adverse award of the Federal Court was defended by Mr. Theodore in his pre-election speech. He then said "the decisions of the Federal Courts are not sacrosanct if they violate the principles of eternal justice."[56] The Government is faced with the problem of reconciling its interpretation of these principles with the economic situation, which has grown worse since the former Government was defeated.

In some respects the new Government must inevitably repeat the history of its predecessor. That Government was returned with a mandate to use the law against social forces too strong for legal discipline. It proved to be impossible to enforce an award of the Arbitration Court which a great number of the people, however wrongly, believed to be inequitable. The late Government had virtually to abandon its mandate and to choose another policy. The new Government was returned with instructions to take legal action against economic forces. It has made itself an uneasy bed of promises, and struggle as it may the stars are against it. Wool has dropped over 30 per cent. in value, involving a reduction of about £20,000,000 in Australian income from that source alone; the wheat harvest is poor, and the overseas market for loans has been temporarily closed. It may also have to abandon its mandate and choose another policy.

The Senate, where the Government has only seven supporters out of 36 members, can at any time force a double dissolution, but it will not willingly be rushed into an election until the Government has lost some of its popularity. This may not take long. The manufacturing interests, some of which were not unfriendly to Labour, have gained all they can hope for from it in the increased tariff, and although this tariff and other expedients to postpone the problem of unemployment may help the Government for a while, they will bring their own reactions. Meanwhile the Opposition in the Senate has declared its acceptance of the popular verdict and will await the course of events.

On the whole, the change of Government may well be of considerable advantage to Australia. The Nationalist Government did not convince, and perhaps could not have convinced the people that the economic problems of Australia were matters for their own solution. It failed to convince employers that something more constructive was wanted from them than mere opposition to Government regulation. A Labour Government may stimulate more enterprise on their part, and it may succeed as no other Government could in making the trade unionists think. It may be that only bitter experience will induce them to abandon the semi-theological disputations which at present befog the conduct of industrial affairs. In any case the responsibility of government will do the Labour party good. It will probably force it to break with the irrational extremists, in which event it may have to suffer a similar experience to that of the Bruce Government in its safe industrial seats. A party breach is not impossible, and there will be exquisite irony in the spectacle of Mr. Theodore having to fight for his seat against the fury of the faithful. The fate of his old Labour Government in Queensland last year shows that such a contingency is not improbable.[57]

The following figures place on record the changes in the representation of Federal parties in the House of Representatives since the war:—

		1919	1922	1925	1928	1929
Labour	..	26	29	23	31	46
Nationalist	..	39⎫ 49	32⎫ 46	38⎫ 51	29⎫ 42	14⎫ 24
Country	..	10⎭	14⎭	13⎭	13⎭	10⎭
Others	..	—	—	1	2	5

December 1929

PART FOUR
1930 – 1942

THE FEDERAL ELECTIONS

March 1932, vol. 22, pp. 407–20

IT is notorious that very few parties can survive a term in office during times of economic distress; this is particularly true of a Labour party, or for that matter of any party of reform. While times of depression are times of curtailment and retrenchment, the popularity of a party of reform depends on the measure of its advance towards more or less unattainable objectives, and its normal programmes are based on the expectation of buoyant revenues. Its supporters are not convinced by the most valiant record of orderly retreats, or even of positions barely held. These considerations apply with peculiar force to the Australian Labour party. Its whole theory of representation subordinates the individual to the group—the Minister is subordinate to the caucus, the caucus to the party organisation outside. To get from the party machine the flexibility that government demands in times of crisis is virtually impossible. It is not surprising, therefore, that the onset of the world economic depression should, in Britain and in Australia, have broken the Labour party in office. But few critics could have expected a collapse so sudden or so complete as has occurred in both countries in the last quarter of 1931.

Mr. Scullin's Ministry came into office at the end of 1929, supported by the largest single party in Australian political history, numbering 46 in a House of 75. Owing to internal dissensions within the party, the Ministry failed to keep its supporters together, and in little more than two years was driven to the country by a defeat in the House, inflicted on a deliberate vote. Mr. Scullin will muster no more than 14 supporters when the new House assembles in February, and will thus have lost some 70 per cent. of his following. When it is remembered that so recently as 1928 Mr. Scullin was returned as leader of an Opposition of only 31 against Mr. Bruce, some idea will be gained of the changes that have taken place in Australian opinion within three years.

The Labour Government was in trouble from the start. To begin with, it had only one real mandate from the electors—to maintain and improve the federal arbitration system; and a strongly Nationalist Senate was by no means willing to allow the Ministry to rewrite the Arbitration Act at its pleasure. But in truth the Scullin Ministry came into office on a wave of feeling almost entirely unrelated to the real task which lay before it—to take measures to meet the economic depression; and it was on those measures that it eventually came to shipwreck. Every fresh development in ministerial policy served only to split the party more hopelessly. The trouble began with the re-appointment of Mr. Theodore to the Treasurership, on the Prime Minister's return from the Imperial Conference, and before the action arising out of the Mungana charges had come on for hearing.[1] That step cost the Labour party two Ministers, Mr. Lyons and Mr. Fenton,[2] who went into Opposition, the former to become Leader of the Opposition. These two were followed in course of time by three other Labour men. Hard upon these events there followed, in February 1931, the Premiers' Conference at which were put forward the three proposals which have become notorious as the "Lang Plan," and Mr. Theodore's counter-policy, an instalment of controlled inflation. Mr. Lang proposed that no interest should be paid overseas until Britain brought Australian interest rates into line with the Anglo-American war debt settlement; that the interest on public internal loans should be reduced compulsorily to 3 per cent.; and that a currency based on production and governmentally controlled should be substituted for the existing bank-controlled currency. These proposals were summarily rejected by the Premiers, but Mr. Lang characteristically refused to abandon them, and the result was a feud between the New South Wales branch of the Labour party, dominated by Mr. Lang, and the federal Labour authorities, dominated by Mr. Scullin and Mr. Theodore. Mr. Lang's group attempted to coerce the Labour members from New South Wales in the Federal Parliament into supporting his views. Mr. Theodore's group replied by asserting that in defying the properly constituted federal committees Mr. Lang's group had forfeited its right to be considered part of the Australian Labour party. Five of the New South Wales Labour members of the House of Representatives, led by Mr. Beasley,[3] eventually formed a kind of "Lang Cave," hostile to, and contemptuous of, the Government and actually holding the balance of power in the House, but unwilling for some time to strike the Government down at the risk of an appeal to the people. Meantime, finding "controlled inflation" unpopular, the Government had reluctantly agreed to the proposals now familiarly known as the "Premiers' Plan," involving a quasi-voluntary conversion of the Commonwealth and State debts, and a reduction in government salaries, wages, pensions and other adjustable expenditure. The acceptance of the latter part of this plan caused further dissensions in the Labour party, just as a similar issue was to split the British Labour party a little later. The Labour Governments had trouble with their own supporters in their respective Parliaments (there was said to be a majority of two only for the plan in the federal caucus), and the party organisations throughout the country were very hostile, especially in South Australia. A great many of the rank and file were inclined to the view that to accept the plan involved a betrayal of vital Labour principles, and that it was the clear duty of true Labour men to go out of office rather than take responsibility for such a policy.

In these circumstances, it can easily be imagined that the Prime Minister had no desire for an early appeal to the country. His position had been greatly weakened in Labour circles, and his record in office had not been such as to retain for him the large body of support from unattached electors which had been accorded him in 1929. His obvious dependence on Mr. Theodore aroused misgivings in many quarters, and so also did his vacillation on monetary policy. These misgivings were intensified towards the end of the year, when it became clear from ministerial pronouncements that, when the election did come, the Government would put forward political control of the currency as the main issue. The time was therefore very unpropitious for the Government when, at the end of November, Mr. Beasley announced his intention of moving for the appointment of a Royal Commission to enquire into allegations that Mr. Theodore was *inter alia* using unemployment relief works in his electorate (at the Commonwealth dockyard at Cockatoo Island and elsewhere) as a means of purchasing votes. It is said that this was a mere pretext—and certainly very little was heard of it during the election campaign—and that the attack was really launched because the Scullin-Theodore group seemed to be making headway in Sydney against the Lang group. The announcement just previously of an amalgamation between the State Savings Bank and the Commonwealth Savings Bank, on terms which would enable the former to make immediate and substantial payments to its depositors,[4] was, for instance, regarded as a triumph for Mr. Theodore. Mr. Beasley pressed his motion, which was duly carried, with the support of the Opposition on November 25, and the Prime Minister advised the Governor-General to dissolve the House of Representatives. In granting the dissolution, Sir Isaac Isaacs[5] took the opportunity of placing on record his understanding of the present constitutional position of a Governor-General in the exercise of the prerogative of dissolution. Formerly it was expected that the Governor-General would exercise his own discretion in the grant of a dissolution, and refuse a request for a dissolution from a Ministry defeated in the House if he thought it in the public interest to do so. In a letter replete with citation of authorities, Sir Isaac Isaacs explained that, in view of the present constitutional position of a Governor-General, as laid down at the Imperial Conference of 1926, he did not feel it his duty to exercise a personal discretion, but contented himself with taking the Prime Minister's advice. Sir Isaac Isaacs added that if he had had to exercise a personal discretion the result would have been the same. But he put it, in effect, that the Governor-General is to stand in the same relation to his Ministers as the King does to his in Great Britain, and that the King would in such circumstances accept ministerial advice. This declaration will probably become a definitive statement of the position of a Governor-General. This sort of thing is one of the by-consequences of appointing a distinguished constitutional lawyer and judge to be His Majesty's representative.

The Government determined on an early election, partly no doubt because it precluded Mr. Lang, and certain other vigorous opponents of the Ministry, from resigning their seats in State Houses in time to contest federal electorates. Polling took place on December 19, a little more than three weeks after the Government's defeat in the House. As usual, an election was held at the same time for the eighteen seats in the Senate (three in each State) whose occupants are due to retire in June, 1932. The Senate, it will be remembered, consists of six members elected from each State voting as a single electorate. Senators hold their seats for six years, and half retire every three years.

The Opposition parties had barely completed arrangements for consolidating their ranks. In order to bring in Mr. Lyons and his ex-Labour followers, and to compose certain other differences, the Nationalist party abandoned its name, and a new party was formed with the clumsy and rather misleading name of "United Australia party," and with Mr. Lyons as leader and Mr. Latham as deputy-leader. (The "alias" party, Mr. Lang's journal calls it; many will regret that the opportunity was not taken to bring to an end the period of more or less "fancy" names and return to the name "Liberal," which grew up and became acclimatised in Australian politics and which stands historically for policies very close to those for which the United Australia party will doubtless become known.) Mr. W. M. Hughes, it may be added, after his abortive attempt to found an independent party of his own, came into the United Australia party. Between the United Australia party and the Country party fairly close co-operation was achieved. They did oppose each other in a few electorates, but nowhere where there was any real danger of losing the seat to Labour by a divided vote.

The federal and the State (or Lang) Labour groups both nominated candidates in most of the New South Wales electorates, in a good many cases not so much with any expectation of success as with a view to testing the strength of the rival groups among Labour supporters. Each group also nominated its three candidates for the Senate election. In addition, the Lang group nominated a few candidates in Queensland, Victoria and South Australia, but this was for purposes of propaganda rather than with any expectation of actually winning seats.

Perhaps because the time was so short and the election so sudden, perhaps because the people have had rather a surfeit of plans and programmes in this troubled year, the election issues were never very clear or distinct. For the best of reasons no party leader was willing to adumbrate a detailed course of future action. The main policy speeches were, of course, those of the Prime Minister and of Mr. Lyons—an odd juxtaposition, for not only had the two men fought the last election from the same platform, but they probably think more alike in politics than almost any other two members of the House. Mr. Scullin put forward the achievements of the Ministry as the principal ground for returning it to office. Mr. Lyons treated the record of the Ministry as his principal ground for urging the electors to reject it. The one positive policy which the Labour party put forward was a change in the monetary system. The Commonwealth Bank—or so it seemed from the rather vague terms in which the policy was discussed—was to become, as the Labour party has always wished it to become, a trading bank in active competition over the whole range of banking business with the private banks; a distinct central bank was to be created and if the intentions of the Ministry were rightly to be gathered from their previous banking proposals, the central bank was to be subject to political control. At any rate its immediate function was thought of by Mr. Scullin in terms of "releasing" sufficient "credits" to put all the workless back into employment.

The policy sketched out by Mr. Lyons was even less precise than the Prime Minister's. He traced the dissensions within the Labour party and the vacillations of ministerial policy; he invited the electors to follow Britain's lead and reject a party which had fallen into discredit through failure to deal with economic necessities. He made no promises, he asked only for the return of a Government which would command confidence at home and abroad. He pleaded, like Mr. Ramsay MacDonald, for a "doctor's mandate."[6]

As the campaign wore on, the United Australia party leaders introduced a little more definition into their policy. Opponents began to recall the stand taken by Mr. Bruce and Mr. Latham in

1929, and to predict the abandonment of the Commonwealth arbitration system if Mr. Lyons were returned to power.[7] Mr. Latham promptly disavowed any intention of repeating the experiment of 1929, and though (like the Labour party at the preceding election) his party was determined to increase the sphere of conciliation in the arbitral system, he declared that they would not introduce any major change without first consulting the people at a referendum. Ministerialists also raised the cry that the tariff would be in danger from a Lyons-Latham Ministry. This attack was parried by a declaration that the United Australia party was definitely protectionist, but that it advocated a sane tariff, based in all cases on the recommendations of the Tariff Board, and adjusted where possible so as to extend the area of Empire trading. The onslaught on the tariff led in the last weeks of the Parliament by the Nationalist Senators did, however, afford ministerialists a colourable ground of attack. United Australia party speakers were able to show clearly enough that the tariff schedules brought in hastily by the Labour Government at intervals ever since it took office bristled with anomalies and even absurdities, and were imposed generally without prior consultation with, and often contrary to the subsequent recommendation of, the Tariff Board. Indubitably the tariff stood in need of revision—as well as validation—at the end of 1931. But Labour speakers pointed triumphantly to the fact that at the time of the dissolution the Senate had dealt with only the first eighteen items on the list, and had reduced thirteen of them. Since this fact alone was quite enough to frighten electors who had any doubts of the United Australia party's firmness on the tariff issue, and a certain loss of support in this issue was inevitable, the leaders of the party might well have taken a bolder line about the tariff, and so kept their hands quite free to do what the situation may turn out to require. But it is easy to say this after the event. To have acted in such a way before polling day may perhaps have demanded a more robust confidence of success than the facts then warranted.

The Country party did not play as large a part in the campaign as might have been expected. Having always had to depend on a number of votes in country districts which would normally go either to the Nationalists or to the Labour party, the Country party has never been able to stand openly and uncompromisingly for farming interests, but has had to make compromises in all directions and steer a middle course, hoping to be able to exercise a moderating influence upon any Government in power, even possibly to hold the balance of power itself. In this election Dr. Page did pronounce definitely in favour of a downward revision of the tariff in order to afford relief to export industries and to facilitate an extension of

Empire trade. (It would, however, be a mistake to suppose that Australia's policy for the forthcoming Ottawa Conference was canvassed in any serious way during the election campaign.) Dr. Page also advocated a number of constitutional amendments, in particular one to facilitate the creation of new States. This has all along been an objective of the Country party. In New South Wales it has recently become a matter of considerable importance, since in a number of rural centres disgust with Mr. Lang's administration has produced movements for separation from New South Wales.

As polling day drew near, ministerialists pushed their monetary policy as much as they could into the background, feeling apparently that it was unsafe ground to fight on. The Opposition, of course, was by no means inclined to let it drop. Opposition speakers dwelt on the evils of inflation, and claimed that the history of the New South Wales Savings Bank showed the insecurity of the people's savings if Governments were allowed to meddle with the banks. Thus, instead of a campaign of promises, it developed into a campaign of terrors. Each side claimed support because of the dangers of putting the other into office. But it is very doubtful whether there was much public conviction on any of these dangers. There was a vast deal of talk during the campaign, but little real excitement. Feeling not unnaturally ran strongest in New South Wales where, in addition to the contest between the Labour and anti-Labour forces, there was a bitter internecine battle between the federal and the State Labour groups, the more bitter since the factions were divided by loyalty to persons rather than by adherence to principles. The federal Labour group denounced the Lang group as wreckers and as the real enemy of the workers, since only in solidarity could the dangers of a Lyons-Latham triumph be averted. The Lang group denounced the Scullin-Theodore group as weak men of compromise, afraid to embrace the only policy that would save the workers from exploitation by the moneyed interests, and borrowing the only valuable elements in their policy from Mr. Lang himself. Mr. Lang's forces concentrated especially upon Mr. Theodore's electorate (Dalley), and only in Dalley was the Mungana affair brought into the foreground during the campaign. "Yes, we have no Munganas," sang Mr. Lang's supporters at Mr. Theodore's election meetings.

It was difficult for an impartial observer to suppose that the Labour Government stood a chance of being returned to office. In its principal stronghold, New South Wales, its supporters were bitterly divided, the country districts were completely disillusioned about Labour policy, the party had lost support everywhere and apparently had not gained it anywhere. Mr. Lyons, whose star had latterly been a little on the wane, came back remarkably into public esteem and succeeded in arousing a good deal of enthusiasm wherever he went. But only the unbounded optimism of Dr. Earle Page, the leader of the Country party, suggested a turn-over of public opinion as great as that which the polls have revealed. On the eve of the election he prophesied that the Labour party would be lucky to have as many as 25 seats in the new Parlioment. He was right. The Labour party has been swept clean out of Tasmania, left with only one seat in South Australia and in Western Australia, and reduced to a handful in Victoria and New South Wales. Only in Queensland did Labour gain any ground. Mr. Scullin went to the polls with 35 supporters. He lost 23 of them (including six Ministers) and even his two gains in Queensland will, as is shown below, give him only 14 seats in the new House. In the Senate election it appears probable that three anti-Labour Senators will be returned in every State except Queensland. Mr. Lyons will therefore have a following in the Senate of about 28 in a House of 36. In the House of Representatives the state of parties will be:

	Old Parliament	New Parliament
Federal Labour	35	14
State Labour	5	4
United Australia	23	39
Country	11	16
Independent (anti-Labour) ..	1	2
	75	75

Mr Lyons will thus have an absolute majority, without needing to rely on the Country party or the two Independents.

The most obvious feature of the voting is, of course, the complete downfall of the Ministry and the heavy anti-Labour gains everywhere except in Queensland. In 1929, on the industrial arbitration issue, a certain number of seats which ordinarily are held by anti-Labour members swung over to Labour. It was only to be expected that these would definitely revert to anti-Labour at the 1931 election. This process has certainly taken place. Mr. Bruce's return for Flinders is the outstanding case. Major R. G. Casey, until recently Australian Liaison Officer at the Cabinet Office in London,[8] has also won a seat in this category. But the turn-over is, of course, very much more extensive than this. Many seats which have been Labour strongholds for years have returned United Australia party members. Perhaps the outstanding instance is the Victorian constituency of Batman in which the Attorney-General, Mr. Brennan, has been rejected after having held the seat since 1910.[9] Even in seats which have still returned Labour members the anti-Labour vote is often larger than it has ever been. It is quite clear from this that there is something more than the usual set of opinion against a Ministry in office. On the other hand, the Labour gains in Queensland are commonly attributed to the unpopularity of the Nationalist Government, which has held office in the State for nearly three years. In Queensland, Labour not only held all its existing seats, but actually gained two and now holds five out of ten seats. Similar developments, however, did not take place either in Western Australia or in Tasmania, both of which have Nationalist Governments, and it is obvious that the general loss of confidence in Labour is very great.

In New South Wales the change is the most remarkable of all. Mr. Scullin now has three seats only, where he had 20 a short two years ago, and 14 when he went to the polls. Mr. Theodore has been overwhelmingly defeated by a Lang group candidate. The Lang group will have four seats—a loss of one. So far as the issue in New South Wales was one between two rival Labour factions the result has been decisive in favour of Mr. Lang. On the primary votes it looked very much as though the Lang group would win nine New South Wales seats. So bitter, however, was the feeling between the rival groups that anything up to half of Mr. Scullin's supporters gave their second preferences to the United Australia party rather than to the State Labour candidates. This explains the loss of several Sydney Labour strongholds to the United Australia party. The voting for the Senate candidates, however, reveals clearly the triumph of the State Labour group over the federal. It has polled nearly 70 per cent. of the total Labour vote in New South Wales. Mr. Lang was believed to cherish an ambition to enter federal politics, and it is understood that the new member for Reid, Mr. Gander,[10] is willing to resign at any time to enable him to contest the seat. But whether Mr. Lang would find the House of Representatives attractive in the new state of parties is at present unknown.

It is always a delicate task to assign afterwards the reasons for action which in many cases was probably quite unreasoning. But some factors, at any rate, which caused the Labour collapse may be isolated with confidence. It has been well remarked that in times of crisis the elector votes not so much for men and policies as against them. The reasons for voting against Mr. Scullin's party were probably very various. Though relatively little was made of the Mungana affair, for instance, it left behind it widespread misgiving and distrust, both of Mr. Theodore himself and of his influence in the counsels of Mr. Scullin. Again, the career of Mr. Lang has undoubtedly lost the Labour party a great deal of support, not only in New South Wales itself but throughout the Commonwealth. The elector was quite unconvinced by the fact that Mr. Scullin and

Mr. Lang were fighting each other; they were both Labour men, he argued, and what is Mr. Lang's policy to-day may very well be Mr. Scullin's policy to-morrow. The history of the State Savings Bank in New South Wales was a telling argument against Labour policy everywhere. Thousands of votes against Federal Labour were votes against Mr. Lang. It is not only in New South Wales that Mr. Lang has smashed the Federal Labour party. But over and above all other reasons for rejecting Mr. Scullin there lay the feeling, which was not altogether fair to him, that he had failed to put the country in the way of prosperity, that the present burden of unemployment is intolerable and that somehow or other a change might do good.

On the morrow of the election Mr. Scullin resigned and Mr. Lyons was commissioned to form a Ministry. Mr. Lyons was anxious to broaden the basis of his administration as much as possible, and accordingly offered three portfolios to the Country party—which had increased its representation by nearly 50 per cent., having swept Labour out of the country constituencies in New South Wales. This offer was refused. The Country party decided that the only terms on which it would enter the Ministry would include the offer of the portfolio of Trade and Customs to its leader. Dr. Page's party will therefore remain outside the Ministry as "benevolent critics." It is quite clear from this that tariff revision will be the grand issue in the new Parliament.[11]

The new Ministry will have a clear enough majority, but very grave problems to face. It is perhaps rather a pity that there has been so much talk since the election of better times ahead for all, and work for the workless. On the other hand the new Ministry comes in on a powerful wave of national support and will doubtless command general approval if it rises above party and faces the problems ahead of it in a truly national spirit. The leaders themselves are vigorously alive to this. Perhaps the most serious element in the situation is the smashing of the parliamentary Labour party. Movements are already afoot to try to heal the breach between the two wings of the movement. In the hour of weakness of the parliamentary party, it is very likely that the industrial section will gain control of the entire organisation, and that during this period of opposition the whole party will swing definitely towards the left. The result of the Senate polling in New South Wales shows how strong a grip the industrial section has, in that State at any rate. If the result of this election is ultimately to eliminate the Scullin group from the party organisation as well as from the House, Australia will have, very soon, to face the issue which New South Wales has had to face in the last few months. The contest will be, not who is to work existing institutions, but whether existing institutions are to survive.

Australia looks to the new Government to show that existing institutions can work, and can bring prosperity to the people.

December 1931

THE TRADE DIVERSION POLICY

September 1936, vol. 26, pp. 843–8

WHILE the tariff proposals of 1935–36 were under discussion in the Federal Parliament, Sir Henry Gullett (Minister without portfolio, directing negotiations for trade treaties)[12] announced the adoption of a "trade diversion" policy. It had been decided to widen the margin of preference for certain goods, and to apply a licensing system over a limited range of imports. The aim of the new policy was declared to be to increase Australian exports of primary produce, expand secondary production, and divert to countries already great customers, and likely to become greater in the future, some of the trade now going to countries that bought little from us. At the same time it was hoped that the new measures would help to place the country's "financial affairs in a sound and enduring position", make "a significant indirect contribution to defence" and hasten the day "when immigration can be resumed on a basis not harmful, but helpful to every industry and worker in the country".[13] In other words, the tariff and the import licences are to be used to accord preferential treatment to the goods of certain nations, especially of Great Britain, and to regulate Australia's London funds. The same instruments, supplemented where necessary by bounties, will also be used to establish or expand local industries.

The trade diversion policy must be interpreted together with the Customs Tariff Act, 1936. The most important features of that Act are the provision for the intermediate rate (actually re-introduced by the tariff resolutions of November 1935), in imposition of specific rates on certain piece goods imported from foreign countries, increased duties on oregon logs and tobacco, and the imposition of duties of 5½d per lb on unassembled motor-car chassis from foreign countries, 2½d per lb on those from Canada, and a further 7d per lb on all imported chassis irrespective of origin.

Under the licensing scheme, the importation of specified commodities (unless of Empire origin) will be prohibited except with the consent of the Minister of Trade and Customs. Licences are to be granted freely for all countries with which Australia has a favourable trade balance, and for others in regard to which, although the trade balance is unfavourable, the Government is satisfied with the position. For other countries they will be granted more freely as and when the trade position improves.

Motor-vehicle chassis are in a special class. They are not to be imported from any country other than the United Kingdom except with the consent of the Minister of Trade and Customs. Until Australia seemed likely to become involved in a trade war with Japan, most of the public discussion centred itself around this proposal.

The Government's decision to give strong and decisive encouragement to the establishment of the motor-chassis industry in Australia was separate from and independent of the general scheme of trade diversion. Its attitude is that the local market is now big enough to support such an industry, raw material and technical knowledge and skill are available, and a large part of nearly every car now in use in Australia is made locally and the rest should be. Whatever objections may be brought against this part of the Government's policy, it can advance a strong case on the grounds of defence.

The textiles mainly affected by the new policy are cotton and rayon piece goods. Here the Minister was obviously concerned at the decline in British imports during the last few years. In 1935 the imports of artificial silk from foreign sources represented nearly 90 per cent. of our total imports, and unless some steps were taken a similar position would exist with respect to cotton goods. The Government therefore decided that it would no longer "look with indifference to the effect upon the Australian interest of these swollen and still swelling arrivals of cotton piece and artificial silk piece goods", and would grant preference to British products.[14]

Before the 1936 tariff was imposed, the duties on cotton piece goods were:

> *ad valorem*:—5% British, 25% Foreign.
> primage:—5% British, 10% Foreign.

The new duties are:

	British Preferential Tariff.	Inter-mediate Tariff.	General Tariff.
Unbleached, per sq. yard. ..	½d*	2½d	2¾d
Bleached, ...	½d*	2¾d	3d
Printed, dyed or coloured, per sq. yard	½d	3¼d	3½d

> * or 5 per cent., whichever is the less.

Primage duties are abolished on British cottons and reduced to 5 per cent. on foreign.

On artificial silk textiles the former duties were:

ad valorem:—20% British, 40% Foreign.
primage:—10% British, 10% Foreign.

The *ad valorem* duties were displaced by specific duties, and primage duties were abolished on British goods and reduced to 5 per cent. on foreign. The new rates are:

	British Preferential Tariff.	Inter- mediate Tariff.	General Tariff.
Per sq. yard	1½d	8d	9d

with provision for by-law admission at the rate of

Per sq. yard	½d	3d	3d

The by-law rates will apply to artificial silk ordered before March 15 last and entered by November 30 next, in respect of goods the value for duty of which is not more than 7d per square yard.[15]

The country most affected by the new textile duties and the licensing system is Japan. For more than a year past negotiations have been in progress for the conclusion of a trade treaty between the two countries, but the Australian Government had almost abandoned hope of agreement when the new policy was announced. The immediate effect of the announcement was an unofficial boycott. Japanese buyers in Australia ceased to buy wool and flour and most of the other products that make up the Australian export to Japan. This was followed on June 25 by an official announcement of an ordinance under the Japanese trade protection law whereby imports of wool, wheat, or flour into Japan were prohibited except under licence and an import duty of 50 per cent. *ad valorem* imposed, in addition to the ordinary import duties, on hides and skins, beef tallow, beef, butter, condensed milk, and casein.

Until the Japanese Government took this action, the Australian Government remained silent as to the course the negotiations were pursuing, but when news of this ordinance was officially communicated to him, Mr. Lyons made an announcement.

I would like you clearly to understand (he said) that the responsibility lies with the Japanese manufacturers and exporters who, during the past two or three years, continuously and drastically, have reduced their prices to levels against which no European country or the United States of America could compete, except upon a diminishing and insignificant basis in this Australian market.

In making these reductions Japan had lead [sic]

the advantage against all other countries of much lower wages, longer working hours, cheaper raw materials, a substantial advantage by currency depreciation, and lower freight rates because of her relative proximity to the Commonwealth.

The extent to which these price reductions have been carried was illustrated by the fact that

in February last the average price of artificial silk imports from the United Kingdom was 14d, from Belgium 14¾d, France 38¼d, Germany 28¼d, United States 14¼d and from Japan 4½d. In 1932 Australian imports of artificial silk piece goods from Japan were 8,400,000 square yards at an average value per square yard of 8·3d sterling. Three years later, in 1935, the Australian imports from Japan were 65,800,000 square yards at an average price of 4·8d sterling. The quantity was increased eight times as the price was almost halved.

When we endeavoured with the Japanese representatives in this country (said Mr. Lyons) to reach a friendly agreement that would have the effect of limiting these imports of textiles to the Commonwealth, but of still leaving them a very large share of our textile trade, they replied after consultation with their Government that they must insist upon the retention of 90 per cent. of our trade in artificial silk, and that there should be no restriction whatever on the quantity of cotton piece goods imported and no alteration in the duties prevailing on these goods.

They went further, and made it clear to us that if their wishes were not respected, and if we varied either the quantity of the Japanese import or the prevailing duties, they would take action against us. In other words Japan attempted to limit our tariff-making powers.

More than that. In correspondence with my Government they have said in effect that useful discussion could take place upon our import of Japanese textiles only when we had given Japan a share of the market in other goods now enjoyed by goods of British origin. So that we have here both a declaration that if we altered our duty rates against Japan we would suffer harmful trade restriction, and a plain proposal that we should jettison our whole policy of reciprocal Empire trade.[16]

Japan has for some years been a very powerful and valuable influence in the Australian wool market, and there is a fear in Federal parliamentary circles that she may be disposed to exploit the fact. Should that fear be well founded, the disposition is likely to grow as her purchase of Australian wool increases, and with the growth of Australian imports from Japan there will be larger interests in that country to support the Government if it should see fit to demonstrate against Australian tariff charges. However regrettable a trade war may be, Australia must insist that her tariff policy is a matter for her own decision.

Not unnaturally many of the graziers are perturbed at the news of the Japanese trade restrictions, but in general there is a tendency to await further developments. As yet it can scarcely be said that public opinion has crystallised.

July 1936

THE TRADE DIVERSION POLICY AND JAPAN

December 1936, vol. 27, pp. 206–11

THE trade diversion policy, announced on May 22 last, raises in the sphere of external affairs, political and economic, even larger issues for the future of the Australian people. A summary account of the steps taken, and of the principal reasons advanced by the Government for taking them, appeared in the last number of THE ROUND TABLE.[17] Present needs will be met by simply recalling the three main elements in the new policy: the diversion to England from Japan, by means of drastically increased customs duties, of a large import trade in textiles; the diversion from America to Australian home manufacturer of a large trade in motor car engines and parts; and the diversion from "bad-customer countries" (chiefly the United States) to "good-customer countries" (mainly European) of a substantial amount of imported manufactures. The technique of the two later diversions has been to prohibit the importation of the goods concerned, save under licence from the Minister.

These steps may fairly be regarded as committing Australia wholly, for the time being at any rate, to the prevailing policy of economic nationalism, trade restrictions, quotas, bargains between governments. Obviously enough, because of her external indebtedness if for no other reason, the Australian economy cannot be self-contained. The question then is, where is Australia to find her complementary units. The policy of May 22 answers this question emphatically, in an imperial sense. Readers for THE ROUND TABLE will be familiar with this theme. The Ottawa agreements were a clear expression of it, and it is thus expressed by Mr. Amery:

It is indeed one of the apparent paradoxes of modern economic development that while the whole conception and structure of the modern state imply a policy of economic nationalism, the technical developments of modern production all demand so wide a range of varied natural products, so large a market to secure the maximum efficiency of mass production, so powerful a financial basis, that few of the existing countries into which the world is divided constitute economic units adequate to modern conditions. The solution of the paradox lies not in flying in the face of the whole tendency of modern thought in order to restore a nineteenth-century internationalism, nor in acquiescing in the stifling of progress by existing national boundaries. It lies in widening those boundaries by bringing together nations in groups large enough to satisfy the technical requirements of modern production, and yet also sufficiently held together by some common ideal, some permanent co-operative purpose, to enlist the forces of economic nationalism on their behalf . . . . For us that wider basis, political and economic, is already given. The British Empire, with the outer circle of economic or political dependencies which are, or may yet come, within its orbit, provides, for us at least, our natural starting point and the object of our main endeavour during this next phase of the world's development.[18]

But is this policy sound for Australia to-day? Fundamentally, the criticism of the trade diversion policy now making itself slowly manifest is that it is neither economically expedient nor politically safe for Australia to adopt towards the countries of the northern Pacific the attitude which the new policy implies.

Misgivings along these lines were widely felt in Australia as soon as the new policy was announced, and they have not since been lessened. The volume of overt criticism, however, has so far been almost incredibly small. The newspapers, even where not supporting the Government, have at least been reticent, the graziers for the most part unconvinced but not vocal. Partly, no doubt, this apparent complaisance is due to pressing party-political considerations. The only effective alternative to the present Government would at the moment be a Labour Government, and the shadow of Mr. Lang has kept many critics silent.

There have been other considerations operating as well, notably the request made by the Prime Minister that interested parties should "keep out of the ring". So dramatic have been the Government's moves, so skilfully have suggestions about defence been introduced, so sedulously has an air of mystery been preserved, that the plain man feels, almost in spite of himself, that there is a great deal more in this business than meets the eye. It will be remembered that the Government announced the new policy, without warning and without opportunity for discussion, only a few hours before Parliament adjourned for the winter recess. In informing the people later of developments in the trade dispute with Japan, the Prime Minister has twice used an instrument of propaganda unprecedented in Australia—a broadcast over all networks in Australia. These tactics have produced a considerable impression, but, in periodicals and in pamphlets, reasoned criticism is growing in volume.

Parliament reassembled early in September, but the Opposition has been in some difficulties about launching any effective challenge. To begin with, the trade diversion involved the promise of a very considerable expansion of employment in Australian secondary industry; in addition, an Australian Labour member would inevitably find himself in an unenviable position in defending the entry into Australia of goods produced by workers under less favourable wage conditions and on a longer working week.

In some quarters the trade diversion policy was regarded as a far-sighted measure, calculated to induce in Japan a greater willingness to accept the import restrictions that the Australian Government had proposed during the previous negotiations. Certainly no realist could have expected any immediate result of the kind. The immediate result was, in fact, Japanese retaliation, as was to have been expected. The Japanese wool-buyers began it by boycotting the Australian sales. Then on June 25 an official Japanese ordinance prohibited the import into Japan, save under licence, of wool, wheat, flour and starch, and imposed a 50 per cent. *ad valorem* surtax on a number of other commodities usually imported from Australia. The list included meat, butter, condensed milk, leather, animal fat and casein. Whereas the Australian customs duties were not to come into full force until December 1, these customs increases were to operate immediately.

The next move came from Australia, in the shape of a regulation, issued on July 8, prohibiting save under licence a wide range of imports from Japan. The Prime Minister explained that this action was not taken in any "retaliatory or punitive spirit", and he accompanied it with an offer to resume negotiations on the basis of a suspension of the measures taken on both sides, with the exception of the Australian tariff alterations of May 22.[19] This was not very promising diplomacy. The Japanese Chamber of Commerce in Sydney urbanely remarked that: "a sporting people will readily realise that Australia thus suggested compromise whilst she retained a hammer lock on Japanese trade".[20] In the alternative, Mr. Lyons offered to resume negotiations whilst leaving all the recent measures to their operation. This offer was accepted, and negotiations so far abortive were resumed. The exact proposals and counter-proposals do not appear to be known. The Ministry has denied a report from Tokyo that the Japanese Government offered to barter cottons and rayons for wool.

In the meantime the wool sales have been proceeding. If the Japanese had hoped for any dramatic slump in prices they were disappointed. On the other hand, it is idle to pretend that the market has been unaffected, though how much it has been affected is very difficult to estimate.

The Prime Minister has put the issue as one that "involves our right to legislate, as we may decide, upon our own domestic affairs, and touches our right to trade as we wish within the British Empire".[21] That is a strong enough point in itself, though of course it is a boomerang argument, and if pressed makes all tariff discussions useless. After all, Japan is doing to Australia exactly what Australia is herself doing to the "bad-customer countries" with whom she has an unfavourable trade balance. The whole point of negotiating trade treaties is precisely to modify the manner in which each country shall exercise its admitted rights.

In any case the insistence on Australia's right to follow this particular policy determines nothing whatever as to the merits of the policy itself, in Australia's own interest and in that of the Empire. The dilemma in which the Government has found itself should be clearly realised. On the one hand, it has been trying to negotiate, as against South American and European competitors, for a larger share of the British import market in meat and in other foodstuffs. In that negotiation, Australia's bargaining counter has been the offer to regain for British textiles, at Japan's expense, a larger share of the Australian import trade. But the very act of making such an offer impairs the success of Australia's efforts to find in the northern Pacific an expanding market for meat, flour and wool, particularly for wool. Australia loses, perhaps, whichever way she chooses.

That means she must choose in the light of the long-distance factors. Possibly not all of them are known to the general public. But those which are known weigh, on balance, against the particular arm of the dilemma that the Government has chosen. The strenuous effort being made to increase British home production and to make the Mother Country more nearly self-sufficient in foodstuffs suggests strongly that Great Britain cannot continue to offer an expanding market for Australian produce. The East can. But the trade diversion policy not only produces immediate dislocation of that market, it threatens ultimate contraction of it, in wool especially.

Arguments for this part of the trade diversion policy based on defence needs are disturbing but not altogether convincing. To provoke the antagonism of Japan is not, obviously at any rate, the best service that Australia can render Great Britain and the rest of the British Commonwealth. The British Government is reported as having disclaimed all responsibility for the introduction of the new policy, and the repercussions of Australia's action may perhaps cause some embarrassment to Great Britain herself in the East. There seems to be some ground for thinking that the diversion of trade may help Lancashire rather than Great Britain, and even that, taking a long view, its advantages to Lancashire are dubious. If the reports are correct that the future of Lancashire depends on courageous reorganisation and re-equipment within the cotton industry itself, the present concessions may well be on a wrong basis altogether.

One aspect of the new policy has been adversely commented upon, and never seriously justified. The Commonwealth Government has, over a term of years, been building up a tariff system based on a sound technique of expert and impartial investigation by the Tariff Board. The introduction of the licensing system, the imposition of new tariffs upon Japanese textiles, and upon motor engines and parts, took place, so far as the public is aware, without any prior consultation whatever with the Tariff Board. When questioned, the Government's answer in each case was simply that this was "a policy of trade diversion", and fell outside the scope of the Tariff Board's operations. Upon this the Ritchie Professor of Economics in the University of Melbourne[22] remarked that "the Government appears to have exposed the whole structure of our tariff policy to the vagaries of future political expediency, and the log-rolling of interested parties".

October 1936

FOREIGN AFFAIRS AND DEFENCE

June 1938, vol. 28, pp. 604-8

EVENTS in Europe during the past few weeks have focused political controversy in Australia on foreign policy and defence. The circumstances surrounding Mr. Anthony Eden's resignation as Foreign Secretary aroused much discussion of the problem of imperial consultation, and there was a certain feeling of disquiet.[23] At the Imperial Conference last year "emphasis was laid on the importance of developing the practice of communication and consultation between the respective Governments as a help to the co-ordination of policies".[24] Mr. Eden's resignation seemed, to many people, to imply a radical change in British foreign policy, which, on Mr. Lyons' own admission, had not been preceded by anything like "consultation" with the Dominion Governments.

Mr. Lyons claimed, however, that the Australian Government had been informed of "the trend of events", and that this was sufficient in the circumstances. For, in his opinion, all that Mr. Eden's resignation implied was that there had been differences within the British Cabinet, differences concerning method, which did not spell any departure from the policy agreed upon at the last Imperial Conference.[25]

This failed to satisfy Mr. Curtin, the Leader of the Federal Opposition.[26]

I deem it the imperative duty of the Federal Government (he said) to summon the Commonwealth Parliament forthwith. In view of the momentous significance of what has occurred in Great Britain recently, Australia needs to know fully and frankly what is the policy of the Lyons Government on foreign affairs. More than a week has passed, and the Prime Minister remains silent. Representative government in Australia is being made a travesty in a matter of supreme national importance . . . . The British Prime Minister informed the House of Commons of the changes that had occurred in British foreign policy, and the House debated the matter. In Australia, however, Mr. Lyons thrusts Parliament into outer darkness, and the people into uninformed obscurity . . . . Sectional action in Australia in international matters is wrong, and could very easily become dangerous, but I am faced with the fact that by lack of candour respecting its own policy the Government has abdicated the field, and, in the absence of leadership, sporadic outbursts can be expected.[27]

To this Mr. Lyons replied by drawing attention to the divided counsels within the Labour party itself concerning foreign policy. Two days later, he announced that he had been authorised by Mr. Chamberlain to state that

the United Kingdom Government still adheres to the policy enunciated and discussed at the Imperial Conference of 1937. There is no change in the attitude of the United Kingdom towards the League of Nations and collective security.[28]

Regret was expressed even in conservative journals, in Melbourne and Sydney, that Mr. Lyons should have regarded as a "challenge" Mr. Curtin's request for an immediate meeting of Parliament, and concern that the issue had been reduced to one of party politics. The Melbourne *Argus*, for example, said:[29]

Surely it is carrying party warfare too far when the Prime Minister of a senior Dominion, in the hope of scoring a polemical point against the leader of the Opposition, solemnly denies a fact which is patent to every observer of world affairs. To say that the difference which arose between Mr. Chamberlain and Mr. Eden was merely a difference of opinion concerning method is to play with words.

The *Sydney Morning Herald*, on the following day, expressed its frank disbelief in Mr. Chamberlain's assurances that no occasion for consultation had arisen. After quoting from the debate in the House of Commons, it concluded:

Surely "fundamental" differences could not arise between a Prime Minister and his Foreign Secretary unless some substantial change were intended in the policy which the latter had been pursuing . . . . In the light of these disclosures it is impossible to accept the view that the issue dividing Mr. Eden and his Prime Minister was too trivial to deserve the attention of the Dominion Governments. Moreover . . . the divergence had been developing for some weeks . . . . It can hardly be held, therefore, that the failure to consult the Dominions on the questions at issue was due to lack of time and opportunity. Mr. Chamberlain may genuinely believe that such consultation was not necessary in the circumstances, but this view will not be generally shared in the Dominions, and it is regrettable that the Australian Government should appear over-ready to accept it. If a decision which, by Mr. Chamberlain's own testimony, was intimately bound up with issues of peace and war is not a proper subject for consultation, it is hard to imagine what is.[30]

This discussion was terminated by the crisis arising from the absorption of Austria within the German Reich. In the light of events, fears that Mr. Eden's resignation showed that there had been a radical change in British foreign policy have largely disappeared. The public therefore no longer regard the incident as a test case concerning consultation. It is assumed that before any reorientation of British foreign policy were to take place, in the light of the present critical situation in central Europe, there would be close and detailed consultation throughout the Empire.

The storm-clouds in Europe have increased the anxiety already felt in many quarters concerning the adequacy of Australia's defence forces. The official opening of the graving-dock at Singapore on February 14 was felt to "increase the security of the Empire from Aden to Hong Kong, and Cape Town to New Zealand".[31] But the warning was clearly given in the press that the immediate value of Singapore could easily be exaggerated. In the future, if and when Great Britain was able to station a battle fleet permanently in Eastern waters, this base would become a real bulwark. Until then, Australians had little reason for complacency. A speech by Mr. Chamberlain early in March aroused further doubts about the present position of the Dominions in the Empire scheme of defence. Mr. Chamberlain indicated that the first concern of the British Government would be to protect the Mother Country, then to maintain her supplies from abroad, and thirdly to defend her overseas possessions. Did this mean that the Dominions would have to rely on their own resources in time of war? Mr. Lyons sought assurances from Mr. Chamberlain, and was able to announce that, although appearing third on the list, the protection of overseas possessions was definitely regarded as of first-rate importance.

The defence of Australia (said Mr. Lyons) and of the trade routes between Australia and Great Britain is an essential part of Great Britain's defence policy, forming as it does part of "the first main effort". For this reason, Singapore, as a pivotal point of the whole system of the naval defence of the Empire east of Suez, is being provided not only with docks, but also with the most powerful guns and air defences of any port in the Empire.[32]

It is indicative, however, of the feeling in Australia that press forecasts that the defence estimates were again to be revised upwards produced scarcely a protest. Indeed, public opinion, including a section of the Labour party, seems anxious to accelerate still further Australia's defence programme. The Premier of Tasmania, Mr. Ogilvie, at the Tasmanian Conference of the Australian Labour party, held early in March this year, sponsored a motion seeking the reintroduction of "universal military training for home defence and universal physical training". Replying to Labour criticism in other states, Mr. Ogilvie pointed out that his motion had been unanimously endorsed, and that the conference was representative of every Labour branch in Tasmania. "It was the Labour party that put compulsory training for home defence on the statute book in the first place, and it is competent for Labour again to enforce it, if it so desires," Mr. Ogilvie declared.[33] The measure was enacted by a Labour Administration in 1909; in 1929 the Scullin Ministry, under stress of economic depression, suspended the obligation to train "in time of peace".

As against this, Labour leaders in New South Wales declared that "conscription is the unforgivable political sin", and in "conscription" they seem at the moment to include compulsory training for home defence as well as military service overseas. Since the crisis over Austria, however, there have been several resolutions in business and pastoral circles favouring universal training for home defence.

A climax to these discussions about defence was reached on March 25, when the Prime Minister, Mr. Lyons, in a "record" broadcast over 106 stations, announced that the Government had decided upon a defence programme involving £24,850,000 of additional new expenditure in the next three years. This, added to the vote for the maintenance of the defence forces as at present organised, would raise the total defence expenditure during this period, apart from the civil aviation vote, to £43,000,000. The new expenditure will be divided as follows: £7,770,000 extra for the navy; £5,500,000 extra for the army; £8,800,000 to complete the Salmond scheme of air defence within the next three years; and £2,800,000 of new expenditure for government munition factories and the organisation of industry. "Acting on the advice of the army authorities," said Mr. Lyons, "it is not the Government's intention to increase the strength of the militia services above 35,000 at present. The experts consider that the most pressing need is to strengthen the material side, while at the same time raising the efficiency of the existing forces to the highest degree possible."[34]

April 1938

AUSTRALIA AND THE CZECH CRISIS

December 1938, vol. 29, pp. 44-9

IT would be misleading to speak of "Australian public opinion" on the Czechoslovak problem during the period of the negotiations, for there was no united, unambiguous national attitude to the crisis, although its phases were followed in an agony of suspense. Some of the organs of public opinion adopted a definite line throughout, but newspaper and other comment mostly reflected the apprehension and indecision of the ordinary citizen, who felt that events were moving in a direction that he dreaded, under the impulse of forces of which he had no control and little understanding. The basis of this confusion was to be found partly in a limited knowledge of the problems of central Europe, and the absence of statements by Australian politicians which might have given a definite lead to public feeling, or indicated the proper rôle of Australia in the crisis. Even in retrospect, the solution of the crisis appears to some as the answer to prayer, and to others as a work of the devil. The most positive effect of the whole episode on public opinion is the marked renewal of attention to two problems—namely, national defence, and the rôle of Australia in British foreign policy.

Although the general level of education in Australia on international affairs has been steadily rising in recent years, the problems of Czechoslovakia remained a closed book to most Australians. Vagueness as to the boundaries of Czechoslovakia, and how the name should be pronounced, were coupled with complete ignorance of the centuries-old conflict between Slav and German in Bohemia. On the other hand, the probable expansion of Germany under Herr Hitler's leadership had been a matter for frequent comment and discussion.

In view of the general expectation that the Nazi Rally at Nuremberg on September 5 would be the occasion for a critical decision by Herr Hitler, the Commonwealth Government, on September 2, cabled to the Government of the United Kingdom, stating that it "strongly supported the policy set out" in the speeches of Mr. Chamberlain and Sir John Simon,[35] on March 24 and August 27 respectively.

The United Kingdom Government was also informed (Mr. Lyons later told Parliament) that the Commonwealth Government urged that the Government of Czechoslovakia should not delay in making a public announcement of the most liberal concessions which it could offer, and that representations should be made to the Czechoslovak Government with a view to securing an immediate public statement of such concession.[36]

As the situation deteriorated, the general tenor of press comment was that the decision as to whether Europe should be plunged into war lay with Herr Hitler. It was with astonishment that Australians learned of Mr. Chamberlain's dramatic flight to interview the German Führer at Berchtesgaden on September 15, and the press united to praise this "courageous and inspired act of statesmanship". The Sydney *Morning Herald*, which, in the curious company of the extremely radical *Labour Daily*, has been advocating a firm line in dealing with dictators, was at pains to argue that Mr. Chamberlain's step did not betoken any weakness in Britain's attitude; indeed, that it provided the opportunity to make it clear to Herr Hitler that Britain would not stand aside if France were involved in war, despite Herr von Ribbentrop's scepticism on this point.[37] The rest of the press, however, did not go so deeply into that issue.

The publication of the Anglo-French proposals, involving the cession of large areas of Czechoslovakia, came as a painful shock to most Australians; Lord Runciman's letter of September 21 was not made public in Australia until September 28, and even then received little attention.[38] The Sydney *Morning Herald* was frankly hostile to the proposals and regarded them as a blow to British honour and prestige. The *Labour Daily* quoted them as proof of Mr. Chamberlain's love of Fascism. But the remainder of the Australian press repudiated the criticism of the British Prime Minister which their cables recorded. "It is to be noted", wrote the Brisbane *Courier-Mail*, "that the most bitter criticism outside Czechoslovakia is offered by those whose words are weighted with least responsibility."[39]

It is difficult to estimate the extent to which editorial comment reflects or, on the other hand, influences public opinion. Nevertheless, it seems certain that there were substantial groups in the community whose views were represented by these newspaper opinions. But in addition there was a large group which felt doubtful as to what its attitude should be, and was certain only of one thing—namely, that the Czechs would not accept such drastic proposals. When they did accept, their action was applauded by all sections of the community for its nobility, although the probability that it was a concession to British and French pressure tempered enthusiasm. Then, as Godesberg followed Berchtesgaden, and hopes for a peaceful settlement faded, the pros and cons of the Anglo-Fench proposals became less important than the question of Australia's rôle in the likely event of war. Most of the press proclaimed that the nation would stand solidly behind Britain, but a discordant note came from some important Labour circles. Mr. Lang had already declared the attitude of his section of the Labour party in New South Wales, on September 16. "Our people", he said, "are determined that Australia must be kept out of European wars at all costs. The Labour party must prepare itself to organise the Australian people against participation in a European war."[40] Mr. Forgan Smith, the Queensland Labour Premier, said he was opposed to all dictatorships, but would not support a war outside Australia.[41] On September 27, the Federal Labour leader, Mr. Curtin, declared in Parliament that the Labour movement would oppose any move to send an Australian force overseas.[42] The industrial wing of the movement, however, both in Sydney and in Adelaide, had demanded a declaration by Australia "of support for Czech independence against Fascist aggression and for peace by collective security", the policy adopted by the *Labour Daily*.[43] This led the Sydney *Morning Herald* to find gold where it had never previously thought of searching.

The real heart of the Labour movement lies, we may feel, not in Mr. Curtin's vain cry for a stay-at-home policy, but in the attitude of the Labour newspaper in Sydney, whose "reply to Fascism's threat of war is to offer wholehearted support to Great Britain in a stand for democracy, liberty and collective security".[44]

Herr Hitler's ultimatum to the Czechs was to expire on September 28 at 11 p.m. (Sydney time), and Mr. Lyons chose this hour for his first Parliamentary statement since the crisis entered the acute stage. His review of events, which received scant attention in the press, was described by Mr. Curtin as "a most extraordinary anti-climax", providing "no additional information".[45] But the Prime Minister did table the text of the documents that the British Government had published.[46]

The following day brought news of the proposed Four Power meeting at Munich, and Mr. Lyons disclosed to Parliament that, prior to the announcement of the Conference, the Commonwealth Government had urged that Signor Mussolini be asked to make a personal appeal to Herr Hitler, and offered the services of the Australian High Commissioner to fly to Rome with a personal message from Mr. Chamberlain to Signor Mussolini. Mr. Chamberlain had intimated "that he was at the moment considering action of this nature". Mr. Lyons further assured the House that the Commonwealth had been kept fully informed of Mr. Chamberlain's negotiations and added, "We have made such suggestions as we believed would be helpful, and which we believe have been helpful at various stages of the dispute".[47]

Meanwhile, the State Premiers had been hurriedly called to Canberra for a Premiers' Conference, but within a few hours of their arrival news came through that the Four Power Agreement had been signed. The criticism of the settlement came from many angles. Some deplored this latest defeat for democracy; some saw a mere postponement of a war less escapable and more horrible because of its postponement; some felt conscious of a betrayal of Britain's honour.

The centre of interest has now passed to the problems that remain. The future of Britain as a world power, Australia's rôle in British foreign policy, the defence of Australia, and her attitude towards refugee immigrants.

Some reflection of current opinion may be found in the debate in the Commonwealth Parliament on October 5, following the tabling of the text of the Munich Agreement. Mr. Curtin again expressed astonishment at the paucity of information from the Commonwealth Government regarding its policy during the crisis, and repeated the official Labour view that Australians should not be recruited for service overseas in time of war. But he drew the moral that "we need to do more in ensuring the impregnability of Australia against attack", and advocated co-operation between all Australian governments "in respect of the civil and industrial side of defence".[48] Speakers from both sides of the House supported this. Mr. Menzies, the Attorney-General, aroused interest by a speech in which he said that Parliament in the past had "had rather too little discussion of foreign affairs", and that while Australia should not set up an independent foreign policy of her own, we should nevertheless "have minds sufficiently informed and sufficiently strong, positive and constructive, to be able to say useful things at the right time to the Government of the United Kingdom". He suggested that there was a trend in this direction. Mr. Menzies also stated again the view that Australia could not be neutral if Britain went to war, but that Australia could nevertheless decide the extent and form of her participation in the war.[49]

Another point was raised on October 6, when the Minister for External Affairs was asked in Parliament whether Australia had been approached concerning guarantees of the new Czechoslovakian frontiers. Mr. Hughes replied in the negative and added that the Government did not intend "to take any part in the matter".[50] But there is still some uncertainty as to what this would imply if Britain had to act to protect Czechoslovakia's frontiers, and the problem of Australia's rôle in British foreign policy is not yet settled.

October 1938

AUSTRALIA AT WAR

December 1939, vol. 30, pp. 190–6

THE news of the declaration of war on Germany by Great Britain was received in Australia on a Sunday evening with a calm which to some extent was the result of a feeling that the development was inevitable. During the previous ten days the public had been kept in a state of high tension as information concerning the dramatic moves in Europe came to hand. The culminating point appeared to bring a certain relief from the tension of the preceding days.

There is no doubt whatever that the principles on which the British and French Governments have taken action have been widely applauded by all sections of the community. Great disappointment was expressed in many quarters at the failure of the Anglo-Russian negotiations, and the signing of the Russian-German non-aggression pact was equally unwelcome. For some months the public had been, through the press and radio, led to expect the adherence of Russia at an early date to the Peace Front. The differences between Communism and Nazism had been so emphasised by many public commentators that many people tended to ignore some of the deeper reasons which, in the opinion of a few students and observers, might cause a Russian-German understanding at any moment. The agreement, however, had a bright side for many Australians as it was considered that Japan's projected military alliance with the Axis Powers was no longer practicable. Undoubtedly the possibility of this alliance had caused concern in Australia and the officially declared neutrality of the Japanese Government has relieved the Australian Government of some pressing anxieties.

The statement of the Prime Minister which was broadcast a few minutes after Mr. Chamberlain's announcement that Britain was at war with Germany at once made the position of the Commonwealth in the Empire unequivocal. "There never was any doubt where Britain stood," said Mr. Menzies, "and there can be no doubt that where Britain stands there stand the people of the entire British Empire ... Britain is at war, therefore Australia is at war."[51] Constitutional authorities in Australia have on the whole considered that when the King is at war all his dominions are at war. There was, therefore, no declaration of war by Australia on Germany.

The leader of the federal Opposition promised the Prime Minister that the Labour party could be relied on to do the right thing in the defence of Australia. The Premier of Queensland, Mr. Forgan Smith, in a statement in Brisbane appeared to go further on behalf of the Labour party in that state. He said "Everything that can be done to promote civilisation and peace has, in my opinion, been done. Principles and liberty mean more than phrases and we must be prepared to do everything possible that the institutions for which we stand may be maintained at all costs."[52]

There was some talk of the possibility of forming a National Government: but the Labour party would not co-operate with the United Australia party for such a purpose. It took the view, which is fairly widely held here, that the real interests of a democracy can be most effectively safeguarded even in war time by the existence of a vigilant Opposition. The Country party has pledged its full support for all measures which it considers will help to prosecute the war in the most efficient and practical manner. Points of difference on other matters prevent at present the formation of a composite Government. Sir Earle Page, who has been leader of the federal parliamentary Country party for nearly twenty years, has resigned the position. This makes the personal antipathy between him and the Prime Minister a less important factor in the relations between the Government and the Country party. Mr. Archie Cameron of South Australia has been elected in his place.[53] A War Cabinet consisting of six of the Ministers has been created. Its chief functions will be to ensure that major policy decisions of the Government are efficiently and speedily carried into effect.

The outbreak of war found the Commonwealth to a certain extent ready for the emergency. Preliminary steps were taken on August 25 to guard important strategic points, and a few days later certain restrictions on the transfer of money from Australia to overseas countries were announced. Precautionary measures were intensified two days before the outbreak of war, and when the fateful decision was taken little remained to be done to complete the emergency plans of the Government. There was commendable co-operation between State and Federal Governments, though defence is the sole responsibility of the latter.

At present the activities of the land defence forces are being concentrated on a programme of intensified training and expansion. The militia has been called up in two batches of 40,000 for a month's continuous training, shortly to be followed by a further three months. This is a welcome decision, for it must be admitted that on September 3 there were very few militia soldiers in the Commonwealth sufficiently trained to meet an enemy attack. The militia is liable for service only in Australia and its territories. But since war broke out there has been a considerable number of volunteers offering for either home or overseas service. Although up to the present the British Government apparently does not desire the dispatch of Dominion forces overseas to the theatre of war, the Commonwealth Government has already begun to raise a special force of 20,000 to be available for service in Australia or overseas as circumstances require. This will be known as the Sixth Division of the Second Australian Imperial Force and is enlisted for permanent service for the duration of the war. The title seems to have been chosen because there were five divisions in the A.I.F. in France during the Great War, and because the militia is organised on the basis of five divisions. The present force was spoken of by the public as the "new A.I.F." from the time its promotion was mooted. The force will be commanded by Major-General Sir Thomas Blamey.[54] The personnel will be drawn principally from the militia. It is expected that their training will commence early in November. The Government has also offered to the British Government the personnel of six Royal Australian Air Force squadrons for service overseas. This contingent will consist for four bomber squadrons and two two-seater fighter squadrons, and they are expected, if circumstances permit, to leave Australia before the end of the year.[55] The total number of this force will be approximately 3,200 men. It has also been decided to raise two garrison battalions for permanent service chiefly from the ranks of the returned soldiers. These will be used to relieve militia units of guard duty at many points where permanent guards are necessary. The Prime Minister has undertaken that there will be no conscription for overseas service. But the Defence Act gives authority for the conscription of man-power for service within Australia and its territories.

The Government's defence programme has been accelerated since Parliament went into recess. Freed for a time from the worries of the parliamentary situation, the Ministry appears to have given the closest attention to the task of establishing the defences of the Commonwealth on a satisfactory basis. Much of the creative organisation of the programme has now been completed, and there remains the more difficult task of giving effect to the principles laid down by improved routine organisation. It is not possible for any person other than those chiefly responsible to judge of the degree of success which is attending these efforts. According to Ministerial statements progress in the manufacture of aircraft and munitions is satisfactory. But it should not be assumed that Ministers are unduly complacent about the position.

A large body of public opinion, both informed and uninformed, will not allow the Ministry to take defence preparations in a casual manner. Since the outbreak of war there has been considerable criticism of the Ministry principally because of its alleged inertia and the apparent delay in making some definite offer of help to Britain. Some of that criticism has been hardly fair and has been made without a full knowledge of the facts. But the pressure of public opinion on Government policy has been for the good of both the Ministry and the country. Although the Government has been pushing ahead with its plans, there are a number of competent observers who consider that the plans themselves are not ambitious enough to cope with the requirements of totalitarian warfare. It has been urged that the organisation of industry means all industry and not merely those sections of it which appear to have a direct and immediate connection with current defence plans. It is likely that more will be done in the future to organise industry so that all of its component parts will function in the most efficient manner in time of war. Something, of course, has already been done in this direction. The oil companies at the request of the Government have agreed to increase their already considerable fuel reserves and it is considered that, together with the expected volume of production of shale oil in the near future, the Commonwealth will have reserves to meet the present emergency without resort to rationing.

Plans have been completed for the organisation of the primary industries. The British Government has bought practically all the exportable surplus of Australia's primary products. Some of this will probably be re-sold to neutrals. Australian primary producers, with the exception of fruit growers, will not have to worry about markets for the duration of the war. Wool, wheat, sugar, flour and meat have all been purchased at prices that will give a fair return to the producer. In a sense the latter may be considered to be fortunate as the result of this development, and their part in the war effort to be rather inglorious. But it must be remembered that the extent of the Commonwealth's war effort will be finally determined by the strength of its economy and that this in return is based on the primary industries.

The National Register of wealth and man-power was taken before the war, but not without some trouble. The boycott which had been decided upon by the Australian Council of Trade Unions was eventually lifted as the result of certain assurances that were given to the Unions by the Prime Minister. The Labour party was anxious to avoid a clash with the Ministry on this issue and the Leader of the Opposition, Mr. Curtin, played a prominent part in the negotiations which led to the decision to lift the boycott.

Before the federal Parliament adjourned on September 21 it passed the National Security Act. This measure gives the Government complete power to deal with any matter which in any way affects Australia's war effort. This is legally justified because of the wide scope of the Commonwealth defence power notwithstanding normal constitutional limitations. There is a power of restricting freedom of speech which, however, can only be exercised by the Minister for Defence. Though most members disliked the Bill and there were various criticisms of some of its details, it was recognised as an essential part of the Australian war effort.

The Ministry had to face considerable criticism because of its decision, made shortly before the war began, not to proceed with the proposal to establish a permanent mobile force. Since the Lyons-Page Government had decided in March to create such a force, the decision of the Menzies Government was a reversal of one already taken. But this matter has become of little consequence, for it is now apparent that Australia is going to have a considerable force for the duration of the war.

October 1939

ADJUSTMENT TO DANGER

June 1942, vol. 32, pp. 416-19

IN the past six months, what happened to Britain in 1940 between the invasion of Norway and the evacuation from Dunkirk has happened to Australia also. By a series of swift and unexpected successes the enemy has overrun almost the entire intervening belt of neutrals and Allies. Until Japan entered the war, our rôle, albeit on a small scale, had been in essentials rather like that of Britain before the fall of the West—an island belligerent but itself inviolate, assisting the common cause by expeditionary forces abroad on land and in the air, by the export of munitions, and by help in keeping the sea lanes open. Now the enemy subjects our own coasts to attack by air, and threatens us with a general invasion.

Of course, the greater distances in the South-Western Pacific do from some points of view lessen our peril. Our large cities in the south-east angle of the continent are as far by air even from Darwin as Alexandria is from London. But this means, on the other hand, that our defence must be organized at a great distance from our main bases. Nor will it be forgotten that, when the Japanese began to sweep through Malaya and the East Indies, some of Australia's finest and best-equipped forces were serving far away from the homeland, on land, at sea and in the air: that by agreement with the rest of the Commonwealth our air efforts here have been concentrated on training men for overseas and on the production of training machines: that, in a word, our entire defence programme had been built (in accordance with the official United Kingdom view) upon the assumption that the British Commonwealth would be able in all probable contingencies to retain control of the approaches to Australia. The Japanese victories confronted us with a situation wholly new, a situation moreover with which Australia's 7,000,000 people, unaided, could not by any possibility deal.

The story of Australia in the first half of 1942 has, therefore, been that of a people painfully adjusting itself to an unimagined danger. Folk in Britain, having themselves so recently undergone a like experience, will understand their kinsmen here. The reactions of public opinion have been crude, confused and sometimes violent. We have had no Churchill among our leaders. Even now we have not achieved the political, social and moral unity of which Britain has given so superb an example. But we have made progress. Internally the Government has been further mobilizing the resources of the nation. There have been misgivings in some quarters, heightened by occasional outbursts of Radicalism from the irrepressible Mr. Ward, Minister for Labour and National Service;[56] but the Government has been able to count on very general support. In external affairs Australia has been establishing new relationships both with Britain and with the United States. The numerous and, at times, rather excited official statements by which this process has been accompanied caused so much comment both in Australia and abroad that a retrospect may be useful. But the underlying strategical problem which has confronted the Australian Government and people must be kept carefully and continually in view, if any fair appraisal is to be made.

The defeats of the Imperial forces in Malaya and the siege and capitulation of Singapore were followed in Australia with grief and amazement. Reports came to hand, among them extracts from an article by *The Times* correspondent, of the inadequacy of the preparations made in constructing airfields and in equipping and training troops, and of lack of co-operation between the different arms and again between the British and Australian commanders— a repetition of the worst examples in the last war as recorded by the official Commonwealth historian.[57] It was felt that the events preceding the final disaster constituted one of the darkest pages in the history of the British Empire—the failure of the British community to win the adherence of the native inhabitants, and the failure of the military, naval and air authorities to prepare for an attack of which they had ample warning. Criticism of these events in Australia did not come only from a small minority which expresses a distrust of all things English, nor is it to be confused with a failure to understand the grand strategy of the war. It sprang from a belief that the forces available had not been handled with energy or reasonable forethought, and that this defeat was in one sense worse than Dunkirk because it showed that the British had failed to learn the lessons there taught them, reinforced as they had been by the campaigns of Greece and Crete. Reasonably minded Australians admitted that their country, like the other democracies, had neglected its own defences, that it had done little for the defence of Singapore, and that it might have done more. But they felt, and many of them said, that their manhood had been needlessly sacrificed, and that in future wars an Australian Government must share responsibility for the leadership under which our forces are to be placed, and for the preparations made for their equipment.

Mr. Churchill's broadcast after the fall of Singapore was a salutary lesson in the conditions of Allied strategy. It reminded Australia of the importance of the Russian front, of the exigencies of the Russian command, and of the strain which the voyage round the Cape imposes on Allied transport. But it did not answer criticism of the Malayan campaign; and, even though nine-tenths of the Australian people acknowledge Mr. Churchill's supremacy as a leader, they still believe that Mr. Curtin was right in demanding for Australia a direct voice in the determination of Allied war policy, and also in urging that help should be sent to this country against the time when it should be threatened by a Japanese armada. The demand for a direct voice in policy was twofold. First, the Government requested the establishment of an Imperial War Cabinet. This was not a novel idea in Empire history, nor was it a party matter in Australia. A similar expedient had been used for like purposes during 1917 and 1918. It was Mr. Curtin's predecessors in office who had revived the idea in 1941. For rather different reasons, Canada and South Africa were known not to favour the plan, but the change in the whole strategical position of Australia on the outbreak of war with Japan forced Mr. Curtin to make a definite and urgent request, irrespective of the desires of other Dominions.

Mr. Churchill was unwilling, it seems, to establish anything as formal as the practice of 1917–18, more especially perhaps because the Dominions were not unanimous on the point. When the Imperial War Cabinet of 1917–18 was in session, all major war matters (except those that concerned the United Kingdom alone) were dealt with by the Imperial body. At the end of January last, Mr. Churchill told the Commons that the Government had decided to invite a representative of each of the belligerent Dominions to sit with the War Cabinet of the United Kingdom whenever matters arose which, in the opinion of the Prime Minister of the United Kingdom, urgently affected the Dominion concerned. This was not quite what Canberra had asked for. As Mr. Menzies had remarked in a press article, it was desired that a Dominion representative should sit constantly with the Cabinet, because "only by doing so will he be able to secure, at the right time, Australian consideration of many matters which would not on the face of them appear to touch Australia at all".[58] On the other hand, the continued political representation of Australia in London by Sir Earle Page, who was sent last year by Mr. Fadden's Government,[58] is anomalous, and is scarcely consistent with the importance which Mr. Curtin attached to the subject. Sir Earle Page is now a member of the Opposition in Parliament, and his personal experience and qualifications have not lain in the spheres either of military affairs or of international matters in general.[60] The unfortunate inability of the Government to send a senior Minister to London springs from the acute pressure on Labour's small group of outstanding men.

Canberra's other request was for the establishment in Washington of a Pacific War Council on which Australia would be directly represented as one of the United Nations, along with the United Kingdom, the United States, China and the Netherlands. This plan, though not at first adopted owing (it seems) to a strong reluctance on the part of President Roosevelt to establish a formal Allied organization on the politico-strategical side, was eventually accepted during the visit to Washington of Dr. Evatt, the Australian Minister for External Affairs.[61] Australian opinion evinced no active interest in these questions of constitutional machinery, but there is no doubt of general support for the course which the Government has taken. The Australian request sprang partly from a feeling, expressed also in some quarters in England, that under existing arrangements the general strategical plan was too much the creation of Mr. Churchill's individual mind and personality, partly from a desire to get arrangements made which would emphasize more firmly the responsibility and initiative of Washington in Pacific affairs. The case for direct representation of Australia was clear. To determine the strategy of the United Nations in the Pacific is to decide the plan for the Australian mainland itself, whether in defence or in offence. Where the fate of the nation was being decided, the nation's voice should properly be heard.

Questions of machinery apart, Canberra also urged both on London and on Washington the importance of sending help to this country against impending or probable Japanese attack. Right or wrong, there has been a strong impression in Australia that the discussions involved matters more general than the desirability or otherwise of making certain specific dispositions, and that the British strategical plan for 1942 was to concentrate the available resources of the Allies primarily upon victory over Germany, no matter what the fate of Australia might be meanwhile, in full confidence of the Allies' ability to hurl the Japanese back, once Hitler's power was broken. Such a plan, in view of the supply problem of the democracies and after consideration of the available alternatives, might have turned out in the end to be necessary, no matter how painful. But no Prime Minister of Australia would be justified in allowing his country to be overrun by Japanese hordes without doing his utmost to obtain maximum assistance from his country's Allies. We have not been adequately guided either by the press or by the Government in understanding the general plan of Allied operations, and it has been hard for us to see our country's peril in true perspective. The Government has been insistent, even perhaps importunate, in stating Australia's needs. But importunacy, in an extremity, may be both necessary and fruitful.

May 1942

ATTITUDE TO BRITAIN

June 1942, vol. 32, pp. 419–21

M R. CURTIN had two especial claims on the attention of the British and American Governments. The first was that Australia had sent overseas, either to the Imperial Air Force or to the armies of the Middle East and Malaya, a picked volunteer force numbering many scores of thousands: the second, that if the democracies were ever to recover the wealth of the Pacific and to protect their ally in China, Australia was indispensable as a base from which an offensive should be launched. Criticism under these two heads has been widely expressed, but it must not be inferred that Australia has ever wavered either in its admiration for the courage of the people of Great Britain, and in particular those of the bombed cities, or that we are insensible of the efforts now being made by the two great democracies. We acknowledge gratefully Britain's willingness to set free enough ships to bring home again a large part of the A.I.F., and her co-operation in the policy of diverting to Australia from the United States men and material that would otherwise have been available for different theatres of war. There may be exceptions, who constitute a blot on our democracy, but ninety-nine out of a hundred Australians are convinced that the cause of the Allies is just and that its defeat is incredible, since it would bring about that darkness of the Middle Ages unilluminated by the mercy of Christ to which the prospect of Nazi domination was once compared by a French Premier.

When war with Germany broke out, Mr. Curtin as leader of the Opposition read a statement of Labour policy drawn up by a party meeting:

"In this crisis, facing the reality of war, the Labour party stands for its platform. That platform is clear. We stand for the maintenance of Australia as an integral part of the British Commonwealth of Nations. The party will do all that is possible to safeguard Australia and at the same time, having regard to its platform, will do its utmost to maintain the integrity of the British Commonwealth."[62]

Since war was declared against Japan, the substance of this declaration has been repeated both by Mr. Curtin as Prime Minister and by Dr. Evatt as Minister for External Affairs. There have been two occasions recently when actions of the Government have been interpreted as showing a desire permanently to weaken the ties between Australia and Great Britain. The first was on the declaration of war between Australia and Japan, the second shortly afterwards when Mr. Curtin published an article in a Melbourne newspaper.[63] These occasions have been seized upon by propagandists in Berlin and Tokyo. When examined, they give little encouragement to the sedulously propagated idea of the disintegration of the British Commonwealth. After the shock of this war and the participation of the United States in the defence of Australia and of British colonies, it is not to be supposed that the relations of the Dominions and the British Government will be exactly the same as they were in September 1939. But there is no reason to believe that Australia will look for a position of isolation, or for a change from its present relationship to that of an independent ally.

When war broke out between Germany and Great Britain, the view taken by the then Prime Minister, Mr. Menzies, was that by virtue of His Majesty's declaration of war at Westminister all his subjects in the Dominions were automatically at war. In the case of the war with Japan a different procedure was adopted, which followed the precedents set by Canada and South Africa in 1939. Dr. Evatt, himself the author of a treatise on the prerogative,[64] was oppressed by a doubt whether the Governor-General would have power to declare war in respect of Australia except by specific assignment from the King. He therefore obtained, through the High Commissioner, Royal instruments expressly conferring upon the Governor-General the power to declare that as from a date to be specified a state of war with Japan, Finland, Hungary and Rumania existed in Australia. These Royal instruments, like the Governor-General's proclamation, were to be countersigned by the Prime Minister of the Commonwealth and, with His Majesty's permission, at Mr. Bruce's suggestion they were sent to Australia by picturegram.

Dr. Evatt, as a Minister, is conspicuous for his energy and ambition as well as for his learning. In his speech on the declaration of war with Japan he expressed views which can hardly be criticized by anyone acquainted with the constitutional developments of the past twenty years. He asserted the privilege of Australia, like other Dominions, to tender separate advice to the King in relation to her external affairs, as a right established by constitutional convention. But he also claimed that his course of action was "a complete answer to those who had maintained that separate action means a weakening of the tie of association between the British nations", and that it illustrated the fact "that separate action by the King's Governments in the United Kingdom and the self-governing

Dominions is perfectly consistent with close co-operation in all matters affecting their common interests".[65]

Mr. Curtin's article was a statement of the dangers with which Australia was confronted and of our determination to hold out "until the tide of battle swings against the enemy". It contained the following passage:

> "The Australian Government regards the Pacific struggle as primarily one in which the United States and Australia must have the fullest say in the direction of the democracies' fighting plan. Without any inhibitions of any kind, I make it quite clear that Australia looks to America free of any pangs as to our traditional links or kinship with the United Kingdom. We know the problems that the United Kingdom faces, we know the constant threat of invasion, we know the dangers of dispersal of strength, but we know, too, that Australia can go and Britain can still hold on."[66]

The article should be read as a whole, but this passage was taken apart from any context. In answer to immediate and emphatic protests against some expressions in the passage, Mr. Curtin explained that his words were a reference to the facts of geography and the needs of Great Britain, and were not intended to convey a separatist implication. He said:

> "It did not mean that Australia regarded itself as anything but an integral part of the British Empire. No part of the British Commonwealth is more steadfast in its devotion to the British way of life and to British institutions than Australia. Our loyalty to the King goes to the very core of our national life."[67]

The extent and depth of British sentiment in Australia has often been remarked on. The fact that our Parliament has not so far thought it necessary or even desirable to adopt the Statute of Westminster indicates a widely prevalent Australian view of our place in the Empire. That Mr. Curtin's outspoken avowal of our present dependence upon the United States should arouse a good deal of anxiety, criticism and even resentment is therefore not surprising. There would probably have been more, but for the restraint which, in view of the grave responsibilities now resting on the Government, is being exercised by the press. Many have feared the separatist possibilities inherent in some things that have been done and said, intrinsically justifiable though they may have been. Nevertheless Mr. Curtin has gained a place in the estimation of the Australian people such that an assurance given by him will be accepted. It is admitted that his choice of language is sometimes unfortunate, his quotations from the poets almost invariably so; but his sincerity and his disinterested desire to serve Australia in her present need have not been doubted. In the substance of his appeals or demands for help to Britain and America and of his claim that Australia should have a voice in the councils of the Allies he has support in all parties.

The reproach of "squealing" should not be directed against a Dominion which has done everything that Great Britain has asked of it.

May 1942

REINFORCEMENTS FROM AMERICA

June 1942, vol. 32, pp. 421–2

PERSONNEL and equipment from the United States actually began arriving in Australia from a surprisingly early date, and no doubt we have received some reinforcements originally intended for the Philippines and the East Indies. The size of the American forces in the Anzac area cannot of course be stated, but it is known that they are large and that they include important technical units, tanks, guns and modern aircraft. The result of their arrival has already been manifest in the increased resistance and striking power of our northern defences. To what extent this reinforcement is the direct result of the representations made by the Australian Government obviously cannot be known to the public at present. Be that as it may, there has been an immense lifting of the horizon for every Australian. We are not under any illusion that our dangers are at an end; but we are girding ourselves for the coming conflict in the spirit of the offensive.

Unprecedented steps have been taken in Australia to secure the fullest co-ordination of the efforts of the United Nations in the Anzac area. The appointment of General MacArthur, the hero of Bataan, as Commander-in-Chief over all arms of the Allies in the South-Western Pacific has been received with enthusiasm by the public, for he is the very embodiment of what in our opinion the spirit of the Allied operations should be.[68] An Allied Works Council has been established under energetic and able direction to ensure the effective handling of the vast programme of public works required for purposes of Australian defence. Perhaps most important of all, the Prime Minister has given an explicit assurance that, as far as the actual conduct of the war in Australia is concerned, neither the Commonwealth Government nor the Commonwealth Parliament will interfere in its military direction.

Of close consultation and co-operation with the British Government in handling political and strategical questions, and close co-ordination in the field with other Imperial forces, Australians have had experience. The relations that have been set up with the Government of the United States and with American commanders of the forces on our own soil are entirely new to us. Their difficulties and complications are as yet unexplored. Mr. Curtin has certainly realized that so intimate an association will bring under the review of able and efficient men our own performance, alike in war administration, in politics and in industry. The public is still naturally in the stage of enthusiastic welcome. We have liked and admired very much the outlook and behaviour of the members of the United States forces whom we have seen and met. They are quite frank with us in disclaiming any thanks for coming to the assistance of Australia. They tell us laughingly but truly enough that they are here because the best place to defend the United States is on distant territory and in somebody else's air. Our responsibility will be to ensure that, so far as in us lies, they will remain convinced that the defence of Australia is the best defence for the United States. Of the ultimate political and economic consequences of the present alignments we have not yet begun to think. The first task is to beat back the enemy's assaults upon the postern gate.

The people of Australia now stand at the crisis of their fate. Like every democracy, they are suffering the consequences of past neglect —neglect of defence, of poverty, of industrial relations and of education. There can be no doubt of their determination to repel the Japanese invasion at whatever cost. Of nine out of ten it may be said that they would rather not live than see an enemy occupy this country, and that when the invasion is repelled they will fight on until assured of the ultimate triumph of the Allied cause.

May 1942

ABBREVIATIONS

Aust.	Australia
Cd	Command Paper
C.L.R.	Commonwealth Law Reports
Cwlth	Commonwealth
G.B.	Great Britain
HR	House of Representatives
MHA	Member of House of Assembly
MHR	Member of House of Representatives
MLA	Member of Legislative Assembly
MLC	Member of Legislative Council
N.S.	new series
N.S.W.	New South Wales
P.D.	*Parliamentary Debates*
P.P.	*Parliamentary Papers*
Qld	Queensland
RT	*Round Table*
S.A.	South Australia
S.M.H.	*Sydney Morning Herald*
Tas.	Tasmania
Vic.	Victoria
W.A.	Western Australia

REFERENCE NOTES

Full details of works cited are in the bibliography.

PREFACE

[1] Sir Alfred Milner, 1st viscount (1854–1925): governor of the Cape of Good Hope 1897–1901, governor of the Transvaal and the Orange River colony 1901–5, high commissioner in South Africa 1897–1905, secretary of state for war 1918–19, secretary of state for the colonies 1919–21.

[2] Further information about the Round Table movement and its origins can be obtained in the following sources: 'The Round Table', *RT*, Nov. 1910, vol. 1, pp. 1–6; 'Lord Milner', *RT*, June 1925, vol. 15, pp. 427–30; 'John Dove', *RT*, 1933–4, vol. 24, pp. 463–8; 'Twenty-five years', *RT*, 1934–5, vol. 25, pp. 653–9; 'Lionel Curtis, the prophet of organic union', *RT*, Mar. 1956, vol. 46, pp. 103–9; 'Edward, Lord Altrincham', *RT*, Mar. 1956, vol. 46, pp. 110–12; 'The new Round Table', *RT*, July 1966, vol. 56, pp. 211–14; D. K. Picken, 'The Round Table movement', *Melbourne University Magazine* (ed. R. G. Menzies), vol. 10, no. 3, pp. 76–8; H. Minogue and E. M. Higgins, 'Australia and the Round Table', *Melbourne University Magazine* (ed. Miss D. Meares Andrews and H. Minogue), vol. 11, no. 1, pp. 14–16; [D. H. Simpson], 'Round Table studies: a tentative checklist', *Royal Commonwealth Society Library Notes*, N. S., no. 56, August 1961; J. Eayrs, 'The Round Table movement in Canada 1909–20', *Canadian Historical Review*, vol. 38, no. 1, pp. 1–20; C. Quigley, 'The Round Table groups in Canada 1908–38', *Canadian Historical Review*, vol. 43, no. 3, pp. 204–24; J. E. Kendle, 'The Round Table movement, New Zealand and the conference of 1911', *Journal of Commonwealth Political Studies*, vol. 3, 1965, pp. 104–17; J. Kendle, 'The Round Table movement: Lionel Curtis and the formation of the New Zealand groups in 1910', *New Zealand Journal of History*, vol. 1, no. 1, pp. 33–50; J. E. Kendle, 'The Round Table movement and "Home Rule all round"', *Historical Journal*, vol. 11, no. 2, pp. 332–53; D. C. Ellinwood jun., 'The Round Table movement and India 1909–20', *Journal of Commonwealth Political Studies*, vol. 9, 1971, pp. 183–209; W. Nimocks, *Milner's Young Men: the 'Kindergarten' in Edwardian imperial politics*, London 1970; J. Kendle, *The Round Table and Imperial Union*, Univ. of Toronto Press, 1975.

INTRODUCTION

[1] The best account and analysis of the politics of the federation is in Sawer, *Federal Politics 1901–1929*. For the period between 1901 and the outbreak of war in 1914 see La Nauze, *Alfred Deakin*; Fitzhardinge, *William Morris Hughes*.

[2] Robson, 'Themes in Australian history: Tasmania in the nineteenth century' (Eldershaw Memorial Lecture 1971), Tasmanian Historical Research Association, *Papers and Proceedings*, vol. 19, no. 1, pp. 14–15.

[3] Robson, *Australia and Great War*, p. 46.

[4] Bean (ed.), *Official History*, vol. 1, ch. 1, passim.

Reference Notes

Reference Notes

Reference Notes

5 The conscription campaigns and their political aftermath are described in Robson, *First A.I.F.*; Jauncey, *Story of Conscription*; Bean (ed.), *Official History*, vol. 11; Smith, *Conscription Plebiscites*.

6 Turner, *Industrial Labour*, ch. 6.

7 Robson, 'Origin of A.I.F.', *Historical Studies*, vol. 15, no. 61, p. 741.

8 Edwards, *Bruce of Melbourne*.

9 Graham, *Country Parties*.

10 Green, *Servant*, p. 37; Edwards, *Bruce of Melbourne*, p. 42.

11 Page, *Truant Surgeon*.

12 Green, *Servant*, p. 40.

13 For New Guinea see West, *Hubert Murray* and Ryan (ed.), *Encyclopaedia of Papua and New Guinea*.

14 Sawer, *Federal Politics 1901–1929*, pp. 284–5.

15 Green, *Servant*, p. 114.

16 Ibid., p. 116.

PART ONE: 1911–14

1 London, 23 May to 20 June 1911.

2 'The Australian situation' (sic), *RT*, Feb. 1911, vol. 1, pp. 182–93. This introductory article outlined the general course of Australian development and discussed attitudes to imperial unity. Australians, the writer believed, were anxious for empire preservation and favoured the development of defence resources within an imperial structure, but there was no concrete public opinion as to any form of imperial federation.

3 Rt Hon. Sir Samuel Walker Griffith (1845–1920): MLA Qld 1871–93, minister, premier 1883–8, 1890–3; chief justice of Qld 1893–1903, lieutenant-governor of Qld 1899–1903; chief justice of Aust. 1903–19.

4 The fifth triennial interstate political labour conference which was held 8–12 January 1912.

5 Here the editor drew attention to 'The constitutional issue: two views' and 'The referenda', *RT*, May and Aug. 1911, vol. 1, pp. 329–43, 500–8.

6 John Anderson Gilruth (1871–1937): veterinarian and pathologist in New Zealand, professor of veterinary pathology and director of the research institute at the University of Melbourne 1908–12, administrator of the Northern Territory 1912–20. Gilruth's administration was marked by a riot in which trade unionists burnt him in effigy when the price of bottled beer was increased. He was twice the subject of royal commissions. Judge Ewing found that Gilruth and persons associated with him had acted unwisely in his administration and that the government had been in error by not granting citizens' rights to the people of the Territory (*P.P.* (HR) 1914–17, vol, 1, 1920–1, vol. 3).

7 Rt Hon. Andrew Fisher (1862–1928): MLA Qld 1893–6, 1899–1901; MHR 1901–15, minister for trade and customs 1904, prime minister 1908–9, 1910–13, 1914–15; high commissioner for Aust. in London 1916–21.

8 The Commonwealth Conciliation and Arbitration Act 1909 introduced penalties against employers dismissing employees because of union activity, and against employees refusing to work because of employers' activity in employers' associations (Sawer, *Federal Politics 1901–1929*, p. 70).

9 Hon. King O'Malley (*c.* 1858–1953): MLA S.A. 1896–9; MHR 1901–17, minister for home affairs 1910–13, 1915–16.

10 Sir Denison Samuel King Miller (1860–1923): first governor commonwealth bank 1912–23.

201

Reference Notes

[1] The Sudan campaign 1885, the China naval contingent sent to the Boxer War 1900–1 and the Boer War volunteers 1899–1902.

[2] The British Association for the Advancement of Science met in Melbourne 13–19 August 1914. The official opening was in Adelaide on 8 August and the final meeting in Sydney on 26 August.

[3] The 1911 census of Australia gave the number of German-born residents as 32 990 of a total population of 4 424 537 whose birth-places were specified. This is 0.75 per cent.

[4] Rt Hon. Sir Joseph Cook (1860–1947): MLA N.S.W. 1891–1901, minister; MHR 1901–21, minister for defence 1909–13, prime minister and minister for home affairs 1913–14, minister for navy 1917–20, treasurer 1920–1; high commissioner in London 1921–7.

[5] At the general election of 5 September 1914 Labor won 42 seats in the house of representatives to the Liberals' 32 seats, with 1 Independent. In the senate the Liberals won only 5 seats, Labor 31.

[6] Rt Hon. William Morris Hughes (1862–1952): MLA N.S.W. 1894–1901; MHR 1901–52, minister for external affairs 1904, 1937–9, attorney-general 1908–9, 1910–13, 1914–15, prime minister 1915–23, vice-president of executive council 1934–5, 1937–8, minister for health and repatriation 1934–5, 1936–7, minister in charge of territories 1937–8, minister for industry 1939–40, attorney-general 1939–41, minister for navy 1940–1.

[7] Rt Hon. Sir George Foster Pearce (1870–1952): senator W.A. 1901–38, minister for defence 1908–9, 1910–13, 1914–21, 1931–4, acting prime minister 1916, minister for home affairs and territories 1921–6, vice-president of executive council 1926–9, minister for defence 1932–4, minister for external affairs and territories 1934–7.

[8] Defence of Australia. Memorandum by Field Marshal Viscount Kitchener of Khartoum, *P.P.* (HR) 1910, vol. 2.

[9] Hon. Sir William Hill Irvine (1858–1943): MLA Vic. 1894–1906, minister, premier 1902–3; MHR 1906–18, attorney-general 1913, chief justice Vic. 1918–35, lieutenant-governer Vic. 1918–35.

[10] Naval Forces. Recommendations of Admiral Sir Reginald Henderson, *P.P.* (HR) 1911, vol. 2.

[11] Lieutenant-Commander C. B. Elwell and Captain B.C.A. Pockley were killed during the Bitapaka advance on 11 September 1914 (Bean (ed.), *Official History*, vol. 9, pp. 59, 63–4).

[12] Though there were persistent fears and rumours about spying, no one was caught (Bean (ed.), *Official History*, vol. 11, ch. 4; Robson, *First A.I.F.*, pp. 152–6).

[13] German interests had been very powerful in the metals industry (Bean (ed.), *Official History*, vol. 11, ch. 15).

[14] British White Paper Miscellaneous no. 6 (1914) Cd 7467, Correspondence Relating to Pre-War Negotiations. Presented to parliament 5 August 1914. This document was summarized in *RT*, Sept. 1914, vol. 4, pp. 748–90.

[15] These writings relate to the situation of Germany in the period immediately before the war and include J. C. Cramb, *Germany and England* (London 1914); Prince Bernhard von Bülow, *Imperial Germany* (London 1914); Lieutenant-General Friedrich von Bernhardi, *Cavalry in Future Wars* (London 1906); Bernhardi, *Germany and the Next World War* (London 1914); C. S. Sarolea, *The Anglo-German Problem* (London 1912); R. G. Usher (sic), *Pan-Germanism* (London 1913).

[16] For the Posen question see H. Holborn, *A History of Modern Germany 1840–1945* (London 1969), pp. 293–6, 351–3. It is not clear what is meant here by 'the blood-tax in Alsace-Lorraine'.

[17] G. Meredith, 'France 1870', first published in *Fortnightly*, January 1871, included in *Odes in Contribution to the Song of French History*, 1898, and quoted by G. M. Trevelyan, *The Poetry and Philosophy of George Meredith*, (London 1906), p. 129.

[18] Lieutenant-General Hon. Sir James Whiteside McCay (1864–1930): MLA Vic. 1895–9, minister; MHR 1901–6, minister for defence 1904–5; commander 2nd Australian infantry brigade 1914–15, 5th Australian division 1916, commander Australian forces in Britain 1917–18.

[19] General Sir Ian Standish Monteith Hamilton (1853–1947): Afghan War 1878–80, Boer War 1881, Nile expedition 1884–5, Burmese expedition 1886–7, Chitral relief force 1895, Tirah campaign 1897–8, South Africa 1899–1901, commanded Mediterranean expeditionary force 1915.

[20] Named from the title of a song current in 1915. This position towards the southern end of the Australian lines at Gallipoli was the scene of intense fighting during the attempted breakout from the Anzac perimeter in August 1915. It was usually known as Lone Pine (Bean (ed.), *Official History*, vol. 1, p. 339, vol. 2, chs. 18–19).

[21] Marshal Liman von Sanders, German commander of 5th Turkish army; Enver Pasha, Turkish minister for war.

[22] This despatch has not been traced.

[23] Brigadier-General Hon. Charles Granville Bruce (1866–1939): served Far East 1888–98, 1916–20; colonel commanding 1/6 Gurkha Rifles Egypt and Dardanelles 1915.

[24] This is an extract from Rudyard Kipling's 'The Return' in *The Five Nations* (London 1903).

[25] 'Recruiting for the Australian army', Sept. 1916, vol. 6, pp. 747–50.

[26] Hughes arrived back in Australia 21 July 1916.

[27] The AIF as a whole voted in favour of conscription but those in the trenches were almost certainly against it (Robson, *First A.I.F.*, pp. 118–19).

[28] The conviction of twelve members of the IWW for conspiracy to commit arson and seditious conspiracy on 1 December 1916 led to a campaign that succeeded in having all but two of them freed in August 1920 (Turner, *Sydney's Burning*; Childe, *How Labour Governs*, ch. 10; Report of an Enquiry under the Police Act (Street Commission), *P.P.* (N.S.W.) 1919, vol. 1; Report of the Royal Commission on the Trial and Conviction and Sentences imposed on Charles Reeve and Others, *P.P.* (N.S.W.) 1920, vol. 1).

[29] These were W. G. Higgs, treasurer, Senator Albert Gardiner, vice-president of executive council, and Senator E. G. Russell, honorary minister (Bean(ed.), *Official History*, vol. 11, p. 352; Robson, *First A.I.F.*, pp. 115–16).

[30] The courts appear to have been given inadequate guidance and directions (Robson, *First A.I.F.*, pp. 108–11).

[31] *P.P.* (HR) 1917–19, vol. 4, p. 1469, report the final figures.

[32] Archbishop Patrick Joseph Clune (1864–1935): archbishop of Perth 1913–35.

[33] Hon. Frank Gwynne Tudor (1866–1922): MHR 1901–22, minister for trade and customs 1908–9, 1910–13, 1914–15, 1915–16.

[34] Sir Ronald Crauford Munro-Ferguson, Viscount Novar (1860–1934): Member of House of Commons 1886–1914, minister; governor-general of Aust. 1914–20.

[35] Hon. William Arthur Holman (1871–1934): MLA N.S.W. 1898–1920, minister, premier 1913–20; MHR 1931–4.

[36] 'The prime minister and the Labour party', June 1916, vol 6, pp. 556–63.

[37] 'The Great Strike in Sydney', *RT*, Dec. 1917, vol. 8, pp. 182–6.

[38] The disputed job and time card system was the subject of a royal commission (Report and Enquiry into the Effects of the Workings of the Job and Time

Cards System in the Tramways and Railways Workshops of New South Wales. *P.P.* (N.S.W.) 1918, vol. 6; Turner, *Industrial Labour*, pp. 141–57).

[39] F. W. Taylor, known as 'Speedy', pioneer of the study of industrial efficiency.

[40] Coal supplies had become dangerously low when Hughes appointed Edmunds as a special tribunal. It was said that the prime minister went over the head of the arbitration court (Turner, *Industrial Labour*, pp. 88–92).

[41] 'Industrial unrest in Australia', vol. 7.

[42] James Bryce, 1st viscount (1838–1922): scholar, college don, lawyer and professor of law, politician, author and historian, he was British ambassador in Washington 1907–13. He visited Australia in July 1912. His remark concerning class hostility has not been traced.

[43] Labour leaders in Australia feared that the ideology and action of the IWW would frighten off voters who might be expected to support the Labor party. Childe, *How Labour Governs*, pp. 143–5.

[44] See note 28 above.

[45] Introduced in December 1916 after the conviction of the twelve IWW members (see p. 53), the act declared the IWW illegal. An amending act in July 1917 added provisions for seizure of property and the imprisonment of members of organizations declared illegal (Turner, *Industrial Labour*, pp. 130–1, 134).

[46] Details of this conference have not been traced.

[47] 'The One Big Union', *RT*, June 1919, vol. 9, pp. 611–19. The writer of this article reproduced the preamble to the constitution of the OBU (officially 'The Workers' Industrial Union of Australia'), outlined areas of opposition to its ideology and, though critical of it, concluded that existing relations between employers and employees needed to be improved.

[48] This had been appointed by H. H. Asquith. In March 1917 it was replaced by a committee of experts with Lloyd George as nominal chairman, and ultimately replaced in turn by a ministry (Marwick, *Deluge*, pp. 239–46).

[49] The Whitley Report recommended early in 1917 the establishment of councils representing employers and trade unions (*P.P.* (G.B.) 1917–18, 18 Cd 8606).

[50] 'Some considerations affecting economic reconstruction', vol. 6, p. 468.

[51] 'The conscription referendum', vol. 7, pp. 378–94, reproduced on pp. 51–62.

[52] Hughes discussed the decision not to attend the imperial war conference in London in parliament on 6 March 1917 (*P.D.* (Cwlth) 1917, pp. 10993–11000).

[53] See p. 9.

[54] *Argus*, 28 Mar. 1917.

[55] Hon. Donald Mackinnon (1859–1932). MLA Vic. 1900–21, minister; director-general of recruiting for Australia 1916–18; commissioner for Aust. to U.S.A. 1923–4.

[56] *Argus*, 13 Nov. 1917. See also Robson, *First A.I.F.*, p. 167.

[57] *Argus*, 13 Nov. 1917.

[58] Ibid., 20 Nov. 1917.

[59] Ibid., 13 Nov. 1917.

[60] Thomas Joseph Ryan (1876–1921). MLA Qld 1909–19, minister, premier 1915–19; MHR 1919–21.

[61] See Robson, *First A.I.F.*, pp. 174–5; *Argus*, 29, 30 Nov. 1917.

[62] Daniel Mannix (1864–1963): consecrated coadjutor archbishop of Melbourne at Maynooth College in October 1912, arrived Melbourne the following March, succeeded Archbishop Thomas Carr in May 1917.

[63] The final figures were: Yes, 103 789; No, 93 910 (*P.P.* (HR) 1917–19, vol. 4, p. 1469).

[64] Clearly the date should read 'December 20, 1917'.

[65] *Age*, 5 Jan. 1918. This quotation should read, 'That this party, in view of the

recent declared attitude of the Official Labor Party on the vital question of the conduct of the war and peace, declares that in the interests of the country and the Empire it will not support any course of action that will hand the government of the Commonwealth over to the official Labor party'.

[66] Irvine's statements are generally referred to in *Age*, 4, 5, 10 Jan., 19 Feb., 4, 14 Mar. 1918, but not in the words quoted by the *RT* writer. Irvine's reported statements in the press reflect disillusionment with Hughes and the prime minister's undertaking not to govern should the plebiscite be rejected.

[67] *Age*, 5 Jan. 1918. For 'That the matter' read 'That this matter'.

[68] Irvine's reported statements here have not been traced.

[69] *S.M.H.*, 9 Jan. 1918. This report gave Joseph Cook, W. A. Watt, W. G. Higgs, A. Poynton, G. H. Wise.

[70] *Argus*, 11 Jan. 1918.

[71] This has not been traced.

[72] P.D. (Cwlth), 11 Jan. 1918, p. 2921.

[73] For an example of such reports see *Sydney Evening News*, 22 Jan. 1919.

[74] 4 Feb. 1919.

[75] For 'while' read 'whilst'.

[76] Here the editor noted 'See [W.E.] Hall, *International Law* (7th edition), p. 26, and for an illustration of the dangers of double or ambiguous sovereignty, see the case of Trieste, described at pages 543–4.' The work was edited by A. P. Higgins and published by Oxford University Press in 1917. The reference to Triest (sic) in Hall is on pp. 544–5.

PART THREE: 1920–9

[1] In each electorate a political branch elected delegates to attend state Labor League conferences which drew up the party platform (*Cambridge History of the British Empire*, vol. 7, p. 493; Childe, *How Labour Governs*, p. 57).

[2] The Western Australia Farmers' and Settlers' Association was formed in 1912 and returned eight members in the state election of 1914. This was the first significant step towards the establishment of a separate farmers' party. Similar political organizations appeared in Queensland in 1917, Victoria in 1918 and New South Wales in 1920 (Graham, *Country Parties*).

[3] An election was held on 25 March 1922. Its effect was to make the Progressive party a Country party and lead to the conclusion that the best way a Country party could influence policy was to support conservative governments in return for concessions (Graham, op. cit., pp. 168–9, 172).

[4] Hughes announced abandonment of the convention on 9 December 1921. He had hoped to strengthen the central government but ran into powerful and successful opposition on the grounds that parliament's sovereignty would be reduced, the method of selecting delegates was unsatisfactory, it would cost too much, and there was to be an election within twelve months (*P.D.* (Cwlth) 1921, 9 Dec., p. 14260, 22 Nov., p. 13019, 1 Dec., pp. 13472–9, 7 Dec., pp. 13951–67).

[5] Hon. Sir Joseph Hector McNeil Carruthers (1857–1932). MLA N.S.W. 1887–1908, MLC N.S.W. 1909–32, minister, premier 1904–7. For details of his scheme, see *Argus*, 20 July 1921.

[6] Sir John Warren Swanson (1865–1924) was a mayor of Melbourne 1920–3. For details of his scheme, see *Argus*, 5 Oct. 1921. Alfred Charles William Harmsworth, 1st viscount Northcliffe (1865–1922): newspaper proprietor.

[7] See L. J. Blake, 'Village settlements', *Victorian Historical Magazine*, vol. 37, no. 4.

[8] Rt Hon. Sir Earle Christmas Grafton Page (1880–1961): MHR 1919–61,

treasurer 1923–9, minister for commerce 1934–9, minister for health 1937–9, prime minister 1939, minister for commerce 1939–41, minister for health 1949–56.

9 At Maryborough Hughes claimed that the Country party was a menace to the interests of both primary producers and good government. He asserted that members of the party were destitute of constructive ideas, that destructive propaganda was their only weapon and that their propaganda was bombast buttressed by gross misrepresentation (*Argus*, 6 June 1922).

10 Stanley Melbourne Bruce, 1st viscount, Bruce of Melbourne (1883–1967): MHR 1918–29, 1931–3, prime minister and minister for external affairs 1923–9, minister for health 1927–8, minister for trade and customs 1928, minister for territories 1928–9, minister without portfolio 1932–3; Australian minister in London 1932–3, high commissioner for Aust. in London 1933–45.

11 The main example of this was in the Canadian wheat-growing areas (Graham, *Country Parties*, pp. 20–30).

12 A no-confidence amendment to the address-in-reply to the governor-general's speech was moved 1 March 1923. Bruce defended the accusation that his party had no policy (*P.D.* (Cwlth), pp. 68–293).

13 *Argus*, 20 Feb. 1923.

14 This part of the quotation should read '. . . believing, as we do, that the formulation of a common scheme of defence is vital to our safety and our whole future welfare. Wrapped up in the question of Empire defence, is the question of Empire foreign affairs . . . We have to try to ensure that any Empire foreign policy for which we must bear responsibility is one to which we have assented.' (*P.D.* (Cwlth) 1 Mar. 1923, p. 81).

15 This conference was held at Melbourne 23–30 May 1923. Agreement was reached on the necessity for the abolition of dual income tax, and resolutions were adopted for co-ordination of borrowing, raising of loans for immigration purposes, provision of a sinking fund and discontinuance of the issue of tax-free loans by both federal and state governments. Arrangements were also made to ensure closer co-operation between federal and state governments with respect to health, collection and distribution of statistics, scientific research, standardization of electrical power and the preparation and maintenance of joint electoral rolls. Agreement was reached on encouragement of the cotton industry, and the Murray River agreement was revised. The question of definite spheres of action for federal and state industrial authorities was not resolved and neither was the federal government's proposal for standardizing railway gauges (*P.D.* (Cwlth) 13 June 1923, pp. 5–6).

16 Rt Hon. Sir William MacGregor (1847–1919): administrator and lieutenant-governor of British New Guinea 1888–98, governor of Lagos 1899–1904, governor of Newfoundland 1904–9, governor of Qld 1909–14.

17 Sir George Ruthven Le Hunte (1852–1925): governor of Fiji 1875, president of Dominica 1887–94, colonial secretary of Barbados 1894–7, colonial secretary of Mauritius 1897, lieutenant-governor of British New Guinea 1898–1903, governor of S. A. 1903–8, governor of Trinidad and Tobago 1908–15.

18 British control was ended by Royal Letters Patent in March 1902 and Australian control was proclaimed on 1 September 1906.

19 See below.

20 Presumably the writer means Burns Philp.

21 William Halse Rivers Rivers (1864–1922): English physician, psycho-physiologist and anthropologist; member of the Cambridge expedition to the Torres Strait 1898. His publications include *The History of Melanesian Society* (2 vols, London 1914) and various papers in the reports of the Cambridge expedition.

[22] The Natives' Taxes Ordinance was passed in 1918. The taxes collected in 1922–3 totalled £16 410, bringing the credit balance of the fund to £45 191. In the field of primary education £5051 was spent on subsidies to missions, £3052 on native plantations and a rice mill, £4562 on medical supplies and £932 on bonuses to mothers with more than four children (*Commonwealth Year Book* 1924, p. 621).

[23] Sir John Hubert Plunkett Murray (1861–1940): first lieutenant-governor of Papua 1909–40. His principal achievement was to establish and extend law and order and hold a balance between native and European interests (*Encyclopaedia of Papua and New Guinea*, vol. 2, pp. 806–8).

[24] 'The seamen's disputes', Dec. 1925, vol. 16, p. 165.

[25] Ibid., p. 163. The Immigration Act (No. 7 of 1925) authorized deportation of immigrants who, after proclamation by the governor-general of a state of serious industrial disturbance, acted to hinder foreign or interstate trade or the provision of federal services, or who had been convicted of offences under federal commerce or arbitration laws.

[26] This should read ' . . . he may make a proclamation to that effect, which proclamation shall be and remain in force for the purposes of this section until it is revoked by the Governor-General.'

[27] This should read ' . . . commerce with other countries or among the States or the provision of services by any Departments or public authority of the Commonwealth and that the presence of that person will be injurious to the peace, order or good government of the Commonwealth in relation to matters with respect to which the Parliament has power to make laws, may by notice in writing summon the person to appear before a Board at the time specified in the summons and in the manner prescribed to show cause why he should not be deported from the Commonwealth.'

[28] Thomas Walsh and Jacob Johnson.

[29] Hon. John Thomas Lang (1876–   ): MLA N.S.W. 1913–46, minister, premier 1925–7, 1930–2; MHR 1946–9.

[30] Hon. Philip Collier (1874–1948): MLA W.A. 1905–48, minister, premier 1924–30, 1933–6.

[31] Rt Hon. Joseph Aloysius Lyons (1879–1939): MHA Tas. 1909–29, minister, premier 1923–8; MHR 1929–39, postmaster-general and minister for public works 1929–31, acting treasurer 1930–1, minister for commerce 1932, treasurer 1932–5, minister for health and repatriation 1935–6, vice-president of executive council 1935–7, minister for defence 1937, prime minister 1931–9.

[32] Hon. John Allan (1866–1936): MLA Vic. 1917–36, minister, premier 1924–7.

[33] Hon. William Neal Gillies (1868–1928): MLA Qld 1912–25, minister, premier 1925.

[34] This riot broke out on 2, not 7, November and reports in the *Argus* and *Age* make it clear that many of the participants did not suffer serious injury as the *RT* writer claimed. One policeman and one arrested striker needed treatment in hospital.

[35] *Argus*, 25 Oct. 1922. See also note 4 above.

[36] These words have not been traced. Bruce was reported to have said that 'the ministry proposes large extensions of the defence policy' (*Argus*, 6 Oct. 1925).

[37] *Age*, 6 Oct. 1925. This summary misrepresents Bruce's policy speech in which the greatest stress by far was laid on law and order and the alleged menace of communism.

[38] Hon. Edward Granville Theodore (1884–1950): MLA Qld 1909–25, minister, premier 1919–25; MHR 1927–31, treasurer 1929–30, 1931.

[39] Matthew Charlton (1866–1948): MLA N.S.W. 1904–9; MHR 1910–28. Charlton's policy speech was delivered in Sydney on 9 October 1925.

[40] Charlton's policy speech promised government assistance to bring in supplies of M. Henry Spahlinger's anti-TB serum. Spahlinger conducted a sanatorium near Geneva and his work was the subject of medical controversy (*Argus*, 10 Oct. 1925; *P.D.* (Cwlth) 19 Aug. 1925, pp. 1523–44). Major-General Hon. Sir Neville Howse (1863–1930): surgeon, soldier and politician; awarded Victoria Cross in Boer War as member of Australian forces; accompanied expeditionary force to New Guinea 1914 and with 1st AIF from the landing at Gallipoli; appointed director medical services AIF 1916, director-general medical services 1921–5; MHR 1922–9, minister for defence and health 1927–8, minister for health and repatriation 1925–9, minister for home and territories 1928.

[41] Presumably the writer means Donald Grant, gaoled as a member of the IWW during World War I (Turner, *Sydney's Burning*, p. 254).

[42] See p. 127.

[43] This concerned the Colonial Sugar Refinery. The high court judgment is in 37 C.L.R. 36 and analysed in Sawer, *Federal Politics 1901–1929*, pp. 251–2. Starke J. cited Lord Haldane's judgment in a case on appeal to the privy council that 'general control over the liberty of the subject is not transferred to the national parliament'. Walsh was born in Ireland and arrived in Australia in 1893 and made it his home. Johnson had been born in Holland but was naturalized as an Australian in 1913.

[44] Here the editor drew attention to articles for Dec. 1922, p. 185, Sept. 1925, p. 799, Mar. 1928, pp. 406–7. These articles trace the history of the commonwealth line of shipping from its inception in 1916, when W. M. Hughes bought 15 tramp steamers for £2 million. By 1922 the line had been enlarged to 43 vessels with 11 more building or on order. At the end of 1921 Lord Inchcape offered to buy out the line on behalf of the shipping conference. In September 1923 S. M. Bruce placed the line under the control of the commonwealth shipping board. The government then sought to sell the line but received no tenders. When Bruce's government again tried to sell the ships, the Labor opposition moved a vote of no confidence. This was lost and the government thereupon treated this as an authorization of sale. Sawer in *Federal Politics*, pp. 284–5, states that the purchaser defaulted.

[45] *P.P.* (HR) 1926–8, vol. 4, no. 1.

[46] Rt Hon. James Henry Scullin (1876–1953): MHR 1910–13, 1922–49, prime minister 1929–31.

[47] Owen Cosby Philipps, created baronet 1923, Lord Kylsant of Carmarthen (1863–1937): in 1927 chairman and managing director of the Royal Mail Steam Packet Co. and the Union Castle Line and their associated shipping companies; president of the British Imperial Chamber of Commerce and past president of the Chamber of Shipping of the United Kingdom; director of the Southern Railway; owner of more than 5000 acres of land in Carmarthenshire and Pembrokeshire.

[48] The previous election was on 17 November 1928. Parliament was dissolved on 12 September 1929 and the subsequent election held on 12 October. The *Argus*, (19 Oct. 1929) reported that Bruce lost his seat by 327 votes, 31 379 to 31 052.

[49] Rt Hon. Sir John Greig Latham (1877–1964): MHR 1922–34, attorney-general 1925–9, minister for industry 1928–9, attorney-general, minister for external affairs, minister for industry 1932–4; chief justice of Aust. 1935–52.

[50] Hon. Sir Littleton Ernest Groom (1867–1936): MHR 1901–29, 1931–6, minister

for home affairs 1905–6, attorney-general 1906–8, minister for external affairs 1909–10, minister for trade and customs 1913–14, minister for works and railways 1918–21, attorney-general 1921–5, speaker 1926–9.

[51] The Commonwealth Scientific and Industrial Research Organization was established in 1926 as the Council for Scientific and Industrial Research to replace the Institute of Science and Industry, founded in 1920. It expanded from research into agricultural and pastoral problems to secondary industry and in 1949 was established as the CSIRO under a federal act.

In 1927 a federal-state agreement on finance was reached and subsequently ratified by the states. Among other things, the central government agreed to contribute to payment of interest on state debts an amount equivalent to the per capita payments made in 1926–7 until state debts were redeemed (Sawer, *Federal Politics 1901–1929*, p. 265).

[52] This statement has not been traced. The budget was brought down on 22 August 1929 and included a proposed 5 per cent tax on admission to entertainments (*P.D.* (Cwlth) 22 Aug. 1929, p. 239).

[53] Scullin's policy speech was delivered on 19 September 1929 at Richmond, Victoria. Protection of industry was not mentioned in reports of the speech but was made in his policy address of October 1928, which he reiterated a year later. The main point in the 1929 speech was arbitration 'which the present reactionary government proposed' to abolish in one fell swoop' (*Age*, 5 Oct. 1928, 20 Sept. 1929).

[54] Here the editor drew attention to the article 'The tariff report', Dec. 1929, vol. 20 pp. 161–9.

[55] This is an extract from the 1928 speech (*Age*, 5 Oct. 1928).

[56] This reference has not been traced.

[57] The Queensland state election of 11 May 1929 led to the defeat of Labor, which had been in office since 1915.

PART FOUR: 1930–42

[1] The imperial conference was held in London from 1 October to 14 November 1930. Scullin returned to Australia early in January 1931, having been away since the previous August. The Mungana charges involved a case wherein a Queensland royal commission found that Theodore when premier of Queensland had been guilty of 'fraud and dishonesty'. Subsequently Theodore was vindicated (Sawer, *Federal Politics 1929–1949*, pp. 6, 7, 9, 19, 21, 29).

[2] Hon. James Edward Fenton (1864–1950): MHR 1910–34, minister for customs 1929–30, postmaster-general and minister for works 1931–2.

[3] Rt Hon. John Albert Beasley (1895–1949): MRH 1928–46, minister for supply and shipping 1941–5, vice-president of executive council 1945, minister for defence 1945–6; resident minister in Britain 1946–9.

[4] The Savings Bank of New South Wales had suspended payment on 22 April 1931 and reopened on 7 September for new business only, allowing no withdrawals from old accounts. When early in December the bank amalgamated with the Commonwealth Savings Bank, which had operated in New South Wales since January 1913, depositors were allowed £10 or 10 per cent of frozen deposits. Full amounts became available in early 1932.

[5] Rt Hon. Sir Isaac Alfred Isaacs (1855–1948): MLA Vic. 1892–1901, minister; MHR 1901–6, attorney-general 1905–6; justice of Australian high court 1906–30, chief justice of Aust. 1930–1; governor-general 1931–6.

[6] M. Muggeridge, *The Thirties* (London 1940), pp. 123–4.

[7] See p. 143.

[8] Richard Gardiner Casey, baron of Berwick (1890–   ): MHR 1931–40,

1949–60, treasurer 1935–9, minister for development and industrial research 1937–9, minister for supply and development 1939–40, minister in U.S.A. 1940–2, member British war cabinet 1942–3, governor of Bengal 1944–6, minister for works and housing 1949–50, minister for national development 1950–1, minister for CSIRO 1950–60, minister for external affairs 1951–60, governor-general 1965–9.

9 Hon. Frank Brennan (1880–1950): MHR 1911–31, 1934–49; attorney-general 1929–31.

10 J. H. Gander was the Lang Plan candidate for Reid (*Argus*, 14, 19 Dec. 1931).

11 Here the editor noted, 'The constitution of the Australian Cabinet was announced on January 3 as follows: Prime Minister and Treasurer, Mr. Lyons; Attorney-General, Mr. Latham; Defence, Sir George Pearce; Trade and Customs, Mr. Gullett; Postmaster-General, Mr. Fenton; Markets and Transport, Mr. Hawker; Home Affairs, Mr. Parkhill; Health, Mr. Marr; Vice-President of the Executive Council, Mr. McLachlan, with Messrs. Bruce, Massy-Greene, Francis and Perkins as Honorary Ministers.'

12 Hon. Sir Henry Somer Gullett (1878–1940): war correspondent and official historian of the AIF in Palestine; director of immigration bureau, Melbourne, 1920–5; MHR 1925–40, minister for trade and customs 1928–9, 1932–3, minister without portfolio 1934–7, vice-president of executive council 1937–40.

13 This should read, 'when immigration can be resumed on a basis not harmful, but helpful, to every industry and worker in this country'. (*P.D.* (Cwlth) 22 May 1936, pp. 2211–26). Gullett placed much greater emphasis on restoration of employment, restoration of prosperity in primary and secondary industries and rehabilitation of national finances than this summary implies.

14 *P.D.* (Cwlth) 22 May 1936, p. 2215.

15 Ibid., pp. 2214–16.

16 Lyons's announcement was broadcast from Canberra on the night of 25 June. The *RT* writer's summary corresponds fairly closely to the *Sydney Morning Herald* report of the speech, 26 June 1936. The first passage should read 'I would like you clearly to understand (he said) that the responsibility lies with the Japanese textile manufacturers and exporters who, during the past two or three years, continuously and drastically, step by step, have reduced their prices . . . ' The price of artificial silk imported from the United States should read 19¼d, not 14¼d.

17 'The trade diversion policy', *RT*, Sept. 1936, vol. 26, pp. 843–8, reproduced on pp. 170–4.

18 L. S. Amery, *The Forward View* (London 1935), pp. 111, 115.

19 The new regulations were announced in a special issue of the *Commonwealth Gazette*. For Lyons's statement, see *S.M.H.*, 9 July 1936.

20 This reference has not been traced.

21 *S.M.H.*, 18 Aug. 1936. Report of a broadcast the previous night. It should read ' . . . upon our own domestic affairs. It touches our right to trade . . . '

22 Lindhurst Falkiner Giblin (1872–1951): MHA Tas. 1912–15; member of AIF; Tasmanian government statistician 1920–8; Ritchie Professor of Economics at University of Melbourne 1929–40; member of various federal government bodies. The source of this statement has not been traced.

23 Eden resigned on 20 February 1938 following cabinet disagreement concerning negotiations with Italy.

24 Imperial Conference 1937: Summary of Proceedings, *P.P.* (HR) 1937, vol. 5, p. 10.

25 *S.M.H.*, 1 Mar. 1938.

26 Rt Hon. John Curtin (1885–1945): MHR 1928–31, 1934–45, prime minister 1941–5.

[27] *S.M.H.*, 1 Mar. 1938.
[28] Ibid., 4 Mar. 1938.
[29] 3 Mar. 1938.
[30] 4 Mar. 1938. 'Moreover . . . that the failure . . . ' should read 'Moreover . . . the divergence had been developing over some weeks . . . It can hardly be held that the failure . . . '
[31] The origin of this statement has not been traced.
[32] *S.M.H.*, 15 Mar. 1938.
[33] *Argus* 10, 11, 14 Mar. 1938. Albert George Ogilvie (1891–1939): MHA Tas. 1919–39, premier 1934–9.
[34] This summary corresponds closely to a report in the *Sydney Morning Herald*, 25 Mar. 1939, of a broadcast made the previous night. The figure for the defence programme should read '£24,800,000' and the extra for the navy should read '£7,780,000'.
[35] John Allsbrook Simon, 1st viscount Simon (1873–1954): chancellor of the exchequer 1937–40.
[36] *P.D.* (Cwlth) 28 Sept. 1938, p. 307.
[37] *S.M.H.*, 16 Sept. 1938.
[38] Lord Walter Runciman, 1st baron (1847–1937): MP for Hartlepool 1914–18; chairman and director of many shipping organizations. Lord Runciman was sent to Prague in July 1938 by the British government at the reluctant request of the Czech government as unofficial negotiator to investigate the Sudeten problem and try to influence negotiations between the German minority and the Czech government towards a successful end. Lyons explained Lord Runciman's mission to parliament on 28 September and tabled with other documents Runciman's report to the British prime minister, dated 21 September 1938.
[39] *S.M.H.*, 21 Sept. 1938; *Labor Daily*, 19, 20, 23 Sept. 1938; *Courier-Mail*, 21 Sept. 1938. This should read 'It is to be noted that the most bitter criticism outside Czechoslovakia of what is termed the Anglo-French plan is offered by those whose words are weighted with the least responsibility.'
[40] *S.M.H.*, 17 Sept. 1938.
[41] Hon. William Forgan Smith (1887–1953): MHA Qld 1915–42, minister, premier 1932–42.
[42] *P.D.* (Cwlth) 27 Sept. 1938, pp. 236–8.
[43] *Labor Daily*, 24, 28, 30 Sept. 1938.
[44] *S.M.H.*, 30 Sept. 1938.
[45] *P.D.* (Cwlth) 28 Sept. 1938, pp. 306–26.
[46] Here the editor referred readers to 'A documentary anthology of the crisis', *RT*, Dec. 1938, vol. 29, pp. 197–225.
[47] *P.D.* (Cwlth) 29 Sept. 1938, pp. 332–3.
[48] Ibid., 5 Oct. 1938, pp. 392–7.
[49] Ibid., pp. 428–33.
[50] Ibid., 6 Oct. 1938, p. 470.
[51] *S.M.H.*, 4 Sept. 1939. This should read ' . . . of the entire British world . . . '
[52] Curtin, *P.D.* (Cwlth) 6 Sept. 1939, pp. 36–40. Smith's statement has not been traced.
[53] Hon. Archie Galbraith Cameron (1895–1956): MHA (S.A.) 1927–34, MHR 1934–56, postmaster-general 1938–9, minister for commerce and the navy 1940.
[54] Field Marshal Sir Thomas Albert Blamey (1884–1951): chief of staff Australian corps 1918 and AIF 1919, served European war 1914–18, Australian defence representative in London attached to war office 1922, second chief of general staff commonwealth military forces 1923–5, commanded 3rd Australian division

1931–7, chief commissioner Victorian police 1925–37, controller-general of Australian recruiting secretariat 1938–9, GOC 1st Australian corps AIF 1940–1, GOC AIF Middle East 1941, deputy commander in chief, allied land forces south-west Pacific 1942–5, field marshal 1950.

55 Here the editor noted, 'The decision to send this contingent to Europe was cancelled in view of the Empire scheme for air-training in Canada . . . ' Broadcasting on October 10, Mr. Menzies described the scheme as "the most spectacular and the most decisive joint effort of the British nations in this war".'

56 Hon. Edward John Ward (1899–1963): MHR 1931, 1932–63, minister for labour and national service 1941–3, minister for transport and external territories 1943–9.

57 This reference has not been traced.

58 This reference has not been traced.

59 Rt Hon. Arthur William Fadden (1895–1973): MHR 1936–58, minister for air 1940, treasurer 1940–1, prime minister 1941, treasurer 1949–58, deputy prime minister 1949–58.

60 Here the editor noted, 'For the period of his short stay in England Dr. Evatt has become Australia's representative at meetings of the War Cabinet.'

61 Rt Hon. Herbert Vere Evatt (1894–1965): justice of high court 1930–40; MHR 1940–60, attorney-general and minister for external affairs 1941–9, chief justice of N.S.W. 1960–2.

62 *P.D.* (Cwlth) 6 Sept. 1939, p. 37. This should read ' . . . Commonwealth of Nations. Therefore, the party . . . '

63 *Herald*, 27 Dec. 1941.

64 *The King and His Dominion Governors* (London 1936).

65 *P.D.* (Cwlth) 16 Dec. 1941, pp. 1088–9.

66 *Herald*, 27 Dec. 1941.

67 *Age, Argus* and *Sydney Morning Herald* reports of 30 December 1941 are similar to that quoted.

68 General Douglas MacArthur (1880–1964): member Vera Cruz (Mexico) expedition 1914, commanded U.S. 42nd (Rainbow) division in World War I, officer in charge of U.S. occupation sector on Rhine, superintendent U.S. military academy 1919–22, department commander in Philippines 1928–30, U.S. army chief of staff 1930–5, commander U.S. and Philippine troops 1941–2, commander allied forces in Pacific World War II, supreme commander occupation forces in Japan 1945–50, commander U.N. forces Korea 1950–1.

SELECT BIBLIOGRAPHY

It has not been thought necessary to list sources used to verify quotations. These include newspapers, parliamentary debates and parliamentary papers. Biographical material has been culled mainly from *Who Was Who*, *Who's Who* and the *Australian Encyclopaedia*.

Bean, C.E.W. (ed.). *Official History of Australia in the War of 1914–18*, vols 1, 2, 10, 11. Sydney 1921–37.

Cambridge History of the British Empire, vol. 7. London 1933.

Childe, V.G. (ed. F.B. Smith). *How Labour Governs: a study of workers' representation in Australia.* 2nd ed. Melbourne 1964.

Edwards, C. *Bruce of Melbourne: man of two worlds.* London 1965.

Fitzhardinge, L.F. *William Morris Hughes: a political biography*, vol. 1, Sydney 1964.

Graham, B.D. *The Formation of the Australian Country Parties.* Canberra 1966.

Green, F.C. *Servant of the House.* Melbourne 1969.

Jauncey, L.C. *The Story of Conscription in Australia.* Melbourne 1968.

La Nauze, J.A. *Alfred Deakin: a biography.* 2 vols. Melbourne 1965.

Marwick, A. *The Deluge: British society and the first world war.* London 1967.

Page, Sir E.C.G. (ed. A. Mozley). *Truant Surgeon: the inside story of forty years of Australian political life.* Sydney 1963.

Robson, L.L. (ed.). *Australia and the Great War 1914–1918.* Melbourne 1969.

—— *The First A.I.F.: a study of its recruitment 1914–1918.* Melbourne 1970.

Ryan, P. (ed.). *Encyclopaedia of Papua and New Guinea.* 3 vols. Melbourne 1972.

Sawer, G. *Australian Federal Politics and Law 1901–1929.* Melbourne 1956.

——*Australian Federal Politics and Law 1929–1949.* Melbourne 1963.

Smith, F.B. *The Conscription Plebiscites in Australia 1916–17.* Melbourne 1965.

Turner, I.A.H. *Industrial Labour and Politics: the dynamics of the labour movement in eastern Australia 1900–1921.* Canberra 1965.

—— *Sydney's Burning.* 2nd ed. Sydney 1969.

West, F.J. *Hubert Murray: the Australian pro-consul.* Melbourne 1968.

Since the preface was written, Professor John Kendle's *The Round Table Movement and Imperial Union* (University of Toronto Press, 1975) reveals details of Lionel Curtis's trip to Australia in 1910.

INDEX

Age (Melbourne): character, 91; on Hughes, 86

Allan, J., 128, 207

Alsace-Lorraine: German policy towards, 45, 202

Amalgamated Society of Engineers, 63

Amery, L. S.: on British empire as economic unit, 18, 170–1, 210

Anzac area, 197

Anzac Cove, 4, 47–50

Anzac Day, 4

arbitration, 201; acts, 30–1; ALP's policy on, 27, 30–1, 33, 147, 150; awards, 8, 67–8, 150; faults, 143–4; Harvester judgment, 144; and industrial peace, 72; international, 33; and maritime strike, 72, 129; and Nationalists, 8, 16, 143–4; revisions, 27, 149–50; Theodore's view, 150; and UAP, 160

Argus (Melbourne): on Eden's resignation, 176

Ashmead-Bartlett, E.: on Anzac landing, 4

Asquith, H. H.: on dominion sovereignty, 94

Australia, H.M.A.S., 42

Australian Capital Territory: sale of alcohol, 30

Australian Council of Trade Unions (ACTU), 148, 186

Australian Imperial Force (AIF): 1st, (created) 3, 41, (demobilized) 9, (and Hughes) 98, (at Gallipoli) 4, 47–50, 55, (losses) 7, recruitment, 8, 54–5, 80–1, 203; 2nd, (created) 20, 185, (recalled) 193

Australian Labor party (ALP): conferences, (1908) 32, (1912) 2, 26, 32, (1938) 177; and Commonwealth Shipping Line, 140; and Country party, 106–7; and defence, 177, 193; and economic depression, 155, 164; federal government (1904, 1909), 31; federal seats (1919–29), 151; federal-state conflict, 156; general elections, (1910) 147, (1914) 3, 41, (1922) 13, 113–14, 116, 147, (1925) 14, 126–7, 130, 132–8, 147, (1928) 147, (1929) 16–17, 143, 147, 151, (1931) 164; and immigration, 110; and Liberal protectionists, 12; losses in New South Wales, 5; and Nationalists, 84–5, 87; origin, 105; policy, 1–2, 26–35; press, 91; trade diversion policy, 171–2; and unions, 31; in World War II, 184; *see also* Charlton, conscription, Hughes, Scullin

Australian Notes Act (1910), 32

Australian Notes Trust Fund, 32–3

Australian Seamen's Union (ASU), 127–8

Australian Workers' Union (AWU), 148

Austria: absorbed by Germany, 78, 176, 178

Bank Note Tax Act (1910), 32

bankruptcy and banking law, 34

Batman electorate (Victoria), 162

Bean, C. E. W., 4

Beasley, J. A., 156, 157, 209

Belgium: Australian gifts to, 44; invasion of, 3, 40, 45; silk exports, 169

Bernhardi, F. von, 45, 202

Blamey, Sir T. A., 185, 211

Boer War, 3, 24, 202

Bolsheviks, 11, 87, 101, 134; revolution, 7, 11, 87

Boxer War, 3, 39, 202

Brennan, F., 162, 210

Britain: Australian imperial sentiments, 1, 23–5; and conscription, 61–2, 81; and Czech crisis, 179–82; foreign policy, 175–8; Gallipoli, 48–9; governor-general's role, 158; immigration